WORKING
ON THE
BOMB

AN ORAL HISTORY OF
WWII HANFORD

WORKING
ON THE
BOMB

Written by
S. L. SANGER

Editor
CRAIG WOLLNER

Continuing Education Press
Portland State University

Continuing Education Press
School of Extended Studies
Portland State University, PO Box 1394
Portland, OR 97207

Library of Congress catalog card: 95-069840

ISBN 0-87678-115-6

Design by Frank Loose Design

Index by William Abrams

Manufactured in the United States of America

Interviews first published by S.L. Sanger as *Hanford and the Bomb: An Oral History of WWII*. Seattle, Washington: Living History Press, 1989.

Portions of this book first appeared in the *Seattle Post-Intelligencer*.

The author is grateful for permission to use material from:

Nagasaki 1945 by Tatsuichiro Akizuki. London: Quartet Books Limited, 1981

Atomic Quest by Arthur Holly Compton. New York: Oxford University Press, 1956

The Curve of Binding Energy by John McPhee. New York: Farrar, Straus and Giroux, 1974

Nuclear Weapons Databook, Vol. 2: U.S. Nuclear Warhead Production by Thomas B. Cochran, William M. Arkin, Robert S. Norris and Milton M. Hoenig, copyright 1987 by Natural Resources Defense Council

History of the Met Lab, Section C-1, Journal of the Years 1942-1946 by Glenn T. Seaborg. Prepared for U.S. Energy Research and Development Administration, Lawrence Berkeley Laboratory, University of California, Berkeley, 1977-1980

TO THE PEOPLE
WHO TOLD THE STORY

Hanford's location in the Pacific Northwest.

CONTENTS

Chapter 4 CONSTRUCTION 67

A job bigger than the pyramids; in '44 the war effort's "most urgent construction project;" 51,000 residents at the construction camp where "it was like Saturday night every day."

Chapter 5 OPERATIONS 147

A scientific mystery baffles scientists; the world's first plutonium plant, a combination nuclear/chemical industrial complex, begins production; four months after startup the first plutonium is ready for shipment.

Chapter 6 LOS ALAMOS — 195

From the producer to the customer; shipments of the syrupy plutonium nitrate in ever-increasing volume to the Los Alamos lab.

Chapter 7 TRINITY — 209

The "Gadget," Jornada del Muerto, the dawn of the age of nuclear weapons; "Batter my heart, three-person'd God."

Chapter 8 EPILOGUE — 217

Fat Man and Nagasaki; "a blinding white flash of light;" radiation worries and the wartime emergency; research experiments with Columbia River fish; early methods of monitoring the environment for harmful effects of plutonium manufacture; Hanford's post-war development.

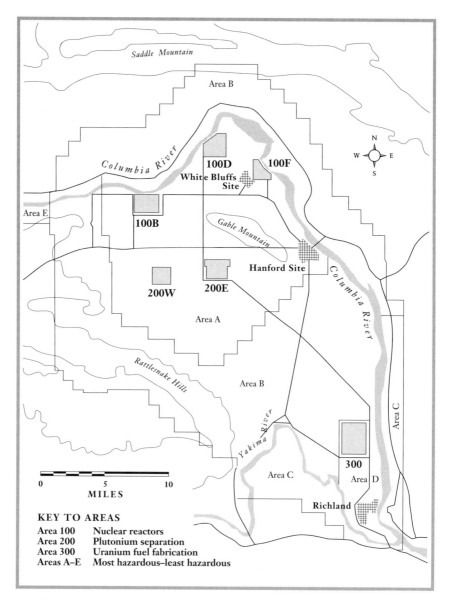

World War II layout of Hanford Engineer Works.

PREFACE

Since the mid-eighties when Stephen Sanger began interviewing everyone he could find with memories of the Hanford Engineer Works in World War II, little has happened to diminish the significance of the plutonium production site in the fastness of eastern Washington. Charges that Hanford polluted the water, air, and soil, of much of the Columbia River basin and was the proximate cause of illness for many of the nearby human inhabitants in the fifty years since the war, however, have created a very different impression from the one that Sanger's interviewees gave voice to. For them, Hanford remains in a certain sense frozen in time, a crossroad of scientific and engineering adventure and moral purpose in a world imperiled.

The Hanford of the forties was an integral element of the Manhattan Project. This massive and astonishing initiative was undertaken by American scientists and engineers to beat their Axis counterparts to "the bomb," that is, to nuclear weaponry, while the fate of civilization hung in the balance. As such, what went on at Hanford was a vital part of the war effort. Because of wartime secrecy, many of the men and women Sanger recorded knew little of the marvels they were helping to perform, nevertheless, decades later they were able to communicate to him the urgency and the excitement of the undertaking to which they contributed.

Their bright memories are, to the greatest extent, currently overshadowed by the thorough study of the damage done to the environment by the radioactive waste and detritus emitted at Hanford over the post-World War II years. This recent release of information put the pernicious effects of Hanford's history in the forefront of public perception.

Still, a knowledge of the Hanford that was critical to the survival of democracy is worth preserving because it so powerfully illuminates the compelling technological history of the war effort as well as the unpredictable mutability of human experience. In that sense, Hanford becomes a foremost case study in the history of unintended consequences. As a World War II western boom town fabricated out of whole cloth to meet a specific wartime need, it is also a fascinating microcosm of life on the home front. Finally, the story of Hanford offers us important insights into the vagaries of history in the arid West, that febrile yet durable land.

Steve Sanger's book thus fills the need to retain the wartime history of Hanford, and the Portland State University Continuing Education Press is pleased to publish an edited version with the addition of essays by two distinguished historians of nuclear technology. As an introduction, Ferenc Szasz, an authority on the Manhattan Project, provides broad reflections on the wartime conditions under which Hanford was born and flourished. In an afterword, Bruce Hevly, an expert in technology history, provides context for what might be called Hanford's post-war half-life.

These brief works are meant to flesh out Hanford's compelling story, not to supplant the intricate web of memories that Sanger wove into a book, published in 1989 as *Hanford and the Bomb*. Taken together, they render a powerful account of the creation and unleashing of an awesome technology in unique circumstances, a technology that left profound changes on the lifeforms, land, and water of the Pacific Northwest.

Craig Wollner, editor
August 1995

AUTHOR'S PREFACE

The interviews in this book, for the most part, were done during 1986. They were tape-recorded and were conducted in an informal setting which allowed the interview subject to talk at his or her own pace. Occasionally the interviewer would ask for clarification or additional information but the interviewee was allowed to tell the story and to express personal emphasis. Usually, the subjects were interviewed at their residence or office.

This material was edited for coherence and conciseness. Nothing was added. In some cases, in the interest of absolute accuracy, technical portions were checked by the person interviewed.

Robert W. Mull contributed to Chapter 2 and to the Epilogue.

S. L. Sanger
August 1995

Leslie R. Groves, the Army general in charge of the Manhattan Project, during a visit to the Hanford Engineer Works.   *U.S. Department of Energy*

INTRODUCTION

By Ferenc M. Szasz
The University of New Mexico

On September 17, 1942, General Leslie R. Groves assumed command of America's secret atomic weapons program, the "Manhattan Project."* The portly, no-nonsense Groves knew exactly what was expected of him. On a salary of less than $1,000 a month, he had to supervise the spending of millions annually (total cost: $2 billion) in the largest organized construction effort since the building of the pyramids. Similarly, he had to oversee complex research/scientific projects in thirty-seven different facilities scattered all through the United States and Canada. All this activity had a single goal: to beat Nazi Germany to the secret of the atomic bomb.[1]

The Manhattan Project drew on virtually every available American resource. It tapped premier university talent at Columbia, MIT, Princeton, California, Minnesota, Iowa State, and Rochester, to name just a few. Gigantic industrial enterprises, such as Stone and Webster, Kellex, Tennessee Eastman, and Du Pont provided essential manufacturing and construction skills. The heart of the Project, however, lay with the creation of three top secret "atomic cities," Los Alamos (Site Y), the Clinton Engineer Works, later termed Oak Ridge (Site X), and Hanford (Site W).

The town of Los Alamos arose amidst the juniper and cedar forests of the 7,000-foot Pajarito Plateau in north central New Mexico. The scientists stationed there were asked to design and fabricate the proposed nuclear

---

* So named because the first headquarters of the Corps of Engineers district in charge of bomb work was located in Manhattan.

1. Notes to this chapter are appended in References, p 243.

weapons. The hamlet of Oak Ridge emerged from the pine forests and hard-woods of eastern Tennessee. The assignment here was to separate as fuel for the bomb sufficient amounts of the fissionable uranium isotope (U-235) from the more common U-238, as well as to initiate a variety of smaller, pilot pro-grams. The community of Hanford was carved from small ranches and scrub land close to the Columbia River in south central Washington. The task here was exceptionally complex. Government officials planned Hanford as the site for several gigantic nuclear reactors, all completely untested and untried, which would produce sufficient amounts of the man-made, fissionable element plu-tonium (Pu). All three communities were surrounded by the deepest secrecy.

Groves selected the location of Los Alamos largely for reasons of isola-tion and security. The choices of Oak Ridge and Hanford, however, were closely intertwined. The buildings proposed for Oak Ridge were to house gigantic electromagnetic and gaseous diffusion operations, the most promis-ing procedures to separate U-235 from U-238. While these methods were not without their radiation dangers, the production of plutonium demanded the construction of an actual nuclear *reactor*. Should a reactor ever malfunc-tion, the resulting explosion could shower radioactive debris over the entire region. The city of Knoxville, about 110,000 in 1940 and only twenty-five miles from Oak Ridge, lay much too close for Groves's comfort.[2]

In addition to isolation for reasons of public safety, the proposed pluto-nium site possessed a number of other requirements. Because time was of the essence, engineers requested a climate that would allow for virtually year-round construction efforts. In addition, the reactor site would utilize an enormous amount of electrical power. Finally, and probably most important, the site needed a large, dependable supply of pure cool water.

This combination of restrictions and demands pointed officials to the trans-Mississippi West, especially to the mostly arid, sparsely populated regions of the great hydroelectric dams that had been built during the previous decades: Boulder, Shasta, Grand Coulee, and Bonneville.[3] Search teams scoured these areas, seriously considering two sites in southern California and one in Colorado. Finally, a search team headed by Colonel Franklin T. Matthias recommended the Hanford site, and in early January, 1943, Groves ordered the commandeering of 670 square miles (about half a million acres) of Washington State land as "necessary to the public interest." "Thus, in only a month's time, and by only a few men," wrote historian Michele Stenehjem Gerber, "one of the most significant decisions in American history was made."[4]

When they first heard the news, Washington state farmers and ranchers were stunned. The fact that no official could tell them *why* their lands were to be taken (most, of course, did not know) only increased their rage. Groves compromised and allowed people to bring in their 1943 harvests, which, because of the abundant yields that year, only intensified their fury. For a person in mid-1943 to admit to being a federal agent meant putting one's life in danger.[5]

In October 1942, Groves approached the Du Pont Corporation of Delaware to oversee the industrial aspect of the proposed Hanford Project. Du Pont officials were initially reluctant, however, for the company had only recently shed the "merchants of death" image that had followed their munitions manufacturing efforts during the Great War of 1914-1918.[6] In addition, a number of corporation executives doubted that the plutonium separation scheme would work.

Groves increased the pressure. Because of Du Pont's long experience with munitions and their excellent safety record, he said, only they could manage this operation. After much arm twisting, Du Pont finally agreed. But they insisted on working at a cost-plus-$1.00 fee, and only for the duration of the war. With this, company executive Crawford H. Greenewalt assumed management of Hanford, with Colonel Franklin T. Matthias as the chief engineer in charge of construction. Scientists at the Metallurgical Laboratory at the University of Chicago, with Du Pont's aid, agreed to design the Hanford reactors. Thus, the unique management team of atomic scientists, the U.S. military, and American industry was set in place for the duration of the conflict.

Then came the construction. The building effort at Hanford from 1943 to 1945 can only be measured in superlatives. Consider the following: Project building crews used 1800 vehicles, including sedans, pick-up trucks, jeeps, and ambulances; 900 buses that had a total seating capacity of over 30,000; 1900 dump trucks and flat bed trucks; 240 tractor trailers; 44 railway locomotives and 460 railway cars; 5 locomotive cranes and 4 stiff leg derricks. The various construction teams built 386 miles of highways, 158 miles of track, poured 780,000 cubic yards of concrete, and erected housing for 5,000 women and 24,000 men. Excavation crews moved 25 million cubic yards of earth in the process. The overall cost was $350 million.[7] Building Hanford has been compared to the simultaneous construction of seven major industrial plants. It would be an immense task even today.

To conduct this mammoth operation, Hanford needed thousands of workers. Consequently, recruiting agents took to the highways with attractive job offers, by-passing only the Pacific Northwest, New Mexico and Tennessee. As a result, virtually all of the Hanford employees were newcomers to Washington. Promises of high wages, free railway tickets, and (probably) exaggerated visions of mountain scenery drew thousands of workers to Richland. During one period, about a thousand newcomers arrived every week.[8]

Recruiting workers often proved easier than retaining them. Because of the strict secrecy surrounding all aspects of the Manhattan Project, officials could not tell anyone what Hanford was producing, only that it was "something to help win the war." Patriotic appeals sufficed for a time, but nagging security restrictions, dismal housing conditions, lack of a family support system (men could bring neither wives nor children), and the often bleak surroundings sent hundreds back home or on to West Coast industries.[9] Every time a severe dust storm swept across the region, workers departed in droves. Locals called such storms "termination powder."[10]

But what were these gigantic buildings *for*? What were all these 40,000 people *doing*? No one knew. Popular Kennewick Texaco service station owner, Walter Knowles, tried for years to uncover the secret, but he never came close.[11] Rumors reached outlandish proportions. One suggested that Hanford was a gigantic WPA "boondoggle." Several workers quit in disgust to move to the Coast where they could engage in a "real" war effort.

From 1943 to 1945, Hanford resembled a western gold mining camp far more than any "typical American city." Everywhere men greatly outnumbered women and fights, brawls, and robbery proved common. Legend has it that the windows of the various bars were hinged so as to facilitate police use of tear gas. One might think that the Hanford jail would loom as the centerpiece of community life, but local police and MPs had firm instructions to get the men back to work as swiftly as possible. Thus, the brawlers were arrested, marched to a holding bin, allowed to sober up, and put back to work as soon as they could function.[12] There was no other American town quite like it.

Everything at Hanford loomed larger than life. The trailer park, which housed 4,300 privately owned trailers (and proved an object of considerable pride for the residents), was probably the largest in the world. The amount of food that the teams of chefs prepared—high in quality and at reasonable prices—rivaled all installations except the largest US Army bases. The attendance at baseball games, where one craft team would play against another, approached that of major league teams. The three reactors at the edge of the Columbia, as well as the chemical separation plants, towered above the landscape like secular cathedrals. Finally, the confiscation of half a million acres from about 2,000 individual owners (although paid for at a cost of 5.1 million dollars) still ranks among the largest forced foreclosures in American history.[13]

Life at wartime Hanford careened from one crisis to another, but three incidents stand out as particularly memorable. Perhaps the most intense moment came in September, 1944, when operators coaxed Reactor B to power for the first time. The sequence of events that followed pointed to both the uncertainty that surrounded the entire Manhattan Project, as well as the pervasive tension between the scientists and the engineers. The element at question involved the design of the reactors.

Based at Chicago's Met Lab, physicist Eugene Wigner's group designed Reactor B as a gigantic graphite cylinder containing about 200 tons of uranium slugs.[14] When these plans reached the Du Pont engineering staff, they insisted on squaring off the cylinder, thus adding a "safety factor" that increased the capacity to 260 tons of uranium. Chicago scientists ridiculed Du Pont's "conservatism" but Groves sided with the company, even though the addition lengthened the construction time and added to the expense.

Finally, the reactor was completed and on September 13, 1944, Chicago physicist Enrico Fermi inserted the first "canned" (i.e., coated in aluminum) uranium slug into the face of reactor B. After two weeks, workers had loaded the entire 200 tons and on September 27, the initial power run began.

For two hours all went as planned. Suddenly, however, operators noted a gradual loss of power, and within three hours the pile had shut itself down. When the process was restarted, the same pattern repeated itself. The reactor would not function.

A perplexed Fermi whipped out his slide rule and concluded that B pile was being "poisoned" by a short-lived radioactive isotope that appeared to be absorbing neutrons faster than the reactor could create them. The culprit turned out to be a gas, xenon 135. But Fermi also calculated that if the extra 60 tons of uranium (Du Pont's "safety factor") could be inserted into the reactor, the total amount of uranium would be sufficient to overcome the xenon poisoning. Purely by accident, the conservative approach of Du Pont's design engineers had saved the entire Hanford production schedule from failure.[15] Not surprisingly, when engineers relate this incident, they devote many pages to it; Eugene Wigner in his memoirs, however, dismisses it in two paragraphs.[16]

At the beginning of 1945, a second dramatic incident occurred. Three years earlier, in mid-April of 1942, America had responded to the raid on Pearl Harbor by launching, from aircraft carriers, a surprise attack by B-25 Mitchell medium bombers on the Japanese Home Islands. Led by Lt-Colonel James Doolittle, this famed raid on Tokyo provoked a desire for revenge among the Japanese military. Consequently, over the next several years the Japanese produced about nine thousand rice paper balloon bombs. Lofted into the air over the Home Islands, the balloons caught the prevailing easterly winds that carried them toward North America. Army Air Force spotter planes shot down as many as they could, but a number reached the North American mainland.

One of these balloon bombs tangled in a power line that stretched between Bonneville and Grand Coulee dams, thus shorting out the transformer, and shutting off power to Hanford. Although the actual power loss lasted less than a minute, it took three days to restore the reactors to full power again.[17] The symbolism of a Japanese balloon bomb halting—even if only temporarily—the production of the plutonium that would eventually destroy the city of Nagasaki cries out for the skills of a dramatist.

In July of the previous year, Hanford had faced still another crisis. From the onset, Los Alamos scientists had expected to utilize the same weapons design for both Oak Ridge's uranium and Hanford's plutonium: a "gun assembly" device that would fire two sub-critical pieces of the fissionable material into one another to produce a nuclear explosion. Indeed, the uranium weapon dropped on Hiroshima on August 6, 1945, was of this gun assembly design.

Further research by Los Alamos, however, concluded that plutonium would not fit into this proposed format. The two sub-critical pieces of plutonium could not be brought together fast enough to avoid "predetonation." With this discovery, there existed the possibility that the plutonium produced by Hanford could never be utilized during the war. The entire Hanford project might, indeed, become a "boondoggle."[18]

For better or worse, however, Los Alamos scientists James Tuck, Seth Neddermeyer, and John von Neumann teamed together to create the concept of "implosion." This involved taking two sub-critical hemispheres of plutonium, surrounding them with conventional explosives and "imploding" (i.e., compressing the sphere) until it reached a critical state. With this discovery, Hanford's production schedule resumed its normal frenetic pace.

The first plutonium shipment from Hanford left for Los Alamos by caravan on February 3, 1945. The world's first atomic bomb, exploded at Trinity Site in central New Mexico on July 16, 1945, had a plutonium core.[19] Three weeks later, a virtually identical plutonium weapon was dropped on Nagasaki, (three days after the uranium-cored Hiroshima bomb). The standard figure for lives lost at Nagasaki is 70,000 by the end of 1945 and 140,000 within the next five years.[20] Although the documents are still classified, historians believe that a third Hanford plutonium weapon would have been available in late September. By that time, however, the Japanese had surrendered and World War II was over.

Of the three secret "atomic cities," Hanford has probably received the least recognition for its World War II efforts. In her 1990 Pettyjohn lecture at Washington State University, Colorado historian Patricia Nelson Limerick complained that American history textbooks were far more likely to index "Mark Hanna" (William McKinley's political advisor) than "Hanford."[21] Richard Rhodes devotes only about ten pages of his majestic *The Making of the Atomic Bomb* (1986) to Hanford, slightly over one percent of the total. After a half a century, there is still only one scholarly monograph on Hanford.[22]

Somehow, the saga of Manhattan Project Hanford has lacked the drama and excitement of Los Alamos or Oak Ridge. Photographs of Reactor B, the chemical separations plants, or the trailer park pale beside the images of the Trinity Site blast or the anxious visage of Los Alamos Lab Director J. Robert Oppenheimer.

Moreover, a number of men and women who served at Oak Ridge or Los Alamos have either written memoirs or been the subjects of biographies. Not so for Hanford. Colonel Franklin T. Matthias wrote little and the career of Crawford Greenewalt is scarcely known outside Du Pont circles. Even the crude doggerel that emerged from Hanford can hardly match the charm of Oak Ridge Cherokee poet Marilou Awiakta, widely known as "the mother of atomic folklore." [23]

Because of this relative neglect, students of both Pacific Northwest and early nuclear history will welcome the reprinting of *Hanford and the Bomb* by the Portland State University Continuing Education Press. It would not be an exaggeration to say that S. L. Sanger's collection of World War II reminiscences has become *the* primary source for our understanding of this period. In the over sixty recollections gathered here, one can discover virtually every aspect of the Hanford saga: The sustained effort, the dedication to an as-yet-unknown task, the bewilderment, the rage, the irony, and the celebration-mixed-with-tragedy that accompanied one of the most remarkable construction efforts of the entire World War II era.

Glenn T. Seaborg, the University of California chemist who was a
co-discoverer of the element plutonium and who directed research which led
to a method of separating plutonium from uranium fuel slugs after neutron
bombardment inside a nuclear reactor.   *U.S. Department of Energy/postwar photo*

CHAPTER 1

BEGINNINGS

I n code, they called the place "Site W." The public name was Hanford Engineer Works. The world's first full-scale plutonium production complex lay in a bend of the Columbia River, on arid tableland between the river and Rattlesnake Mountain. Hanford produced the plutonium used both in the first atomic bomb, which was tested at Trinity Site in New Mexico, and in Fat Man, the military nickname for the bomb which devastated Nagasaki.

The Hiroshima bomb was fueled by uranium, which came from the bomb-building Manhattan Project's other great production complex, called Site X, at Oak Ridge, Tennessee. Hanford and Oak Ridge manufactured the nuclear explosive, and the people at Site Y, Los Alamos, New Mexico, designed and built the bombs.

Fission, the splitting of the nucleus of the atom which results in release of practically unlimited energy, was discovered in 1938 by two German chemists, Otto Hahn and Fritz Strassmann. By the time America entered World War II, scientists knew there were at least two likely ways to achieve a nuclear explosion. The fissionable materials could be either uranium, which existed in nature, or plutonium, which would be created in a nuclear reactor.

At first, the emphasis was on using the highly-fissionable U-235 isotope of uranium. U-235's drawback was that it would have to be isolated from natural uranium before it would be usable in a bomb. This separation process would be overwhelmingly difficult.

Natural uranium is almost entirely composed of U-238, a slightly heavier isotope than U-235. There are 140 times more U-238 atoms than U-235 atoms in natural uranium, and separating these "sisters" would be necessary before a bomb could be made. Since the two isotopes were of the same element, separation could not be done chemically, only physically. For this task, the early nuclear scientists came up with four possibilities, all of immense difficulty: gaseous diffusion, thermal diffusion, electromagnetic separation and separation by centrifuge. Oak Ridge, Tennessee, became the center for U-235 separation work.

The other possibility for a nuclear explosive, although something of a late starter in the race for the bomb, was plutonium, specifically the isotope Pu-239. As early as mid-1940, before plutonium even had been identified as an element, Prof. Louis A. Turner of Princeton had suggested that in a chain reaction of uranium a new element, atomic number 94, could be formed when neutrons freed by the fissioning of U-235 were captured by U-238. This new element, Turner theorized, might be capable of undergoing fission.

This possibility was described in technical detail in a government document published in 1945, popularly called "The Smythe Report:"

> Suppose that we have set up a controllable chain reaction in a lattice of natural uranium and a moderator—say carbon, in the form of graphite. Then as the chain reaction proceeds, neutrons are emitted in the process of fission of the U-235 and many of these neutrons are absorbed by U-238. This produces U-239, each atom of which then emits a beta particle, becoming neptunium (93Np239). Neptunium, in turn, emits another beta particle, becoming plutonium (94Pu239), which emits an alpha particle, decaying again to U-235, but so slowly that in effect it is a stable element. If, after the reaction has been allowed to proceed for a considerable time, the mixture of metals is removed, it may be possible to extract the plutonium by chemical methods and purify it for use in a subsequent fission chain reaction of an explosive nature.

Plutonium was first identified in 1940 at the University of California in Berkeley by chemist Glenn T. Seaborg and four co-workers. In March, 1941, the group demonstrated that plutonium was fissionable "with a large probability," which meant it was a potential atomic explosive. Seaborg and his colleagues named the new element after the planet Pluto. Pluto itself was named for the Greek god of the underworld, the lord of the dead.

In mid-1941, physicist Ernest O. Lawrence, a University of California faculty member and a leader of the inner group of atomic scientists, recognized that possibly plutonium could be produced in relatively large amounts inside an atomic reactor, using purified natural uranium as the fuel. One major uncertainty was the question of achieving a sustained nuclear chain reaction.

In addition, a method would have to be developed to separate the plutonium by chemical means from the irradiated uranium fuel.

Scientists sensed that plutonium was material for a super bomb. Later, it was determined the amount needed to make a bomb is only one third the amount needed than if U-235 is used—a far more elegant solution.

On December 6, 1941, Arthur Compton and two top White House science advisers, Vannevar Bush and James Conant, had lunch at the Cosmos Club in Washington, D.C. They had attended a morning meeting of the S-1 Committee, a pre-Manhattan Project committee formed during the investigative stages of the bomb-building effort. During the meeting, various jobs had been assigned having to do with the separation of the uranium isotopes, but nothing had been mentioned about plutonium.

In his book, *Atomic Quest* (Oxford University Press, 1956), Compton, a Nobel Prize winner and physics department chair at the University of Chicago, wrote that he suggested during the luncheon that more thought be given to plutonium production as another way of obtaining fissionable material. Perhaps, said Compton, plutonium eventually would be "a worthy competitor" to U-235.

Compton's afterthought at the Cosmos Club led quickly to formation of the Plutonium Project, headquartered at the University of Chicago under Compton's direction. Chicago's most dramatic single accomplishment was Enrico Fermi's success in achieving the first controlled and sustained nuclear reaction, on December 2, 1942.

Before the suggestion that plutonium could be manufactured inside a nuclear reactor, a reactor had no military purpose. Reactors were linked to either atomic research or to the possibility of generating electricity by using the heat from the fission process. But, the reality of Fermi's success meant the nuclear reactor had become a machine of war.

In June, 1942, the Army Corps of Engineers had assumed general supervision of the new Manhattan Project. Plans were underway for the massive uranium separation facilities at Oak Ridge, and for a remote laboratory north of Santa Fe at the former Los Alamos Ranch School. Finally, the Du Pont Company agreed in November, 1942, to build and operate a plutonium works for the Army.

Manhattan Project leaders, until November, 1942, had assumed the plutonium operation would be located at Oak Ridge. After more thought, however, it was decided there were too many unknown aspects to plutonium manufacture, and that it would be more prudent to locate in an area where an accident or other unforeseen event would not threaten either a nearby city or other Manhattan Project plants. These apprehensions led to a search for an isolated place with access to electric power and water. Hanford, Washington, was chosen by the War Department in February, 1943.

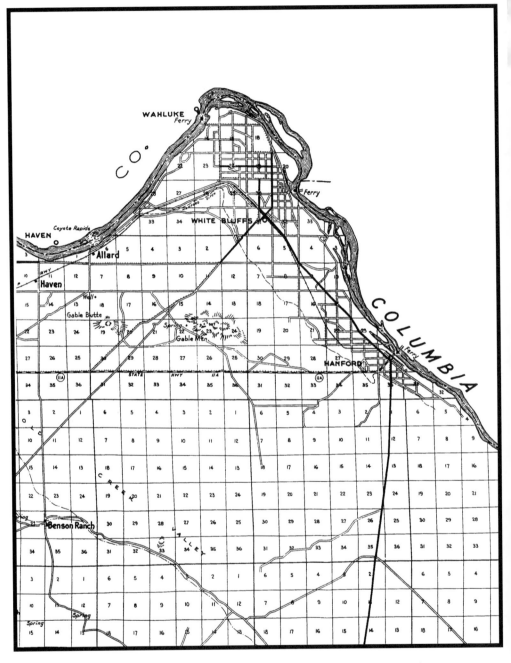

The White Bluffs-Hanford area before the Army came in 1943 to begin construction of the Hanford Engineer Works.

Metsker Maps/Washington State Historical Society, Tacoma

CHAPTER 2

THE SITE

*"Located in the south-central portion of the State of Washington, it lay
on an undulating tableland, composed chiefly of a desolate region of sand,
sagebrush and dried water courses."*

DU PONT'S HISTORY OF THE HANFORD ENGINEER WORKS

The land was downstream from Priest Rapids, an area of sagebrush
barrenness and isolation, gentled in places by fruit orchards and
ranches. Two villages, White Bluffs and Hanford, were home to about
300, and Richland, about 30 miles downriver, had a population of 200. Perhaps 1,000 others farmed and ranched where the Columbia made its sweeping
bend before meeting the Yakima River near Richland.

In all, about 625 square miles (some 400,000 acres) were taken by the
Corps of Engineers, on both sides of the river. Officially described as mostly
"low-grade sage brush grazing land," the project also included about 50,000
acres of farmland, mostly irrigated fruit orchards. Half of the total had to be
purchased outright, the rest was leased or already owned by either federal,
state or county governments. The federal government, using authority under
the War Powers Act, offered the residents compensation and ordered them
to leave, in some cases within 30 days.

Land acquisition became, in some instances, a matter of bitter controversy between the evicted owners and the government. Some compensation
cases were not settled until after the war.

This area, for centuries, had been roamed by a nomadic tribe of Indians,
the Wanapums, or "river people." These Indians declined to participate in

negotiations during the 1850s which would have resulted in their traditional lands being turned over to white settlers in return for life on a reservation. Mother Earth, said the Wanapums, belonged to all and no one had the right to impose restrictions.

A spiritual leader of the Wanapums was called Smohalla, "the Dreamer," who learned great truths, sometimes foreboding ones, during his long journeys into the spirit world. One of Smohalla's visions possessed an eerie accuracy. White men, he said, will come to claim this land and river and to force their ways upon his people. Smowhalla said do not give up the old ways, but await the day when the white man's tide would turn and the Wanapums would again be free to roam and take the salmon.

In December, 1942, officials of the Manhattan Project met with representatives of the Du Pont Company in Wilmington, Delaware, to decide on requirements for the as-yet unchosen plutonium producing site. These included a plentiful supply of electricity and water, no town of any size could be within 20 miles, and no major highway or railroad within 10 miles. Preferably, the weather should be relatively mild. In addition, the site had to be in an area where the population and economy would not be disrupted. Washington, with its open spaces, the Columbia River and its great hydro-electric dams, very early captured the attention of the plutonium planners.

Shortly before the end of 1942, a site selection team headed by Lt. Colonel Franklin T. Matthias of the Army Corps of Engineers was dispatched to the West Coast by Brig. General Leslie R. Groves, chief of the Manhattan Project.

COL. FRANKLIN T. MATTHIAS

Fritz Matthias, a civil engineer, had been a close associate of General Groves since the beginning of the Manhattan Project, and later Groves would appoint him officer-in-charge at Hanford. Matthias and two Du Pont representatives looked quickly at possible sites in Montana, Oregon, and California, as well as Washington. Their first stop was western Montana, then to the vicinity of Grand Coulee Dam where they found three likely spots, but decided against them because of some problems with water availability. They saw two possibilities in eastern Oregon, and then flew north to check the Hanford area.

University of Chicago physicist Arther H. Compton, left, director of the Plutonium Project, and Col. Franklin T. Matthias, the Army Corps of Engineers officer in charge at Hanford. *U.S. Department of Energy*

I thought the Hanford site was perfect the first time I saw it. We flew over the Rattlesnake Hills up to the river, so I saw the whole site on that flight. We were sure we had it. I called General Groves from Portland, and told him I thought we had found the only place in the country that could match the requirements for a desirable site.

I said we had found a place with a spur line railroad, The Milwaukee Road, right into the place where we thought the facilities would be built. And that our property probably would include the switch station between Bonneville and Grand Coulee. Right on that 230-kv line. It had so much in favor of it. An area with almost no people, very undeveloped, it was obvious it had been built by the Columbia River in early times working across the valley leaving gravel behind it. And there's nothing better than gravel, deep gravel, for foundations, for earthquake protection, anything you want. It had all the advantages.

I told General Groves "I don't see any point of going down to Southern California because there are too many strikes against it." Groves said, "Well you better go ahead with your program. It will only take a few more days." So we did. We came to San Francisco on Christmas Eve, we didn't do anything Christmas day except go to a Chinese restaurant for Christmas dinner. We went to Sacramento, to the district engineer there. We pumped him about what there might be in Northern California. There didn't seem to be much prospect of the combination of lack of people and development, and water and power. We went to Los Angeles, and we drove clear out to the Arizona border. We spotted some good possiblities. But the only water source would have been the Colorado River or one of the aquaducts. They were almost out of the question from the point of view of what hell would be raised if we tapped into either of those. We stayed overnight at Blythe, and spent most of the next day driving around the region.

We went back to Los Angeles, and I called Groves again and said I thought we had done all we needed to do. He said, "All right, come on back." We wrote our report on the plane on the way back to Washington, D.C. We got there New Year's Eve. We talked to Groves the next morning, the first day of 1943, and he quizzed us at length about everything but was very well pleased at what we had found. Before the end of the month we had authority to acquire the site.

(Matthias' interview continues in Chapter 4, p 76)

ANNETTE HERIFORD

The Manhattan Project may have found the ideal spot, but the cost was high for the orchardists, ranchers and villagers who lived in the rich, irrigated, agricultural lands of the Priest Rapids Valley. Annette Heriford was deeply nostalgic about her girlhood years near the village of Hanford.

From the time I first remember, I loved those apple orchards. I remember the orchard adjacent to us, the Jay Smith family. He dearly loved that country.

I remember him and my folks talking on our screened porch one evening, and he said of all the places he had ever been he loved that valley more. I always liked him for saying that.

I remember the fruit orchards and the apple blossoms. The orchards were mainly Red Delicious. We also had what we called winter bananas, a yellow transparent apple. We had Jonathans, they were my favorites because they were juicy. We had Winesaps. We had 30 acres at the Hanford place, part of it was in alfalfa. Our fruit was sent overseas, to the East Coast. The fruit was excellent, it was the earliest fruit-producing section in the whole Northwest.

When I was a child economic conditions were fine. But then of course the crash came in '29. It started to get better just before the government came. I started to college in 1939 and there wasn't any money. I know my father went to work for a dollar an hour, as a guard, up at the substation at Priest Rapids, when the war first broke out. He would write me letters at college while he was there. He still had his orchard, but they weren't making any money.

In March, 1943, when I was about 22, we received a letter from the government saying that we would have to move in 30 days. It was a terrible shock. I can't describe it. It was unbelieveable. The only thing that made it credible to us was because of the war. Our town had been chosen for the war effort. We were so patriotic. Although we could go along with that idea, it was still a terrible blow. Even to think about it now, I can't even describe it. In spite of our patriotism, I remember one man stood there with a shotgun and said they would have to move him.

They appraised my father's 30 acres at $1,700, and the final settlement was $3,200 after the fruit loan of $500 or $600 was paid off. We also had 40 acres at the base of Rattlesnake Mountain, which my uncle and father purchased as an oil investment. They had a geologist friend who thought this would pay off in future years. For this land we were offered 25 cents an acre. We later received $1 an acre or $40 in all, with no mineral rights.

For the 30 acres, $3^1/_2$ miles from Hanford, they offered us $1,700 at first, and the pump and well alone cost $1,900 plus the cost of concrete pipe throughout the 30 acres. The price offered for both acreages was ridiculous.

Ridiculous!

We loved that Columbia River and the bluffs, that was a unique spot. It was beautiful, it's still prettier than Richland.

In 1944, I returned to the ranch and that was a mistake. The grass was high and beginning to dry and I sat and wept like a baby. That was the last time I visited our home site until 1967. By that time, the house had been moved. A wagon wheel, old wood stove, sink and my brother's wagon, that's all that remained.

I've told so many people, when I was going to college at the University of Washington, I would say I was from Hanford and they would say "Where's that? It isn't even on the map, is it?" I got so tired of hearing it that I said "Don't you worry, one day Hanford will be so famous the whole world will know about Hanford."

KATHLEEN HITCHCOCK

Another casualty of the 1943 government invasion was White Bluffs, a few miles upriver from Hanford and considered one of the prettiest towns on the Columbia. Kathleen Hitchcock was the daughter of Tom and Jane O'Larey, who owned the local newspaper, "The White Bluffs Spokesman."

We came from the Waterville area. My parents moved down to White Bluffs to develop a fruit orchard. They bought a 10-acre place that had been planted to apples. They really pioneered. This had to have been 1910.

When we first went out there, it was pretty difficult. There was a man who had the newspaper by the name of Angus Hay. My father bought the paper from him, knowing nothing about the business. The post office went with it. That was the way we grew up, helping in the post office and the print shop. The paper had a circulation of three or four hundred, mainly because it went upriver to Priest Rapids, Wahluke and all the little towns, then downriver to Hanford, some to Richland. It was delivered by mail. My father and mother would write the articles. They enjoyed the newspaper. Sometimes Rufus Woods from Wenatchee and Colonel Robertson from Yakima (newspaper editors) would come by and stop and it would be a big day.

Our first house was just kind of a tent, then we added to it as we could. We were going to build a nicer house, my father had started the basement, when we bought the newspaper. We moved from the ranch house into a house close to the river. That was fairly nice. We kept the ranch and always harvested the fruit.

My dad did the paper for a while, then of course, the war started. My mother took the evacuation very hard, they had always expected to live there the rest of their lives. And it was pretty hard when the Army engineers came

Boarded up buildings in White Bluffs after the village was purchased by the Army and the residents evacuated. Building at right housed "The White Bluffs Spokesman" newspaper.   *East Benton County Historical Museum.*

in and told them to, you know, get out. Gave them maybe a week to get out, maybe they had their farm and animals and no money. No cash! Nobody had cash in those days.

It was a pretty hard thing. Some of them ended up at Medical Lake (a state mental hospital), you know, couldn't quite face it. My mother never really adjusted to it. The fact that the government could come in and take your home away. We were in the war and they felt like they were donating as many young men as any other place to the war effort. It was really sad. They didn't know what for, they only knew it was for the war effort.

All of a sudden this little town would have the Army come in and stop a car and see who you are and what you're doing. They resented the whole thing, even knowing that it was for the war effort, whatever it was. They felt it was too great a sacrifice.

C. MARC MILLER

Miller was involved in Army site selections during World War II. In early 1943, he was asked to prepare an area in the Priest Rapids Valley for acquisition.

The sight of military vehicles cruising through the valley started the talk. Upriver, a large parcel of land had been acquired for an artillery range and down at Pasco there was a Naval Air Station. But, the backroads connecting the orchards and tiny villages in between had never been thoroughfares for anything in the war effort. Nearby newspapers caught on to the story, but it didn't seem to rate the space that news from the front did.

They called in the Federal Land Bank appraisers to appraise the project. I was asked to stay as an adviser. The Federal Land Bank had had a very poor experience in the Priest Rapids Valley because they had made loans to soldier-farmers after World War I who failed in their loans. They had the attitude that the Priest Rapids was not a successful farming area, so when they made the appraisals, the appraisals were very low.

Well, then it was a matter of negotiating with the property owners for the acquisition of the land. The negotiators for the Corps of Engineers had offices in Prosser. They had great difficulty in negotiating for the acquisition of any of the land because of the very low appraisals. Much of it went into litigation. And because this was a very serious and important project, the U.S. Attorney in Oregon who had been handling many condemnation matters was brought to Yakima.

Now at that time, since I was under Civil Service and could no longer handle the acquisition, I resigned from the Corps of Engineers. After I resigned and after this negotiation was going on for the tracts, many property owners came to me and wanted me to help them in their sale to the government. I did join with them and I appraised much of their property and I appeared against the government and for the farmers who went to court.

We were quite successful and the U.S. Attorney was quite aware of the fact the prices were too low and the federal government finally reviewed the matter and asked that the old appraisals be thrown out and to reappraise all of the remaining tracts at the Hanford Project. I was employed to do that. I reappraised the Hanford tracts and we settled almost all of the claims.

LLOYD WIEHL

Wiehl's father homesteaded a fruit and livestock ranch out of sagebrush, and later operated a ferry between his ranch and White Bluffs. When the Manhattan Project arrived in Priest Rapids Valley, Wiehl was an attorney in Yakima and represented affected landowners.

It came like a bombshell. They announced they were taking the whole valley. For what? We didn't know. At that time, the farmers were short of money and didn't have any place to go, really. So eventually the government appraised it and put the money in escrow for the landowners to draw on. This was estimated as their just compensation.

What they did, they brought in Federal Land Bank people from clear out of the state, like Montana or elsewhere. They didn't understand the valley or fruit and they didn't think much of the valley and they brought in terribly low appraisals.

Highway robbery!

One case I handled, they went to a guy that had had a heart attack and was in his bed. Got him to sign off on property for what wouldn't even pay for the crop that was growing on it. I actually took it on the basis of fraud with the federal judge and he set aside the whole deal and awarded the family what was proper. The fellow was half dead when they got him to sign up. Then they bragged about it.

Charles Powell, later a federal judge from Kennewick, and I got together and we took most of these land cases to court and the verdicts were so much over the appraisals. We had them reappraised. It was so ridiculous that the government finally confessed that they were wrong. We settled nearly all of the cases out of court. If they'd gone ahead with that original deal and everybody had signed up, it would have been a tremendous injustice.

They didn't need to do that with all the waste I saw here that occurred after they started the project. They bulldozed good walls, they wouldn't let the farmers pick the good crops on the trees. They brought convicts from Walla Walla to pick them off the ground. It was ridiculous.

So we later went to court over the crops. Some of the crops brought, in court, more than what they had appraised the land for. One year's crop. We had to educate them, that's all.

It was a tremendous shock to these people who had lived here, then moved out with practically nothing. Not knowing what for. They wouldn't tell you a thing.

FRANK BUCK

By 1984, at the time of this interview, the Wanapum Tribe numbered two full-blooded survivors. One was Frank Buck, 16 years old when the Army came to build the Hanford Engineer Works. He was the son of Chief Johnny Buck, who became a friend of many Hanford project people. Frank worked at the Wanapum Dam information center, upstream from Hanford, talking to visitors about the history of his tribe.

We used to live in the tules (reed huts) until spring, then we take them apart, put them away and we move. First we move after the root feasts, clear up to Soap Lake and Waterville. Then down to Ellensburg. Horn Rapids for fishing. Naches Pass for berries and more fishing for several weeks.

After this we come back to Priest Rapids, where our home was for winter. We just went over this year after year. We just circle the same way every time.

When the Army came into Hanford, they said we can't go in there. Some years when this is all over, you can come back and fish again whenever you want to. But, now we can't do that.

Col. Franklin Matthias with two Wanapum leaders, Puck-hyah-toot and
Tamahl-wash, photographed at Hanford.   *U.S. Department of Energy*

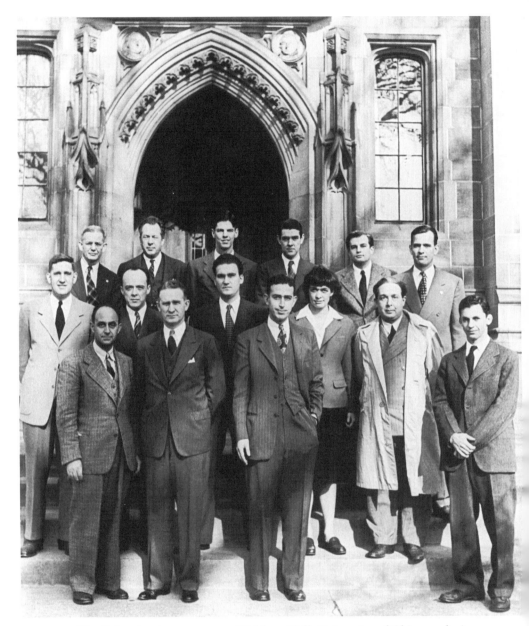

Met Lab scientists on steps of Eckhart Hall, University of Chicago, during a 1946 reunion. *Back row, left to right:* Norman Hilberry,* Samuel K. Allison, Thomas Brill, Robert G. Nobles, Warren Nyer* and Marvin Wilkening.* *Middle row:* Harold M. Agnew, William J. Sturm, Harold V. Lichtenberger, Leona Woods Marshall* (later Libby) and Leo Szilard. *Front row:* Enrico Fermi, Walter Zinn, Albert Wattenberg and Herbert L. Anderson.*

Argonne National Laboratory

* Interviewed for this book.

DESIGN:
THE MET LAB AND
DU PONT

W orld War II Hanford was built and operated by E.I. du Pont de Nemours & Company, Inc., a giant chemical and explosives firm with headquarters in Wilmington, Delaware. Hanford's scientific direction came from the Manhattan Project's code-named "Metallurgical Laboratory" at the University of Chicago. Officially, the Met Lab was called the Plutonium Project, but this name was too provocative for public use. Overall supervision at Hanford, as throughout the Manhattan Project, was by the U.S. Army Corps of Engineers.

Chicago's Met Lab scientists provided the theories that designers and engineers at Du Pont would transform into concrete and steel. Met Lab chemists did the laboratory work which led to successful separation of plutonium from the uranium fuel rods after the rods had been irradiated inside the reactors. Some 2,000 persons were employed at Chicago and 3,000 more worked for the Met Lab at other labs and facilities around the country.

Not long after he was appointed chief of the Manhattan Project in September, 1942, Leslie Groves agreed with Met Lab director Arthur H. Compton that an industrial firm with a "big job" history would be needed to assist in the emergency program for the production of plutonium. General Groves and Compton quickly realized Du Pont was the firm they wanted. Du Pont definitely was an unusual company. With a tradition of building its own plants, the firm had the resources for all aspects of manufacturing, from ground breaking to final product.

In Chicago, some scientists, most of them physicists, objected to the argument that a private firm would be needed to build and operate the plutonium plant. These scientists were suspicious of large industrial concerns and thought nuclear affairs should be left to nuclear specialists. But these objections were overcome by Du Pont's position as a world leader in the production of chemicals and explosives, and its wide experience in the construction of large production plants. The firm, founded in 1802 to make gunpowder, also had a reputation for conservative judgment and safety of operations. In the fall of 1942, the Manhattan Project turned to Du Pont and asked the company if it would design, engineer, construct and operate a large plant for an undertaking that was of utmost importance to the war effort.

Du Pont was uneasy about assuming responsibility for a project so far from its usual field. The firm remained skeptical of even basic aspects of the Plutonium Project until after Enrico Fermi demonstrated the chain reaction. Two days after the successful experiment, Du Pont was encouraged further by the issuance of the government's Lewis Committee report which said the Fermi pile process for making plutonium might provide "the possibility of earliest achievement of the desired result," referring to fissionable material for an atomic bomb.

In a stockholders' bulletin and a message to employees, both issued in August, 1945, after the war, Du Pont's president, W.S. Carpenter Jr., elaborated on the reasons for the company's lack of quick and positive response three years before. The company, he said, was burdened with other urgent war jobs. By the end of World War II, Du Pont had built 54 war plants at 32 locations, and had manufactured products varying from munitions and chemicals to synthetic rubber. Another reason for reluctance, Carpenter said, was that the company's speciality was chemistry, not nuclear physics.

But Groves had told Du Pont executives the stakes were high, and even though the government agreed with Du Pont that the project "was beyond human capability," the work had to be done. Groves said it was assumed the Germans were working on an atomic bomb and that there was no known defense against atomic weapons. His clinching point was that successful completion of the atomic bomb project would shorten the war and prevent many thousands of American casualties.

The company agreed to sign a contract, but only with certain conditions. The first was that the company would earn a profit of $1 on a cost-plus-fixed-fee basis. The company said any patent rights that developed would become the property of the government. In addition, because of the unknown and hazardous field it was entering, Du Pont wanted the government to provide protection against all costs, expenses, claims and losses. One unstated reason for Du Pont's insistence on $1 profit was to avoid a recurrence of the "merchants of death" accusations that followed World War I after allegations the company had engaged in war profiteering.

Du Pont's specific Plutonium Project responsibilities were to design and construct a small-scale research facility at the Clinton Engineer Works (Oak Ridge) in Tennessee and to design, construct and operate a large plant at Hanford. The Oak Ridge "semi-works," including the air-cooled X-10 reactor and a plutonium separations plant, would be operated under the direction of the University of Chicago. A large number of Du Pont people would be involved, and would help train personnel for future service at Hanford. The plutonium work was assigned to the Explosives Department, which created a new atomic energy division within Du Pont code-named "TNX."

Hanford was by far the biggest project Du Pont had ever built and operated. In mid-1944, Acting Secretary of War Robert Patterson wrote in a letter to Du Pont's Hanford project manager that Hanford "is still the most urgent construction project being carried out for the war effort…"

In his 1945 message, Carpenter made sure there was no confusion on one point: "The Du Pont Company did not, and does not, make atomic bombs. Our part in the project has been to produce one of the essential ingredients used in the ultimate construction of the weapon which helped to bring the war to an end."

All along Du Pont had insisted it was not interested in making plutonium after the war. After 1945, the company was eager to leave Hanford and return to its main business, which was chemicals and new product development, such as nylon and other man-made fibers. Consequently, in 1946, Du Pont left Hanford and General Electric took over as the government operations contractor. In 1950, however, Du Pont came back to the nuclear weapons business when it signed a contract to build the Savannah River, South Carolina, nuclear complex as part of the emergency program to build the hydrogen bomb.

Eugene Wigner, a refugee from Nazi Germany who led the scientists and engineers who designed the reactors built at Hanford.

Princeton University (postwar photo)

Leo Szilard, brilliant physicist, and colleague and friend of Wigner, was a key figure in early nuclear weapons history.

Argonne National Laboratories, 1960

EUGENE P. WIGNER

Professor Wigner and fellow Hungarian physicist Leo Szilard went to Albert Einstein in 1939 and convinced him of the need for America to develop an atomic bomb before Nazi Germany. Einstein's concerns eventually reached President Roosevelt and helped spark government interest and research which evolved into the Manhattan Project. After the Manhattan Project was underway, Wigner, who had done important work earlier on neutron absorption, moved to the Met Lab in Chicago as head of the theoretical physics group.

In his mid-eighties when interviewed at his Princeton University office, Wigner was physically small and a bit stooped, but jaunty with his black beret and energetic manner. His office was large, with many books and papers piled on tables and filing cabinets. The old physicist was unpreten-

tious and unfailingly polite, almost humble, although not in the least self-effacing. During a walk to a campus eating place and during lunch, he talked of his days in Berlin and of his friendships with Einstein, Szilard and mathematician "Johnny" von Neumann, another Hungarian who worked on the atomic bomb.

Wigner had known Einstein in Berlin and also at Princeton. At Princeton they took long walks together because both spoke German, which Einstein preferred in conversation. "He was not very talkative, not very quick in conversation, but he was a very deep thinker and a very friendly man," Wigner said.

In 1935, Wigner began teaching fulltime at Princeton after he was fired at the Institute of Technology in Berlin because his mother was Jewish.

When Wigner was 17, his father asked what he wanted to be and Wigner replied, "A physicist." His father wanted to know how many physicists there were in Hungary. "Four," Wigner replied. Following that conversation, Wigner studied chemical engineering and after getting his degree worked in a tannery for a time before going to Berlin to teach. Wigner said he never took a formal physics course in his life, except for the time he sat in on one to learn English. In 1963, he shared the Nobel Prize for physics.

I shouldn't boast but it is generally said, you see, I was in charge of the group which designed the reactors built at Hanford, and these reactors really worked. Fermi constructed the first nuclear reactor that really was reacting, but it had virtually no energy. And Alvin Weinberg, he designed almost alone the Oak Ridge pilot reactor. But the bigger reactors, we all designed together.

Really, there was no invention at all (with the Hanford reactors). There were only decisions to be made. To decide what kind of reactor to build, and how to extract the heat. But such a thing has many many factors in it, that the uranium should be put into aluminum, for instance, is an important thing. How the water should be pushed through, how the uranium fuel slugs should be located. The form of the inner structure of the (fuel) tubes. Many, many little things.

You see, I was educated as an chemical engineer, which came in very well, because I learned a lot of chemistry and that was very useful. I remember an instance, I don't know whether I should tell this story, but the Du Pont Company felt we should put some chromate, potassium bichromate, in the water to destroy the hydrogen peroxide, and they didn't realize the result of such reaction is the production of chromium hydroxide. It would deposit on the aluminum and decrease heat conductivity. I told them they should not do that. There are many, many little things, not little things, many things they were in error about because they were not at all familiar with nuclear reactions.

With Du Pont, the rule was this, they made the drawings but they submitted every drawing to us at Chicago to review, and we reviewed them, Weinberg, Gale Young and I and another man. We worked together and we discussed everything, but we had no conflicts. If somebody made a mistake, we tried to point it out and said, "Well, we'll change it." We felt when Du Pont took over it will delay things and it did, although it didn't matter as much as we were afraid it would.

The design of the Hanford reactor was submitted for typing just about a week after the Fermi chain reaction. Well, the Hanford reactor was an easy, a relatively easy, calculation. I carried it out. If I want to build a gate, we'll say, I always can do it and be confident it will work.

It is right I was in conflict at times with Du Pont, because it took much longer than reasonable and we were certainly afraid the Germans were ahead. But the Germans surrendered and they were not as close as we thought. But we thought they must be.

Du Pont had to learn so many little things which we knew already. That delayed things very badly. They sent every drawing to us in Chicago to review. We did that and many had serious failings. They did not understand the details of why we designed in a certain way. Why pipes had two ribs, why the sides of pipes were as we proposed, and we had to explain. I think it (Hanford reactors) could have been built probably nine months earlier.

The site was not unreasonable, but it doesn't matter where it is. Water is very important, but I think it should have been built on the Potomac, at the end of the Potomac River. General Groves felt a remote site was best. We did not object. We objected, at least I strongly objected to the Du Pont Company, which had no knowledge at all of nuclear physics, and very little knowledge of the other engineering problems. Otherwise we did not feel it was important whether it was at Hanford or close to Washington, D.C. The way I remember it we wanted to put it close to the end of the Potomac River. Chicago had two disadvantages. It had no fast river going through and second, eventually Lake Michigan would be contaminated. The Atlantic Ocean is much bigger than Lake Michigan, and the radiation was not much but just the same a significant amount.

Well, eventually Hanford worked, and Du Pont learned a lot. They did not close their eyes to facts of physics or engineering.

You know, I don't remember very well my visits to Hanford. I saw very little, and you see, when you see a nuclear reactor in operation, you see very little. They invited me, I think, principally out of politeness. It was a well-working reactor, unquestionably. Of course, it was our design. I was a little surprised at how large Hanford was, how much money and energy they put in. I thought it could have been done much cheaper, and much faster, much faster. Du Pont learned a great deal about nuclear physics at Hanford.

We were very much afraid of Hitler and I don't know the exact date but in Chicago we received a paper written by a friend, a German friend working on the German atomic effort and he was sent to Switzerland to do something. He was against Hitler and he told us, "Hurry up, we are on the track." You see, they were on the track theoretically, but in practice they were not. Hitler said Germany will win the war before this (atomic) weapon will be effective. Very few German physicists were really enthusiastic. In America, we thought it was very important to maintain freedom in the world and not a dictatorship of Hitler.

Perhaps I should mention that when the Germans surrendered and it was very evident it would be used against the Japanese, several of us felt it was unreasonable to destroy many Japanese lives in order to demonstrate it. We wrote, actually James Franck formulated it, a petition. We were practically all in favor of demonstrating the bomb in the presence of Japanese scientists and government men over uninhabited territory, hoping this will convince them. General Groves was very much against it. I don't know if the Nagasaki bomb was necessary, the first one apparently was necessary. I read a book by Feis (historian Herbert Feis), and he said it saved a million Japanese lives and perhaps 200,000 American lives. This struck me, and I asked my Japanese friends if an explosion as we proposed would have demonstrated the same thing and made it unnecessary to explode over a city. With one exception, they said it would not have convinced the Japanese emperor. You see, though, it is not a question which interests me because we can't change the past.

ALVIN M. WEINBERG

Alvin Weinberg joined the Met Lab in 1941 and became Eugene Wigner's neutron multiplication expert.* A small, forceful man, he was interviewed in Chapel Hill, North Carolina, where he delivered a memorial address for the late Henry Newson, a Duke University physicist and associate from the Manhattan Project. Weinberg was director of the Oak Ridge National Laboratory from 1955 until 1974.

I was working in mathematical biophysics at the University of Chicago. One of my professors asked me to help him out for six months at half-time on the uranium project which he had got involved in, and I began in 1941. We both were rather skeptical it would amount to very much. He asked me because it turned out there was quite a bit of analogy between the mathematics used in calculating how nuclear reactors would work and how cells work. So, with my biophysics background, I had a little bit of a head start.

Eugene Wigner came to Chicago as head of the theoretical group and I became one of his assistants. The job he gave me was to estimate and keep track of the value of the neutron multiplication factor in the reactors. You must realize since we were trying to make a chain reaction with natural uranium and graphite that it was a very close thing whether it would work at all.

---

* When the uranium isotope U-235 fissions, or splits, particles of the atomic nucleus called neutrons are ejected. In nature, if uranium fissions, most of the ejected neutrons are captured by the atoms of another uranium isotope called U-238, which is not readily fissionable. The fission process then stops because not enough additional U-235 is split to sustain a chain reaction.

If, however, the speeding neutrons are slowed by a substance physicists call a "moderator," such as graphite or heavy water, and refined natural uranium and graphite are arranged properly, the chance they will strike other U-235 atoms and cause fission is much increased. In the early days of nuclear physics, this arrangement of graphite and uranium in a lattice-like configuration was called an atomic pile because, in simple terms, it was a pile of uranium lumps and graphite blocks.

Physicists used the symbol "k" to indicate the average number of neutrons generated or multiplied in a given pile design, and also to measure the quality of a pile's U-235-splitting effectiveness. In order to keep the chain reaction going, "k" must be 1 or greater. When a U-235 atom fissions, on average it emits more than two neutrons. But not all are available for further fissions because some are lost through escape from the reactor, and some are absorbed by the graphite or other neutron-absorbing impurities inside the pile.

It wasn't until May, 1942, that the experiments were sufficiently successful to demonstrate quite clearly you could make a chain reaction.

It was simply this. If everything absolutely went in the very best possible way, then the multiplication factor that we calculated was about 1.08. But things would never be that good. There would be impurities, which captured neutrons, and you would have to put coolant in and have cladding on the fuel elements and so on, all of which absorbed neutrons, and the multiplication constant might turn out to be 1.01. If it were only 1.01 the reactors would have to be miles big, the bigger the multiplication the smaller the reactor. In a bomb, the multiplication is around 2.0 and so the bomb is small. The bomb, of course, had a high multiplication factor because it was made of almost pure U-235 (or Pu-239). In a reactor, we were working with natural uranium, of which fissionable U-235 is only $1/140$ of the whole.

But Wigner was very confident it would work. He played the absolutely central role in the Hanford reactors. He was really the inventor of the Hanford reactors. The original direction was to use helium as the coolant. Wigner objected because he said the materials problem would be difficult to solve in a short time. The helium-cooled reactor was a very high temperature device and he said you should shift to a lower-temperature reactor and cool it with water and clad the uranium with aluminum. By the spring of 1942, long before the first chain reaction was demonstrated, he had begun design studies on a plant with water cooling. I was doing the estimates of the multiplication factor, the theoretical work, and Herb Anderson, among others, was involved in the experiments.

Wigner convinced Arthur Compton it was a good idea to pursue water cooling seriously and it became more and more important. When the Du Pont Company was brought in, later in 1942, they made a study of the different possibilities of helium and water and decided Wigner was right.

Wigner had his little group. His primary assistant was Gale Young, I was there, a fellow from Belgium, an engineer, and Miles Leverett, now very prominent in atomic engineering, designed the reactor mechanism, Leo Ohlinger, who drew pictures and did some of the design and Ed Creutz, a physicist, who suggested the actual cooling arrangement for the fuel slugs. In something like three months, between September, 1942, and January, 1943, Wigner and his little group worked at a feverish pace, you wouldn't believe, we worked every single day, including Sunday, actually working out the detailed design of the reactors built at Hanford.

When I say detailed design, I really mean that, how the connections would go, bringing the cooling water in, how you remove the irradiated slugs, whether to make it vertical or horizontal, the size of the reactor.

Wigner and I decided what the lattice spacing would be. I remember clearly doing the calculations and going into his office one day and we looked at the numbers, and we said, "Well, should we make it this or that? Let's make it more like that." The lattice spacing was 8 3/8 inches, that was close to the optimum and happened to be the size the graphite blocks came in. We did all the details, how the slugs would look, how they would fit in the tubes, every single one of these details was essentially controlled by Wigner, and some very able people helped him.

The Hanford design culminated in a report, called process design for a water-cooled plant, and the number was CE-407, January, 1943. It was probably the second-most important report of the Manhattan Project, the first being the report on the first chain reaction. The remarkable thing was that Wigner had the nerve to design a big reactor, and had the design essentially complete before the first chain reaction was established. In fact, Wigner would sometimes say, he wasn't quite serious about it, that he was so confident the chain reaction would work that he wouldn't attend the first one. But he did, and he broke out the bottle of Chianti to celebrate.

The unique thing about Wigner was that he was the only one on the project, and in this he actually exceeded Fermi, who had such a complete understanding and interest both in the physics and the engineering. Fermi was mostly interested in the physics but if need be would get involved in engineering. It was Wigner who did both. In any design, you have to make compromises, you have to be very confident of your knowledge.

Du Pont, with Crawford Greenewalt as contact man, took Wigner's preliminary process design and made it into the actual engineered device. It was very close to Wigner's design. The Du Pont blueprints were sent back to Chicago and examined in detail by Wigner. One of the foremost theoretical physicists in the world during the war did the most detailed kind of engineering. It was that sense of responsibility he had that was so extraordinary and important.

The Du Ponts also did something which was relatively important. The question was how big to make the reactor. We said 1,500 fuel tubes was okay, which meant the reactor was like a big cylinder with a circular cross-section. But it was built with corners and the Du Pont engineers, who were rather conservative, said, "Let's fill in the corners with fuel tubes." We didn't make a big fuss, so they made the actual reactor with 2,004 tubes, which turned out to be really quite helpful because of the xenon poisoning, which occurred with the first reactor at Hanford. We didn't think the poisoning would happen, although John Wheeler had looked at all the fission product possibilities. It was theoretically possible, but it was a sheer fluke it turned out to be xenon, which decays with a rather short half-life, so it didn't screw up the whole project.

Wigner likes to say I designed by myself the X-10 reactor at Oak Ridge in early 1943, but it really wasn't much of a thing. There really wasn't much design that had to be done there. I was responsible for deciding what the lattice spacing was (the geometry of the nuclear pile). You see, the multiplication constant depends on what that lattice spacing is. That really was what he meant by design.

The X-10 at Oak Ridge was simpler than Hanford because X-10 was air cooled. The question of the multiplication was much less sensitive. Wigner objected to the X-10's air cooling because he said it wouldn't be an adequate prototype for the Hanford reactors because Hanford's were to be water cooled.

The significance of the X-10 to Hanford was that nobody had ever extracted plutonium on a large scale, separation had always been done on a micro-scale. This was the first time in human history that mankind was handling radioactivity on this enormous scale. That was what Oak Ridge was set up for, to see if this whole thing would work when you had this intense radioactivity. X-10 was the first reactor that produced significant amounts of heat, a thousand kilowatts. Secondly, it was the first reactor in which sizeable amounts, meaning gram quantities, of plutonium were produced, about one gram a day. The Hanford reactors each one initially produced about 250 grams a day.

Side by side with the X-10 was an elaborate chemical plant quite a bit like the Hanford chemical plant. It was more like the Hanford chemical plant than the X-10 was like the Hanford reactors. Clinton Labs (Oak Ridge) was mainly set up to practice extracting plutonium. Du Pont people destined to go to Hanford stopped in Oak Ridge for several months or as long as a year, learning the chemical plant and practicing on the reactor.

There was always a bit of tension between Wigner's group and the Du Pont people. Wigner at the time thought Du Pont wasn't moving fast enough. He was wrong on that. He was wrong to think the scientists could build the reactors themselves. Wigner threatened to leave the project. On one occasion, he was like Achilles, sulking in his tent. But when he sulked in his tent, that didn't mean he wasn't working. He stayed home and worked three times as hard.

You see, Wigner and his friend Leo Szilard really had more or less first-hand contact with the Nazis. They lived in mortal terror of them. One interesting sidelight is that at Christmas time, 1943, Arthur Compton asked Fermi, Wigner and myself to come to his office. What we were supposed to do was estimate when we thought the Germans might have an atomic bomb. This estimate would be passed on to James Conant, who was in the White House as a presidential adviser. Wigner always hedged his estimates in the most pessimistic way. If it turned out better he would feel good. Wigner wrote on the blackboard it would take the Germans two months to build a reactor, three months to take the plutonium out, two months to make the bomb, by Christmas of 1944, they would have the bomb. That scared us shitless, I guess you would say.

Szilard was always sort of the gadfly. He was always marvelously imaginative. He really didn't have the scientific power that Wigner had. Szilard had a certain kind of genius in that he was extraordinarily imaginative and original. Wigner had that, but he also had enormous scientific power. I mean by this, that any problem that was solvable, Wigner could solve. Szilard didn't have that capacity. Wigner is not known well by the public because he is rather retiring. Among physicists he is known totally. Fortune magazine described Wigner as the quiet genius who singlehandedly invented much of modern physics. So much of modern physics' structure and so on goes back to Wigner. His role in the Manhattan Project is not fully appreciated and the entirely central role he played. You would not have had Hanford on the time schedule you did had it not been for Wigner.

When it comes to my own ideas on nuclear weapons, I wrote a paper which appeared in the Bulletin of the Atomic Scientists (Dec., 1985) about what I called "the sanctification of Hiroshima." What I said, although I signed the Franck Petition suggesting that a demonstration be made of the bomb in an uninhabited area, was that I never have been concerned about dropping the bomb because I tended and still tend to believe that on balance you probably saved lives by dropping the bomb. The point of my article was that the 40th anniversary of Hiroshima was almost what one could describe as a religious outpouring of concern over the Hiroshima incident. It seemed to me the bomb at Hiroshima was beginning to acquire a kind of transcendent significance which can almost be described as having semi-religious overtones. I think that is a very important, very proper and desirable development. We're going to live with nuclear weapons forever, or the next 50 years, 100 years, 1,000 years.

The significance of Hiroshima is being made somehow part of the myth of mankind, in somewhat the same sense that the Holocaust is becoming a myth among Jews today or the crucifixion, if you like. I said I did not believe a test of the bomb could ever be made into a religious myth. Only because 100,000 people or more were killed can that event be mythologized, or canonized.

I don't think the second bomb, the Nagasaki bomb, was necessary. No, that was strictly General Groves. In fact, I was drinking whiskey with Groves one night in a hotel bar in New York after the war and he more or less agreed the second bomb was not needed. He didn't say why. Groves was first of all a military man.

NORMAN HILBERRY

Physicist Norman Hilberry was Arthur H. Compton's righthand man at the Metallurgical Project, the associate director who handled administrative chores. Thin and frail at 86-years old, yet forceful in his recollections, he was interviewed in 1985 at his residence in Tucson, where he was a professor at the University of Arizona.

I was teaching at NYU and Ann and I had gone into our first faculty party just before Christmas '41. Our babysitter called and told us a telegram had come. It was from Compton. "Have important war job for you. Please report earliest possible moment." I got on the train and went to Chicago, PDQ. He told me what he could. I went to the Physical Society meeting to recruit and reported back to Chicago in January of '42.

Our first meeting was the first weekend in January. All physicists. There was Fermi's group and Szilard's group from Columbia. There was Wigner from Princeton, John Wheeler was in that group, there was the Chicago group. At that meeting every reactor type was discussed. The decision was to use a gas-cooled reactor purely for neutron absorption reasons. The fact was that when we got the first Chicago pile running and found how much excess reactivity we had, then water made so much more sense than gas as a cooling agent that we ran a set of experiments using paraffin as a stand-in for water and obviously it would work. Later on, the design for a gas-cooled one was almost complete and Du Pont made the decision and said the simplicity of the water-cooled design is so much greater than the complex mechanical engineering for loading and unloading the gas cooled one that we think there is no real reason for a gas-cooled reactor, it has to be the water-cooled machine.

Compton ran the operation by commune procedure because these longhairs, well, this was the only way you do it. We gathered every Wednesday and they chewed the rag and expressed their differences of opinion unmistakably. Colonel James C. Marshall of the Army Corps of Engineers (temporary chief of the Manhattan Engineer District) was in one meeting and after the meeting was over he came over and put his arm around my shoulder. He said, "Look, Hilberry, it sounded to me that these guys were saying they think a single bomb, or two, is all that's necessary." I said "Yes, quite definitely that's what most of them would believe."

He said, "Look, let me just sketch you in on the basic military mind and ethics and philosophy. You never use a weapon that you cannot continue to use once you use the first. We are not talking about A device, we are talking about the construction of production facilities to make these in whatever quantities it turns out are necessary for national protection."

Well, this just sent cold chills up and down my back because when you start talking about production facilities I knew enough about this to know that this is going to take a very very different slant.

Well, when it became clear this was a production matter, Groves sized the thing up in a hurry and he said as far as he knew there is only one organization in the country that in his opinion can handle this kind of thing and that's Du Pont. Groves said we simply have got to get Du Pont to do this.

Groves said that this had to be a production operation, and we've got to have a production outfit do it. Folks like Wigner, in particular, just blew their tops. "This is absolutely impossible. Just terrible." I went into see Wigner one day and he jumped up and down, and said "Give me some hacksaws and a couple of hammers and we'll do better than any damned Du Pont Company."

Du Pont was approached, and said, "Look, the last war left us called 'merchants of death.' We are damned if we are going to get in this situation again. This is just utterly impossible." Groves said, "Well maybe it's impossible but you're going to do it." "Says who?" says Du Pont. We had a meeting with the Du Pont executive committee. Groves, Compton, I was there, and went over this thing. And boy, that bunch, you understood why Du Pont was the company it was. They were the hardest-nosed, sharpest bunch of characters you ever ran into.

They even made Compton mad. You see this must have been in October or early November of '42. The guy that was head of the committee turned to Arthur finally, and he said, "Look, now be realistic. You haven't even proved the scientific feasibility of this business, yet you are asking us to undertake engineering on something you haven't even gotten out of the laboratory. I don't think you stand more than a three percent chance of getting it out of the laboratory." A.H. just went through the roof. He said, "If you have no greater faith than that, it's proof that you don't have the policies necessary to carry it out." Finally, they said, "We'll do it on one condition only. That the Du Pont Company take be $1 and that we have a signed letter from the President of the United States ordering us, essentially, to do it." Groves said, "You will have it in the morning," and they did. That was the start.

Du Pont took absolutely no responsibility for the basic science. That's yours, they said. We will take full responsibility for the engineering development, for the construction and for the operation. The cut was clean. A straight, clean operation. When they agreed to do it, okay they took over. The shift supervisors, when we got to operations, most of them, were at least assistant plant managers, they hadn't done shift work for years. Du Pont said everything hangs on this. When we play, we play for keeps. They did, there wasn't any question. They put the best people they had on at every point.

The physics went along amazingly well. There were four projects to obtain fissionable fuel at the start. Our first instructions in December of '41, were that we were to do the reactor business, but also the fast neutron work, which meant designing the bomb, a job taken over later by Los Alamos. That summer, the boys at California had come up with the fact, okay, you could make plutonium if you had lots of neutrons, and plutonium was probably a better fissionable material than uranium 235. So, our instructions had been changed to do all things possible to produce plutonium in quantities of military significance.

I went to Hanford the first time in July, '44. Then very shortly, the group went in to test the effects of the Columbia on the fish (see Chapter 8). It became clear that if anything happened to the salmon, the hell with the United States.

Du Pont had said at one time to give me a good title. In the Du Pont Company, titles count, they said. If he's got a good title it will help in many ways, so I was made assistant director of the overall project. I went back and forth from Chicago on the railroad so often that one of the porters said to me one day, "Boss, us porters has decided youse the only guy who rides this train more than we do."

Really, at Hanford, there was no sense the production or separations process might not work, as far as I know. Before the development work, before the process started at Oak Ridge, perhaps yes. But Seaborg's first separation at Chicago, the sample that's in the Smithsonian, I guess, now, indicated quite clearly that you can recover plutonium from uranium used in a chain reaction.

One difference I continually had with Groves was his belief we were perfectly safe because none of the other countries in the world had our great engineering, our technological knowledge. I told General Groves to remember that our dye industry was constantly struggling to keep its head above water against the German industry. There's always more than one way of killing a cat. You don't have to choke it with hot butter. A group of senators came out once to Chicago to look at our operation. I said don't let Groves give you a cockeyed picture that other folks can't do what we are doing, because anybody that is willing to do it can do it.

The thing that impressed us was that when we carried out a review of four major systems of getting fissionable material—plutonium reactors, gaseous diffusion, electromagnetic and centrifuge—all four systems looked as if they would work. Instead of being able to say it can't be done, you had to say it is almost impossible for anybody that really wants to do it to go wrong because anything he does will work.

One thing you should ask Fritz Matthias. He was noted for a story he told the business people in Kennewick and Pasco who were continually trying to find out what on earth was going on at Hanford. Fritz finally gave in and went to a luncheon and talked about the project, then he said I understand all of you folks are curious about what we are making. He told them he didn't want anyone to pass it on, but what we are making out there are wheels for miscarriages.

HERBERT L. ANDERSON

Herbert Anderson was completing his graduate studies in physics in 1939 at Columbia University when he began a close scientific and personal association with Enrico Fermi that was to continue until Fermi's death in 1954. Anderson assisted Fermi in early research on nuclear fission, including Fermi's direction of the first chain reaction. Anderson himself, early in 1939 at Columbia, performed the experiment which resulted in the first observation of fission in the United States. The two men worked together at the Argonne Forest near Chicago on design features of the Hanford reactors.

Fermi went to Stockholm with his family in late 1938 to accept the Nobel Prize for physics. Afterward, instead of returning home to Italy he emigrated to the United States to escape Italy's anti-Jewish laws, which had put his wife, Laura, in jeopardy. Fermi accepted a professorship at Columbia University in New York City.

At the time of the interview in Los Alamos, Anderson was a professor emeritus at the University of Chicago, but had retired to Los Alamos where he was doing protein biology research. He was a small man, and rather curt in conversation. He spoke fondly of Fermi, and on the wall of the office was a small painting of his friend. Next to it was a photograph of the Trinity shot, taken by Anderson using a hand-held movie camera.

I think I could tell you a little bit about the very early days when I was working with Enrico Fermi. I remember I had gotten my Ph.D and I was wondering what I would be doing, and Fermi persuaded me to continue to work with him. He felt, although I don't think he had at the time a clear idea of what was involved, that if you worked on the chain reaction, that would be the quickest way to producing a bomb.

There was a question of who thought of plutonium first, and the credit usually was given to Prof. Louis Turner of Princeton, who wrote it up in an article. He pointed out that if you captured neutrons on uranium-238, you ultimately made plutonium-239. I don't want to claim that Fermi already had that idea but the idea was taken seriously by Turner and that was a start. It had been presumed plutonium-239 was fissionable because of the Bohr-Wheeler theory that if the isotope was an odd number instead of even it would behave similarly to uranium-235. People were fairly convinced of that.

Hanford itself was a factory. The basic process had been worked out at Chicago and, to some extent, at Oak Ridge. Hanford was always referred to as the production plant. I was never at Hanford. I spent a lot of time at Wilmington [Du Pont's headquarters], in fact that's how I got to know Crawford Greenewalt (Du Pont's technical liaison with the Met Lab, and later president of the company). He wanted a scientist in Wilmington to consult and to help and give advice about the nuclear physics involved. I went there for not quite a year. I spent time designing the Hanford test reactor and looked over the plans for the big reactors to see if the design was sound.

A characteristic thing about Hanford is that the site is enormous, but the reactor is a very small thing and all the rest is water treatment. Most of the money went into water treatment. It isn't clear to me, but the weight of evidence is that it was more economic to build a water-cooled reactor than a gas-cooled one. Wigner and his group at the Met Lab designed the water-cooled reactor, and the Du Pont people took that design and turned it into a realistic engineering design and then Du Pont did the construction design.

Friction between the Du Pont people and the Met Lab scientists was always a problem. It was handled beautifully by Greenewalt. His key engineers learned a lot, worked hard, asked lots of questions. They weren't bashful about asking questions. Of course, there were always academic types who were very suspicious of big industries. They thought industries were out for themselves, making profit and so on. The fact of the matter is that the Du Pont Company, according to its contractual agreement, said it would be reimbursed for all costs and $1 profit. They certainly didn't make any money out of it. I think they looked at the whole enterprise from beginning to the end as a public service, and didn't want any suggestion it was anything but a public service.

I remember discussing it with Crawford Greenewalt when I traveled to and from Wilmington with him. I said I bet Du Pont will go into nuclear energy after the war and make a big thing of it because you know so much more than anybody else. He said, "No, we are going to go into nylon, and make nylon stockings. We can make more money that way."

You know, I discovered, it was a great eye-opener for me, an academic type with all the suspicions academics have about industry. It was an eye opener to discover how competent these guys were. How important it was to have not only the competence but also the number of people who got involved in this planning, that really was necessary. So many details have to be followed, and only by having a huge engineering organizatioin can you attend to that. I think the idea that Wigner had that he could manage that is just unrealistic. There is no way an academic can learn quickly how to handle a vast engineering organization. I remember there were 300 engineers designing things, and attending to procurement problems, knowing whom to call, how to get the cement and the other things. That takes a vast experience, that Du Pont had. To General Groves' credit he realized that.

Nuclear weapons, well, that's a complicated question. On the one hand nuclear weapons are a disaster, and a major concern for all mankind and we would be better off not to have them. But we do have them. They do exist. You have to deal with that. It is unfortunate. Right after the war, I played a role with my associates to tell people how dangerous they were and that there ought to be some kind of international agreement. That never worked out. It is easy enough to say we don't need nuclear weapons. I guess I am sufficiently a hawk to feel that if you don't have a strong position militarily, nobody talks to you. I believe if you aren't strong, you don't have a voice. I believe we have to be involved in the decision-making process. You can't delegate political dominance to somebody else.

I did not work on nuclear weapons after 1945, but I don't turn my back on the weapons. Nuclear weapons are a great anomaly. Spending so much money on something you never will use.

JOHN MARSHALL

John Marshall lived in a low, rambling white house on the edge of the mesa in Los Alamos. Athletic and tanned, he was a hiker and cat lover, and spent a lot of time in his greenhouse. A close associate of Enrico Fermi and Herbert L. Anderson, Marshall also had worked with physicist Leo Szilard, one of the most influential figures in the history of atomic energy.

It was Szilard who applied for a patent in 1934, in England, which described the physical laws governing a chain reaction. The year before, while walking in London and waiting for a red light, it occurred to Szilard that "if we could find an element which is split by neutrons and which would emit two neutrons when it absorbed one neutron, such an element, if assembled in sufficiently large mass, could sustain a chain reaction." He said the thought "became sort of an obsession with me."

Working with Albert Einstein, and two fellow Hungarians, Eugene Wigner and Edward Teller, Szilard was a key figure in alerting President Roosevelt to the possibility Germany would build an atomic bomb. Marshall met Szilard in 1941.

During the Manhattan Project years, Marshall was married to physicist Leona Libby, the most well-known of the few women scientists in the bomb project. They went to Hanford together in 1944.

I got my doctorate in physics in 1941 at the University of Rochester. At that point, the group under Fermi and Szilard was at Columbia University. They were trying to answer some questions, to carry the investigation further. Szilard was a very bright guy, but not very good with his hands. He wasn't an experimentalist in any sense. Well, he wasn't a hands-on experimentalist. He was looking for somebody to be his hands and he must have asked Victor Weisskopf who was at Rochester if there were anybody around who would be available and Weisskopf gave him my name. I visited Szilard at Columbia and he gave me a long rambling account of what the problems were. Next thing I knew, I was hired.

The project was in full swing at that point. They were interested in finding out whether it was possible to make a chain reaction in a pile. There had been a series of experiments and new experiments were coming up. There was an effort being made to find a source of graphite which was pure, had less boron in it or whatever other neutron-absorbing impurities there might be. Also, they were looking for pure uranium and making it suitable for putting in a reactor. There was a system worked out by I guess mostly Fermi, called an exponential pile, which generally consisted of a stack of graphite in the shape of a prism, higher than it was wide and deep.

I did whatever needed doing at Columbia. For instance, Szilard was doing some experiments on spontaneous fission, photo-neutrons, photofission, gamma ray induced fission. All of which would be relevant to a chain reaction. I was still Szilard's hands, to some extent. Szilard tended to do things he was interested in, then he would switch over and be interested in something else with great enthusiasm.

Somehow, I found myself measuring neutron distribution in exponential piles, then in the construction of them. Getting the graphite machined, pressing uranium lumps that went into it. All this was in the fall of 1941. Along about Christmas, well, there was a group at Princeton, there was Sam

Allison's group at Chicago, and isotope separation at Berkeley, us at Columbia, and they wanted to bring the thing together. They wanted someone to head it up and that was Arthur Compton, so the chain reaction group was moved to Chicago shortly after Christmas, 1941.

At Chicago, again I got mixed up with one of Szilard's enthusiasms which was to try to get uranium metal for fuel instead of uranium oxide. For quite a while I was busy trying to figure out how to cast uranium, making vacuum furnaces and trying to melt some small samples that Szilard had managed to scrounge up someplace. Metal was somewhat better in the pile, it was denser and tended to enhance the lumpiness of the geometry of the system. You just don't mix the uranium or the heavy water and the uranium, whatever it is, but you put the uranium in lumps. That was probably Fermi's idea.

Fermi was a marvelous guy, I liked him very much. He was an extremely productive person. He had an active imagination and he didn't waste time. If he was doing something, he would do it, instead of wandering around thinking of what he ought to be doing. He was very much a hands-on physicist, but he also was a very competent theorist. When he built experimental apparatus, it was no better than it had to be, in fact, it was downright sloppy at times. But it would get the work done. If a new idea came into his mind, he would work on it very rapidly until he got sufficient stuff to come to some sort of conclusion. Then he would publish immediately. If somebody else got the same idea he did from the same source at the same time, Fermi would be there a month ahead.

I was in rather close contact with Szilard until the end of 1942. Szilard was one of these guys who is a little bit too bright. He had the right conclusion as to what should be done but it would turn out in practice to be something that couldn't be done for 20 years. Like he was insisting that the Hanford production reactors should be liquid metal-cooled. Now that is the way you do high-performance reactors nowadays but to try to have done that in the time available then was not possible. He was irritated by what he called quote engineers sneer unquote, particularly the Du Pont engineers. At one point, I'm told he went to Arthur Compton and said the engineers were getting intolerable. Either they had to be fired or he was going to quit. Compton said, "You have just resigned." After half an hour Compton cooled off and came back and said, "I didn't mean that, Leo."

For a while, I was at Indiana University, with Louis Slotin, to run a cyclotron experiment, measuring temperature co-efficients, to find what effect temperature of the uranium lumps would have on reactivity. I went back to Chicago, and they were moving the original pile out to the Argonne site. We were happily doing experiments of various sorts, Fermi, Wally Zinn, Leona, measuring neutron cross-sections and god knows what. We used that reactor as a source of neutrons. By then, it was 1943.

Well, I was interested in staying with the reactors, to see them going, and the Du Pont Company was in charge at Hanford, so I got a job with Du Pont in January, 1944. I stayed at Argonne for six more months, mostly working on dull stuff figuring out all sorts of procedures of how to start up a reactor and how to operate it. In June Leona and I went to Hanford.

(Marshall's interview continues in Chapter 5, p 159)

MILES C. LEVERETT

When World War II came along, Miles Leverett was a young Ph.D chemical engineer working for Humble Oil & Refining Co. in Houston. One day his boss, who had disappeared from Houston not long before, telephoned from Chicago and asked Leverett if he wanted to work on a war project. Leverett did, and eventually became associated closely with the helium-cooled reactor proposal at the Met Lab. In addition, he was part of design engineering for the mechanical aspects of the Hanford reactors, and was initially in charge of the engineering group attached to X-10, the small air-cooled reactor at Oak Ridge.

After the war, Leverett continued a distinguished career in nuclear engineering, a field he pioneered, with an emphasis on reactor safety. He was interviewed in his office at the Electric Power Research Institute at Palo Alto, Calif.

When my boss T.V. Moore asked me if I wanted to come to work on a war project, the whole thing sounded pretty flaky because he couldn't tell me what I would be doing or where I would be located. I told him I would need some time to think it over. So, a couple of weeks later he called again. He said you've had time to think it over now, and I want you to come up to Chicago and meet me at the Miramar Hotel on 63rd Street in south Chicago, by a certain date, which I think was May 18 of 1942. I did. That evening, when I got to Chicago, he met me and took me to the hotel where he was staying, and he and Dick Doan, R.L. Doan, told me what the project was all about. He went into enough detail to say it was an atomic weapon, describe its power, what the Metallurgical Lab was trying to do, what its role was, an idea what I would be doing. Of course, that was a tremendous shock, the idea there could be anything that big, and that powerful, and the chance of working on it was obviously something I couldn't pass up. I stayed.

We knew Germany was working on the same thing. That was a strong motivation. I remember T.V.'s remark "If some morning you wake up and read in the newspaper that half of Germany has disappeared, well, you'll know what the reason was."

My first assignment at the Met Lab was to work on the helium- cooled reactor. Chemical engineers are supposed to know something about heat transfer, fluid flow and this reactor was supposed to be cooled by flowing helium, so the job was to work on heat transfer and to some extent on the mechanical aspects of it.

It wasn't long after that that the Army brought Du Pont into the picture, late '42. Also, the physicists were pushing the idea that the reactors should be water-cooled. I think not because they thought it was inherently better but to have a second string to the bow. The more we went into the helium-cooled thing, the more we realized high temperatures were going to be a big problem. When Du Pont came in they looked at the helium-cooled reactor and said we can get it loaded and we can get it unloaded once, we can't guarantee that it will be more than that. Because of mechanical problems. The fuel handling mechanism in the helium-cooled design was located in the bottom of the reactor which was the highest-temperature location. They felt very uneasy about the long life of that part.

There was an advantage to helium because it is a chemically inert gas, it doesn't combine with anything so it would not corrode the graphite which was to be used as the moderator, would not corrode steel, would not corrode uranium or the coating on the uranium. Those were the principal reasons. As gases go, it was a good coolant, and provided a low absorption rate for neutrons, much less than water, in fact essentially zero. But, people felt so much more at ease using water-cooling and aluminum tubes. We had succeeded in cladding the uranium in aluminum shells. It was not long before everyone agreed that approach probably should be the main line.

There was some doubt at first that water would work because it is a fairly good neutron absorber, the hydrogen atoms in water are good neutron absorbers. But water also would moderate the neutrons, which we wanted. The experiments that were done indicated you probably could make a chain reaction with water cooling and aluminum tubes. There would be enough reactivity to make it work. I think basically it was Du Pont's decision. They were brought in to do the engineering work, and this was obviously an engineering decision.

It was my job primarily to review the Du Pont designs as an engineer, from the point of view of the Metallurgical Laboratory. Du Pont knew nothing about nuclear engineering, in fact there wasn't any nuclear engineering.

My direct connection with the Hanford reactors essentially ceased when I moved to Oak Ridge, in September '43. Before that, it was a matter of working on the cladding of the uranium, looking at the preliminary drawings of the Hanford reactors. There was additional heat exchange work to be done, but Du Pont had people who were quite capable in that area. There was a lot of corrosion work which had to be started.

I don't recall there was a great deal of worry that the Hanford reactors wouldn't work. If there were a deficiency of neutrons, if "k" were not quite big enough, you'd simply have to build the reactor bigger. If "k" got to be less than one, of course, no matter how big, it still wouldn't work. I don't think there was much concern it would be that bad. In fact I have a joint patent with Fermi in which the very ingenious solution we came up with was, if you don't know how big to build a reactor, build it bigger than you think you have to. Put in some extra holes. Fermi, incidentally, was a very nice person to work with. He was meticulous in his work, but there was nothing pretentious about the man at all. No pomposity or anything of that sort which you saw in some of the scientists, particularly the Europeans.

DALE BABCOCK

Dale Babcock was a physical chemist and colleague of Crawford Greenewalt, himself a chemical engineer who married a Du Pont and eventually became president of the company. Greenewalt had been working in the development of nylon, but had to put that aside when he became technical director of the firm's Manhattan Project contracts. Greenewalt took Babcock and a few other close Du Pont colleagues with him into the new world of atomic energy. Although Babcock eventually became an expert on nuclear reactors, he also did research on heavy water, an expensive and difficult alternative for graph-ite in reactor operation.

One of Babcock's concerns after the Manhattan Project began in earnest was how to keep the neutron count high enough in a reactor to keep the reaction alive. In addition, Babcock studied "fission products," substances formed during the atom-splitting process, some of which might absorb so many neutrons that the nuclear reaction would be "poisoned" and "die." In fact, this dreaded event did occur at Hanford and years later Babcock wrote the definitive article on it for the journal "Nuclear News," (Sept., 1964) giving credit for solution of the reactor riddle to physicist John A. Wheeler.

During the interview in his residence at Cokesbury Village near Wilmington, Babcock was dignified and meticulous, and careful to explain any point that might be confusing. He was proud of Du Pont's part in the Manhattan Project, particularly the competence and speed displayed in the construction and operation of the Hanford Engineer Works.

I went out to the Du Pont Experimental Station in 1929, after I received my doctorate from the University of Illinois. I was a physical chemist and rather long-haired I would say. Working with chemical engineers was, well, something outside my field. After I learned that the only real difference between a physical chemist and a chemical engineer was that they spoke in pounds and we spoke in grams, there was no problem.

My first assignment was under Crawford Greenewalt, who was directing a modest-sized group of chemists working in organic synthesis and separation of products. Crawford went up the ladder relatively rapidly and soon became assistant director of the laboratory. Then the war was coming on, it was 1939. When Du Pont got into atomic energy, Crawford Greenewalt was one of the top people, and he took certain of us along with him, people he knew and had worked with.

In November of '42, Crawford called a few of us together, Lom Squires, Monte Evans, Hood Worthington and myself, some others, and said, "I am going to describe to you people something that is heresy to chemists. We are going to make a new atom, on a scale of pounds per year. That new element is plutonium." To persons who were chemists all their lives, that was heresy, absolute heresy. If he had said micrograms, it would have been no problem. He described what had been done by Seaborg and Compton and Fermi and the whole works. But, nothing would be done for now, go back and continue working in nylon, he told us. Crawford saw the Chicago reactor go critical in December and he came back all excited, and about at this time I was taken out of nylon and put on this development full time as the liaison between Du Pont and the Chicago group in the area of physics and reactor control.

That's when I met Fermi. He let me run the reactor in Chicago after I expressed an interest in control, how we could keep things from getting out of hand. Control is no problem, Fermi said. "Sit down here at the controls," he said. I leveled it out after three or four minutes and his words were, "You are indeed a very careful young man." I wasn't much younger than he. I was 36.

Things happened rapidly after that. Du Pont was asked to build a plant and operate it. In Wilmington, I was directing a group of physicists and engineers, including John Wheeler. We were greatly concerned about criticality, which was related to the number of atoms that were inside a reactor that didn't contribute to the nuclear reaction itself. Obviously, we had to have water in there, and aluminum, we had to have control rods. We were operating on a very thin margin of criticality. "Excess k" is a term I will bring in now and that is the percent of neutrons that are in excess of those needed to maintain the reaction. That number must be a small positive number if the reaction is to sustain itself. .001 is enough but you won't do very much at that rate. It has to be over 1.0, enough over 1 to take care of the materials that absorb neutrons without contributing to fission.

John Wheeler was concerned about the effect of fission products on the nuclear reaction. If these substances formed when the U-235 atoms split, they would stop the reaction because they absorbed too many neutrons. We had a way of measuring that probability of capturing neutrons, called a cross-section. We called that measurement unit "barns." The largest cross-section known at that time was about 50,000 barns. I am jumping ahead of the story but xenon-135 formed in the first nuclear reactor at Hanford had a cross section of about 3.5 million barns. Completely unheard of, and unpredicted.

The first nuclear reactor at Hanford died almost right away. John Wheeler decided it probably was caused by a fission product. He selected three pairs of decay products, and he decided we should calculate how these would behave if they had a high cross section. We divided into three teams. I certainly was low man on the totem pole as far as knowing how to do it was concerned. It so happened I was part of the group which had the fission product that caused the problem, but we were so slow John and Charlie Wende finished up their products and they came over and worked over our backs. It was the xenon-135. We were starting to figure it out and would have gotten it by sundown. John, of course, had it, I'm going to say in 15 minutes. If we had not been able to add more fuel, I'm certain we would not have been able to produce plutonium at the rate we had calculated, which was 250 grams per day per reactor.

Earlier, when the reactor was in the final design stage, George Graves, Greenewalt's assistant director, and I were chosen to carry the news to the manufacturing director that there was a large probability that the reactor that was considered at that time would fail to operate at the design power of 250 megawatts. We suggested enlarging each one of the 1,500 fuel assemblies so that they would contain more uranium and expanding the number of fuel assemblies to 2,004. This required prompt action because the shield blocks through which the fuel was inserted were just ready for shipment to Hanford. Fortunately, this change could be made and the lost time was acceptable. The added fuel assemblies were what allowed us to overcome the later poisoning by xenon.

The first thing that gave Wheeler international attention was the development of the so-called Bohr-Wheeler theory. Niels Bohr of Denmark was one of the world's top physicists and John had worked under him. After Bohr brought the news of fission to America in 1939, Wheeler saw Bohr and they decided this thing needed theoretical attention, and they put out a theory relating to atomic stability, a beautiful piece of theoretical physics. I'm biased, but I think John Wheeler's analysis of the xenon poisoning at Hanford was in the Nobel Prize category. The problem appeared, it was solved, and we were going again.

I will give you an example of my social life during the time I lived at Hanford. John Wheeler and I decided to go to Priest Rapids and three of us walked to a point 16 miles from where we started. All we got to was a little knob of a hill. We started at 6:30 in the morning and got back at 8. We were in pretty good shape. That was a high point of my social life. We worked seven days a week. Another time John and I were out on a hike and I lost him in the lava fields. We got separated. I waited, thinking I have the brains of the entire organization with me and I lost him. Finally, I saw John walking about half a mile away. That was the most uncomfortable 90 minutes I ever spent.

Another little story. Enrico Fermi and I shared an office in the 700 Area of Hanford for two months. You know when two people work in the same office they don't always talk about work. Enrico one day pushed whatever he was doing aside and looked over at me and said, "Dale, did I ever tell you about how I got to come to the United States?" "Well, no, not really," I told him.

When he was in Italy, he said, "I was a BEEG SHOT!" He was what amounted to education minister in Mussolini's cabinet. He had gotten word that he would win the Nobel Prize. He also knew his wife was one-fourth Jewish and he was afraid for his family and was looking for a way out. He went to Mussolini and said he was getting the Nobel Prize and this is a wonderful thing for Italy. It was like setting off a bomb under Mussolini, who asked if Enrico needed money. He said he had money and might sell some of his things, but would ask if he needed more. Enrico left Rome and took everything with him he could take, including his family. He got the Nobel Prize and the $50,000 check or whatever it was, got on a boat and came to the United States. End of story. That comes right from Enrico.

About the supposed friction between the academics and Du Pont. I am going to say there was absolutely none, but that isn't quite right. The boys down the line, who had just gotten their Ph.Ds, with very little experience, were more inclined to be critical. I knew Wigner quite well, we got along famously. I'll skip ahead several years. I was at Oak Ridge to see Alvin Weinberg. We were eating in the cafeteria and Eugene came in. I saw him standing there. I went over and said hello. He said, "Dale, I saw you sitting there and I was going to come over and say hello but I was afraid you wouldn't remember me." As sincere as could be. As if I could forget a Nobel Prize winner. The friction between the academics and Du Pont was about as important as that.

I didn't see the Trinity test. I have never seen an atom bomb explosion and I am just as happy I haven't. I know that after the bombs were dropped on Japan, I told my friends I would not have dropped it on a civilian population. I would have gone to the big mountain outside Tokyo and dropped one near the top and dropped another one about at the snowline where everybody in Tokyo could see it. I talked to Fermi about that and he said it was considered, but the reason they didn't was that they didn't have any extra bombs. They only had two and they would drop them where they meant business. I am not disagreeing but at the time I would not have done it if the decision had been mine.

GEORGE GRAVES

George Graves was so famous at Hanford he inspired a poem.

> *We'd called up a tight design*
> *Hewn strictly to the longhairs' line.*
> *To us, it looked almighty fine —A honey, we'd insist.*
> *But Old Marse George, with baleful glare*
> *And with a roar that shook the air,*
> *Cried, "Dammit, give it stuff to spare —*
> > *The longhairs may have missed.*

This doggerel by Du Pont engineer Charlie Wende referred to Graves' critical role in the decision to add more uranium-bearing tubes to the Hanford reactor design, done at the urging of physicist John Wheeler. This decision saved the day when the xenon poisoning incident stopped the first reactor from operating.

Wheeler has called Graves "the hero of the story," a man who asked him questions like, "What in the hell are fission products." Once Graves became knowledgeable he insisted on a margin of error, even though the decision took courage and was costly. At Du Pont, in the old days, they called him "the bearded one." Graves was interviewed by telephone at his residence at Port Charlotte, Florida.

Yes, I am "Marse George" in the poem. There's some mythology connected with all that business with the tubes. As I pictured the situation, Du Pont was under contract to design and build this equipment following the basic data provided by the group in Chicago. So therefore when the group at Chicago gave us what to us was official data we simply had to follow it. Now it happened several times during the design and construction of this place that they recalculated things, see, this was all very new, new physics. They were breaking ground all the time. They recalculated the situation a few times for certain design changes. Well, we proceeded to make them. Then, finally, as time was going, for one reason or another, Du Pont felt we should put a stop to this if possible, and the chief engineer, Slim Read, said he wasn't going to accept any more changes.

Of course, that is a position you can take but you can't hold it. So when the Chicago people came through with another change, we had to make it, even though we said we would not make any more. And that is exactly what happened, they came through with another change, and unless we had made it we had every reason to suppose the plant wouldn't work. That was the change to add some extra tubes. It seems the plant was designed to have a certain driving power in terms of the capacity of the plant to permit the fission reaction. If anything were to happen so that the capacity were diminished, then of course the plant wouldn't run. We had decided that we keep a 10 per cent safety factor on this driving power, 10 percent excess "k" if you want the jargon.

We made the change Chicago specified, but we insisted there still be a 10 percent excess "k" as a safety factor, and that's what saved the day, because lo and behold when they tried to operate the place some unexpected things happened and unless we had had this excess it wouldn't have run. We were glad we had the excess, and the excess was provided in the design by changing certain dimensions and setting the number of tubes of canned uranium in the pile. The net of it was that more tubes were made available than the design called for, to the extent of 10 percent, and that let us operate even in the face of this unexpected phenomenon that occurred on the startup. After that, about the end of '44 or early '45, the technical group I was part of was disbanded. My contact with the Manhattan District was terminated I guess even before the Hiroshima job.

RAYMOND P. GENEREAUX

Ray Genereaux, born in Seattle in 1902, a graduate of Stanford and Columbia, was design project manager for the chemical separation facilities at Hanford. He was the man responsible for designing the massive buildings and innovative machinery that separated the plutonium from the irradiated uranium fuel elements after they were taken from the reactors. Several times, however, during an interview in the living room of a beach house at Rehoboth Beach, Delaware, Genereaux refused to take credit for the designs, saying his engineers were responsible.

A courtly, tall man wearing a soft beige cashmere sweater, the veteran Du Pont executive said World War II Hanford was an intense place. Still, he and his friends found time at night for poker, dances and dinner parties.

"Well," he said, "I can tell you I had nightmares all the way through design, because of what I thought the consequences of this thing would be. I thought the bombs were devastating, but we were in competition with the Germans and the bombs were a winning weapon." He said the use of the bombs against Japan was "a 1-2 punch, and it's a long time ago, and a lot of people fail to think in terms of what was going on then."

Genereaux emphasized they were dealing with forces no one had ever worked with, but he didn't seem surprised that everything worked, from dissolving the fuel elements to the purification of the recovered plutonium. Hanford, he said, was supposed to be "the biggest scale-up in history. From atoms to chunks."

I started with Du Pont in 1929, in chemical engineering research, then plant design. In 1929, before the Crash, jobs were a dime a dozen. I had 10 offers, two from Du Pont. I started at the experimental station, working on the flow of fluids, my main research topic. After 1935, I began designing chemical plants, including some chemical warfare plants. Along came Oct. 5, 1942. I was called into the head of the design division and given the works, that the Du Pont Company had been asked to design a plutonium separations plant at Oak Ridge. This was before Du Pont got into the pile end of it. I was to be in charge of the design. I designed the Oak Ridge separations plant but it was smaller and much simpler than Hanford because of the vastly smaller amounts involved. In fact, we had the basic design of the Hanford project done before we started at Oak Ridge. That is the reverse of what generally happens. Usually, you do a semi-works in order to get some dope for a major plant.

I went out to the Met Lab that month. It turned out they didn't know what chemical process they would use, wet, dry, you name it. We realized immediately we had to design flexibility into it if we were going to move ahead and get any designing done before we knew for sure what we were doing, before we knew what the process would be.

We came up with a building, eventually it was the 221 or canyon building, with 40 cells for processing, all designed exactly the same. All the same connectors, for liquids, electricity, steam, air, lubrication, instruments. That was a key, standardization of cells.

Incidentally, do you know why we called the main separations building a canyon? Originally we were going to build them with walls, no ceiling. It became apparent there would be radiation to the sky, then reflected. We added a roof, three feet of concrete. We built three canyons, T, U, and B, and used two. Two were 810 feet 6 inches long by 102 feet and 85 feet two inches from bottom to top. The other one was 65 feet longer because we added a lab for handling hot materials. One day some workmen were at one of the 221 Buildings, our designation for the canyon buildings, and the building was just up to grade. The bottoms were about 50 feet into the ground, and one of the workmen said, "I don't understand anything about it." The other guy said, "Yeah, I think they're building it upside down."

Are you familiar with the interior of the canyon building? Well, let me tell you. You have a cell, rectangular, lids six feet thick, 40 cells in a row, each 17 feet by 8 inches by 13 feet by 20 feet deep. Maximum flexibility was to be achieved by the installation in each cell of 42 pipe and electric connections. These pipes and conduits were to be buried within the concrete walls and to have their cell connections located to rigid tolerances to permit interchangeability of equipment. Connections not used in any particular cell were blocked off awaiting possible use in the future. A key to the whole operation was that we had a mockup building. In it, we had, I forget, but I think three or four cells that were not surrounded by concrete, but had the same shape, floor, same piping locations. Every bit of equipment and piping that went into a cell was put together first in a mockup, to make sure it fit and to make it possible if something went wrong in, say cell 5, it could be taken out and another set mocked up in the same mockup and put in. This was like a Meccano set. If you didn't have the right dimensions for everything, forget it.

We standardized connections so when we put a vessel in, it would sit there perfectly in position and then pipings and connections and so forth would go in by the crane, lowered and connected. The connector had a big nut on top and we had an impact wrench, with three lugs around it and we clamped the flange with a Teflon gasket. We made the real first use of Teflon, it was a secret, so we dubbed it GX, for Genereaux.

In order to put the flanges together to make a joint, in piping, say, or electrical or for grease, you had to be able to put the flanges together remotely because later there would be radiation. This was one of the critical things, the connector. We devised it and tested it at the Wilmington shops. What it consisted of was three hooks that would engage on the under side of the lower flange, and a big nut on top which the impact wrench would tighten. The wrench would be lowered by the crane. We had to design it so it did not put too much pressure on the gasket. It was a lot of development. My engineers designed it. I had engineers of every calling on my team, mechanical, electrical, civil, metallurgical, chemical. It was that combination of people and talent that you needed. Assigning the right guy to the right job. But, we were very cost conscious. You know why? I told my people when we get done with this, we go back on Du Pont process design, and I don't want you spoiled when it comes to spending money.

There were several steps in the separations process. For example, you first dissolved the fuel elements that came from the reactors. Then you, I forget, but I think we centrifuged next and we had tanks with agitators.

The drives for these agitators, well, the fabricator didn't follow my admonition that everything must be absolutely perfect. Twenty of these were delivered to Hanford and I happened to be out there when they arrived. I had a mechanic take one apart and I found mistakes. Too much grease, no fan blade in a motor, etc., etc. I called the company's head man in Philadelphia, and said, "Send your top mechanic out here. We are going to take every damn one of these apart at your expense." That is why we were successful in not having any failures. Why? BECAUSE WE PAID ATTENTION TO DETAIL. The key to safety and success is strict attention to detail. Not that we overdesigned. We tried to have everything as simple as possible. The least you have in a design, the better off you are. It's a matter of probability. The more pieces, the greater probability of something going wrong.

As I said there were various steps. Rail cars from the reactors, storage of the fuel to let it cool down some more, dissolvers, decontamination, neutralization of the waste chemicals. In the canyon building, all fluid moved through piping. There were no pumps. We wanted as few moving parts as possible. Moving parts have problems. They jam, wear out, fail. What we used were steam jet ejectors.

At the end of the 221 canyon building, where the bulk of the irradiated uranium fuel and other products were separated from the plutonium, we pumped underground to the 224 building, where the plutonium was concentrated and purified further. By then, the activity level of the plutonium residue was lowered, radioactivity decreased as the product was purified, but it remained sufficiently high that direct contact was avoided. There were concrete walls, remote controls and careful ventilation. Any leaks or spills had to be recovered and decontaminated, regardless of how minute. All surfaces had to be smooth and free of pockets and pits.

At the end of the canyon building decontamination cycle, at the 221 building, the product from a ton of uranium was in the form of plutonium phosphate and nitric acid, together with about 75 pounds of bismuth phosphate carrier. Specifications said it should be separated as a pure compound before acceptance by the government. Therefore, before the final isolation steps could be attempted, it would be necessary for the decontaminated slurry to be about eight gallons, from 3,000 gallons to eight gallons. The overall result of this concentration would produce a reduction of solution by a value of about 400.

More processing was necessary for purification and storage, but by then we were down to small quantities. The last process was on a laboratory scale, with low radiation and high toxicity. We designed hoods, with surface pits and blemishes hammered out. Ventilation was done with extremely efficient filters on hood exhausts to prevent contaminating discharge air.

I never saw any plutonium at Hanford. My job was pretty well done near the end of '44. We were ready to run before the first pile was done in the fall of '44. I started on the design in October, '42. By March of '43, we had the concept done.

The construction people had some unusual problems. One of them was in the bottom of the floor of these cells. The floor had to have a certain slope, so any spills would go down the drain. That floor had to be within a strict tolerance of flatness and it had to slope. They said we can't do it. We can't come within that tolerance. But they did it. That was the teamwork out there. One of the greatest benefits of the whole project was we had research and design and construction and operating people, all in Du Pont, who knew each other. We had communications. But don't forget the terrible urgency to beat the Germans.

At Hanford, two elements involved were different from what we were used to. One was radiation, the other was critical mass. With respect to radiation, Johnny Wheeler came down to Wilmington from Princeton and he and I sat up in my office and I said, "Johnny, I need to know how thick to make the concrete in this canyon building in order to protect the people. We had a lot of fun. Finally, he said six feet of concrete. Well, I made it seven. We came up with a simple little thing, which is the radiation protection depends on the density of the material, the shielding. Lead of course is one of the densest of metals.

These are the equivalents to one foot of lead: one yard of steel, one fathom (6 feet) of concrete, one rod (16 1/2 feet) of earth and a mile of air. That's what Johnny Wheeler and I cooked up.

Then, I told him, "Johnny, we are going to have a crane with a cab with people in it, for work inside the canyon building, so we have to protect them. The crane cab was mainly made of steel, but we used some lead. Up where this was, we didn't need as much lead because the people were farther from the material. The crane was to be above the cells and the cab was back of a five-foot thick concrete wall. The cab was protected by the wall. On the crane we mounted a periscope.

Also at that time I heard RCA was developing something that turned out to be television. I went up to Philadelphia and saw it. They had a camera out on the Benjamin Franklin Bridge and I could see bridge detail. We didn't know whether the radiation would make it inoperable or if radiation would harm the lenses in the crane periscope. The radiation didn't harm them. These television cameras were the only means that we had for the crane operators to see what they were doing. The television camera was mounted on the crane, so the operator could watch from a screen. As far as I know, that was the first industrial application of television.

Now, the crane operators could see what they were doing at the mockup building. We didn't have to shield them. When they got to the 221 building, they didn't know they had to do anything different. So, I got two or three of the top operators into the cab, of course there was no radiation yet, and I said, "Gentlemen, I'm not a crane operator. You are. I think we have to get together and learn how to use what we've got." Oh, they thought that would be terrible. The first thing you know they were getting the biggest kick out of looking through the periscope, with this great big hook going down and hooking on to a wheelbarrow or something down there in the cell area, picking it up and gently putting it down. They had a ball. They were fantastic. The crane operators learned in 10 hours or so. Once they got onto the idea, they could do it. They were like kids. They thought I was nuts.

After the process began, and it was radioactive, they lifted cell lids, which were six feet thick. Each cell had about four, they were stepped because you couldn't have a straight crack. Radiation would escape. Each of the lids had a bale on it for the crane hook. The lids were installed after the equipment was in. Each came on a railroad flat car. They were balanced. Nobody was down there saying, "A little this way, or that way."

We installed the equipment remotely, even at first when there was no radiation, because we didn't want workmen in the cells. That would violate the whole principle. You would eventually have to replace equipment and you could not put anybody in the cells then. So, you had to know how to do it ahead of time. Sometimes during construction, somebody would want to do things faster and not use the mockup building. We had some battles and we had fun, but we were all friends.

On the operating side of the wall, in the canyon building, you have people behind seven feet of concrete. All their instrumentation is on the wall and they can't see a thing. They can't see what is going on inside a cell. We did arrange for them to be able to hear when there was a motor or centrifuge running. That helped. If you heard a rough noise something was wrong. If it was humming you were okay.

Getting back to critical mass. The process went through various stages on down the canyon, from cell to cell. You eventually get to a point where the concentration of plutonium was getting greater and greater, getting closer to a chain reaction. You don't want a critical mass in one vessel. That meant we had to design the equipment to be smaller and smaller. You couldn't have a great big tank at the end, and take a chance. Two things we never put up with before, radiation and critical mass. And we never have had people operating something they couldn't see, and fuss around with, or put together in a normal construction fashion.

We put considerable emphasis on handling the waste. Consideration was given to designing a waste concentration facility but the urgency of getting the plutonium meant we had to put that idea aside. They said we will reduce the volume and store it in underground tanks. We spent days and days going over the specifications for those. We had three degrees of protection, and we x-rayed every weld. The tanks were steel, with concrete surrounding, and we had monitoring devices around them. We put air coolers on top because of the heat, which would come up and we would condense the vapor into liquid.

We never intended that these underground tanks be the final storage. I proposed designing another building, like the 221 building, to concentrate the waste. But I was told, "No, we can't afford the time." I said I would like to do it, and on the earliest plans I included a plant for waste concentration. You don't do away with it, what you try to do is reduce the volume until you've got something that is significantly small enough to encapsulate in some way and then bury it somehow.

Did you know I'm the Holy RPG? Everything on Du Pont construction projects gets a number. Everything ordered from Wilmington gets a half number, like 1 1/2, and everything ordered from the field gets a whole number, like 100. But there is always a three-letter symbol ahead of the number. At the normal plants the symbol is something to do with the department, but on government jobs they pick the initials of the first guy put to work on it. So that's why RPG was on everything out there at Hanford.

Construction at one of the mammoth plutonium separation plants, 1944.
Three of these chemical plants were built for the purpose of separating
plutonium contained in the radioactive uranium fuel from the Hanford
reactors.   *U.S. Department of Energy*

CONSTRUCTION

'Twas on a hot and dusty day
In August '43
I saw a cloud of Hanford dust
Blow high to welcome me.

ANONYMOUS POEM

They came to Hanford by the thousands, some stayed for the life of the job, and beyond into their retirement years. Others didn't last any longer than the wait for the next train out of Pasco. Most had no idea what was happening at the Hanford Engineer Works, only that something was going on there that would win the war.

Recruiting pamphlets circulated nationally were plain spoken: "There's a job for you at Hanford. It's not a short job and it's not a small job. We can't tell you much about it because it's an important war job, but we can tell you that it's new heavy industrial plant construction."

"Life here is a little on the rugged side," recruiters said, and prospective workers were told of semi-desert conditions with occasional windstorms. That was an understatement. The windstorms were really sandstorms, disagreeable events which sometimes caused workers to quit their jobs at Hanford in large numbers. Workers were advised to bring a padlock, towels, coat hangers, a Thermos and the tools of their trade, as well as lots of clothing because laundry service was slow. A radio was all right, but no firearms and no cameras.

A two-person barracks room cost $1.40 a week rent per person, and that in blankets, linen, janitorial and bed-making services. Mess hall meals —served family style, all you could eat—were 60 cents. The normal work week was six days, 54 hours, with overtime paid above 40 hours. Pay scales were at prevailing rates, which were about $1 an hour for laborers and up to $1.85 or more for skilled workers such as plumbers, steamfitters, electricians and bricklayers. Leadburners, the elite of construction workers in those days, made $2.

Recruiters, who advertised Hanford as a "Pacific Northwest construction project," concentrated on men who were not liable to be drafted, such as men 38 years of age or older with children, or men who had physical or occupational draft deferments. Almost any kind of laborer or craftsman was needed, because in addition to heavy building construction, 345 miles of permanent roads and 125 miles of railroad were built.

The first major construction was Hanford Camp, a sprawling temporary city for construction workers which surrounded the hamlet of Hanford along the Columbia River. Hanford Camp began with tents in April, 1943. Eventually, it included 1,175 buildings, most of them living quarters, varying from the 131 H-shaped barracks with beds for 190 persons, to some 900 huts holding from 10 to 20 men. The camp was a full-service town with banks, hospital, eight messhalls, taverns, movies, an auditorium for sports and dances, fire and police departments, baseball fields and a swimming pool.

Du Pont's unpublished company history of Hanford, on file at the Hagley Museum and Library at Wilmington, Delaware, said that some 137,000 persons moved through Hanford, during the two-year construction period from March, 1943, until February, 1945, when Hanford Camp was abandoned. Peak construction payroll was 45,096 in June, 1944, with more than 51,000 residents at Hanford Camp, counting family members at the trailer camp of 4,300 privately-owned units. At its peak, Hanford Camp, said one resident, "was like Saturday night every day."

Eight mess halls each served 2,700 persons three times a day, and the taverns sold 12,000 gallons of beer a week. Hanford Camp had the largest general delivery post office in the world.

The camp was segregated by sex and race.* The trailer camp also was segregated by race, and was the only place in the Hanford Camp itself where

---

* By actual count in July 1944, there were a total of 52,709 persons at Hanford Engineer Works, which presumably included people in Richland. The breakdown was 34,007 white men; 13,044 white women; 4,650 "colored" men; and 796 "colored" women

Hanford construction camp for worker housing and administrative operations with Columbia River and bluffs in background. The barracks camp and trailer park, with more than 51,000 residents in 1944, was built in 1943 and abandoned in early 1945 when the construction period ended. Nothing but a few faint remnants of the giant camp remain today. *U.S. Department of Energy*

married couples—black or white—could live together. Generally, the mess halls and taverns were segregated by race, but not as rigidly as the barracks. The camp had quarters for some 6,000 black men and 1,000 black women, with an additional 76 spaces for blacks in the trailer camp.

In 1946, the camp was dismantled. Nothing was left in the cheat grass, rabbit brush and sage except for remnants of asphalt streets, bits of lumber and rusty tin cans.

Building the workers' camp was a warmup for the three main heavy construction jobs: reactors, chemical separation buildings, and the fuel fabrication facility. In order, Du Pont designated them the 100, 200 and 300 areas. There were seven separate processing units: three reactors, three chemical separations plants and one fuel fabrication facility.

Reactors and separations plants were built at the north end of the project, with the reactors adjacent to the Columbia but six miles apart, and three separations plants six to eleven miles south of the reactors. In addition, there was an area called "lag storage," that was designed for the temporary storage of "hot" irradiated uranium metal from the reactors. Fuel fabrication, since it was the least likely unit to experience a serious accident, was constructed about seven miles north of Richland. The more dangerous reactors were about 30 miles from Richland, and the less risky separations facilities about 20 miles from the town.

Although the immediate emphasis was on plutonium manufacturing aspects and the creation of a construction workers' camp, Du Pont also had to build simultaneously a new town to house some 6,000 operations workers and 11,000 family members who would be in residence after production began. In early 1943, before the federal government purchased it, Richland was a farm country village of 200 persons along the Columbia, upstream from the tiny town of Kennewick, population 1,918 in 1940, and across the river from Pasco, county seat of Franklin County, which had a 1940 population of close to 4,000.

By early 1945, Richland had been transformed, with 4,304 new housing units, and sufficient stores, shops, schools, churches, medical facilities and government services to support the mushroomed population. The 2,500 conventional wood-frame houses were of eight different styles, from two-bedroom one story duplexes to four-bedroom two-story single-family houses. In addition, about 1,800 small prefabricated houses were shipped from Portland, Oregon, 300 miles away.

In heavy construction, top priority at first went to the 300 Area because its job was to fabricate the uranium fuel for the reactors and to serve as a laboratory for testing materials. A small, very low-power reactor was constructed in the 300 Area for evaluating fuel elements and other materials, such as graphite.

Du Pont called the reactors "process units" and designated the three locations 100-B, 100-D and 100-F, with the reactor building in each of the three complexes called "105 building." Each 100 Area was about one-square mile in size and virtually identical, the only major difference being that D and F included refrigeration units for cooling the river water during the summer. B was started first and had priority. Initial work at 100-B began in March,

The new town of Richland, 1944. More than 4,300 housing units were constructed ranging from small duplexes to four-bedroom two-story residences. Hundreds of these structures were pioneering examples of prefabricated housing.   *U.S. Department of Energy*

1943, but construction of the reactor building itself did not begin until December. It was completed June 1, 1944.

Each 100 Area, in addition to the reactor building, contained enough equipment to provide electric power and water for a small city. Included were a retention basin, pump house, chemical and gas storage, water purification building, river pump house and reservoir, filter plant, power house, water de-aerating building, water treatment plant, water tanks, main pumphouse, three electrical substations, waste processing, fire department, storehouses, oil storage, patrol headquarters, shops and a storage building for "fresh" uranium metal.

A large and steady supply of cool, clean water was needed to run the reactors and the Columbia provided it, with an average flow of 121,000 cubic feet a second.

In addition to the main task of cooling the reactors, a complete backup system also was required in case of failure of the pumps. Water was stored in giant tanks for gravity feed in case of emergency, and coal-fired steam turbines designed to respond within 25 seconds were on standby to provide power if the electricity supply failed. The scientists figured the worst that could happen at the reactors would be a failure of the cooling system, which would result in a steam explosion that would rupture the building and scatter highly radioactive fuel assembly pieces.

Construction of nuclear reactors was unprecedented, except for the ones at Chicago and Oak Ridge, and the plutonium production machines at Hanford were mammoth by comparison. Du Pont described the pile as a cube-like structure approximately 37 feet by 46 feet by 41 feet high, consisting of an interior cube of graphite approximately 31 feet by 40 feet by 35 feet surrounded on top and sides by laminated walls of steel and masonite.

The structure stood on concrete approximately 23 feet thick. Between the graphite and laminated walls on the top and sides was a cast-iron thermal shield, about 10 inches thick at the top, front, back and bottom, and eight inches thick on the right and left sides. The entire reactor was enclosed by three to five feet of concrete. Horizontally, through the graphite, were more than 2,000 holes containing aluminum tubes approximately one and one-half inches in diameter. The side of the reactor where the tubes were inserted, and loaded with 70,000 uranium fuel slugs, was the charge or front face. At the other end, where the slugs were pushed out after use, was the discharge or rear face. From front to rear through the cast-iron thermal shield there were 208 holes containing cooling water pipes.

Vertically, through the graphite, there were 38 holes for safety rods (27 were used) for stopping the reaction. Horizontally, there were nine holes for the water-cooled control rods, which allowed reactor operators to raise or lower the reactor power. Front and rear faces were equipped with elevators for loading at the front and for assisting in unloading at the rear. The entire reactor was gastight.

Laying the graphite was a delicate job because of the need for very close tolerances and extreme cleanliness. Graphite blocks were of varying sizes, from about 40 inches long to five inches square to ones half that length. Some blocks were solid, some had drilled holes or were slotted, others were beveled. Machining was done at Hanford, most of it on converted woodworking equipment. Tolerances ranged from plus or minus .005 inches to plus .003 and minus .000. Installation was intricate, with four different types involved in complicated designs. Each block was marked according to heat and quality ratings. All men working on laying graphite wore special uniforms and as

Construction work for the 100-B reactor area began in March, 1943, and was completed June 1, 1944. The reactor produced its first plutonium in November, 1944. The reactor, which is at the right, was the first large-scale plutonium producer in the world.   *U.S. Department of Energy*

each layer was laid, it was vacuum cleaned to insure that no dirt or other neutron-absorbing contamination was present.

Serious delays occurred during the reactor construction period, and the worst problem was scarcity of labor. Until March, 1944, only 50 to 70 percent of needed manpower was available, a condition which resulted in shift work and overtime. Welders and millwrights, especially, often were in short supply. Du Pont turned to subcontractors for specialized jobs.

By spring, 1944, the adverse conditions improved, and at the end of September, 1944, 100-B was loaded and began making plutonium. B's production start was followed by 100-D in December, and 100-F in February, 1945.

The plutonium separation plants, the 200 Areas, were begun at about the same time as the reactors, but their completion was not as urgent. The first plant did not have to be finished and ready for operations until about two months after 100-B was done. It would take that long for the uranium fuel to be processed through the reactor.

Separations plant design was slowed because the specific chemical process for separating the plutonium from the irradiated uranium fuel was not determined until later. During 1943 not much was done except preliminary preparation of the building sites. Each of the separation areas, 200-West and 200-East, was about 2,000 acres. 200-West, usually called 2-West, contained two separate separation plants, 200-T and 200-U. 200-East contained one plant, 200-B.

The largest buildings in each were the 221 "cell" buildings, so huge they resembled gray aircraft carriers on a sagebrush sea. 810 feet, 6 inches long, 102 feet wide and 85 feet 2 inches high. 221-T was 65 feet longer than U and B because of an added laboratory. About one-fourth of each was below finished grade. Other buildings in each area were more like the usual laboratory and processing support buildings Du Pont was familiar with at its chemical plants.

The 221 buildings, though, were special. Because of their size, and the necessity to protect workers from the extreme radioactivity present inside them, they presented special problems of construction. Each 221 building was divided into two main parts. Narrow galleries on three levels, like hallways, ran along one side, heavily shielded from the rest of the building, which was called the canyon. The canyon floor contained 40 recessed cells, heavily lidded, which contained the apparatus needed to accomplish plutonium separation, the isolation of plutonium in solution from dissolved uranium and the highly-radioactive fission products.

The lowest gallery was in the basement and held electrical gear and control cabinets, and another on the first floor held piping for steam, water, chemicals and air. The second floor gallery was where the operators ran control panels for the equipment inside the cells.

A three-foot thickness of concrete was required for the canyon roof, and placing this much concrete over an area 60 feet across without intermediate support posed a construction problem. Du Pont built traveling forms similar to those used in tunnel construction, and moved them in sections on a crane track along the entire 800 foot length.

Exterior concrete building walls varied from five to three feet thick, with a seven-foot concrete barricade wall between the operator gallery and the canyon cells.

An overhead traveling 75-ton capacity crane was installed in each canyon, to be used for lifting the 30-ton cell lids. Auxiliary hooks were added for more delicate repair and maintenance work inside the cells.

A great deal of waste material, much of which was radioactive, had to be disposed of at the end of the separation process. Liquid waste was stored in underground tanks or held in reservoirs. During the wartime period, each plant had twelve 75-foot diameter tanks and four 20-foot tanks, each reinforced concrete with a steel lining with condensors designed to prevent fumes from escaping into the air.

At the reactors, cooling water was held in concrete retention basins until radioactivity had diminished. Some of this retained water went into the ground, the rest into the river.

200-West construction was completed in December, 1944, and began its first run-through later that month of irradiated uranium metal from the first operating reactor. 200-East was completed in February, 1945, and began plutonium separation in April.

Sixteen workers were killed on the job during the construction period. Eleven of the 16 died in two accidents. A tank collapsed at one of the separation plants, killing seven men, and four died in the collision of two locomotives.

Construction costs for the main plant were $253.52 million, and special construction, such as Hanford Camp service areas and maintenance shops, came to $51.9 million. Richland Village cost $44 million, bringing the total to about $350 million. Overall cost of the Manhattan Project was about $2.2 billion, which would be $20 billion in 1995 dollars.

COL. FRANKLIN T. MATTHIAS

Colonel Matthias' superior officer wrote him a letter in February, 1946, as Matthias was about to return to civilian life. He thanked Matthias for his "brilliantly outstanding performance in driving through to completion the Hanford Engineer Works, the most difficult, the largest, and the most isolated single job in the entire Atomic Bomb Program."

Matthias was in at the beginning of the Manhattan Project because of his association with General Groves, whom he had known since they worked on Pentagon construction. Groves liked and trusted the young civil engineer and reserve officer from Wisconsin, and appointed him to be officer in charge at the Hanford plutonium works. This title meant he ran the entire operation, with authority over civilian operations as well as military.

In April, 1943, he wrote an open letter to military and civilian employees: "This is a 24-hour a day, 365 1/4 days a year job. Hanford was the biggest construction job of the war even though no one ever would be able to step into the spotlight and enjoy the glamour associated with fighting troops."

During several interviews at his ranch-style house in Danville, California, near San Francisco, Matthias, usually friendly and good-humored, would be annoyed by a certain line of questioning, specifically any misunderstanding of the "context" of the Manhattan Project years.

"We didn't think much beyond the general consciousness that it would contribute to the end of the war. There was a lot of discussion about the moral side of it, but we were firebombing Japan and many more were killed by that than by those two nuclear explosions. By and large, knowing about the forecast that a million Americans and two million Japanese would be lost in an invasion, that was the overwhelming thing to consider in the environment of the time. If the Manhattan Project hadn't done it, by now someone else would have.

"I am always reminded of something I heard Fermi say. He came very close to discovering fission while he was still in Italy in the early 1930s. He used to say, 'I was eternally grateful I failed in making this discovery because if I had, I think the Germans and Italians would have been able to start the war with an atomic bomb instead of us ending it with one.' "

Matthias thought the Manhattan Project was unique in its total and successful coordination by one man. But even Groves, the master organizer, was not always sure of success. Before the startup of the first Hanford reactor, Groves told him, "If the reactor blows up, jump in the middle of it, and save yourself a lot of trouble."

Matthias left the Army in 1946. He didn't think atomic energy would amount to much in peacetime, and nothing appealed to him as much as the excitement of big construction jobs. Until he retired in 1973, Matthias built dams and hydroelectric projects, tunnels and powerhouses, in Brazil, Canada and the United States. Among the many dams he helped build were two on the Columbia River, Wells and Wanapum, both upstream from Hanford. Wanapum held special significance, since it was named for the tribe of old Johnny Buck, an Indian he knew and liked during the Hanford years.

I think there were two real critical things during the construction period. One thing that occupied the attention of a lot of high-ranking people was the question: Would it be possible to build an operating system that could handle the loading and unloading of the chemical separation cells and to do whatever they might have to do, could you build a system that would let you put an operating unit that was bigger than this room down into a cell and connect it to pipes, maybe a hundred connections? These cells were built completely pre-fabbed as one piece, to a precision where they could drop it in place, and with equal precision have fittings around the outside to connect it up.

The other difficult thing that caused a lot of concern was the canning of the uranium fuel slugs for the reactors. It was such a critical thing if one of these slugs exploded. And we tested some that did explode, like a hot dog. Solid uranium popped out with jagged edges just like a busted weiner. That might have contaminated the whole process. We never knew for sure if a reactor would operate with some of these slugs exploded. We subjected the slugs to a degree of stress that would not be encountered inside the reactor, and we tested them with high-pressure steam which did not exist inside the reactor.

There were not a great number of scientists at Hanford. Maybe Du Pont had half a dozen top-ranking people, and we had quite a number of visitations from Met Lab people. Fermi, Wigner, Franck came, but Szilard didn't visit. He was kind of sour because they hadn't followed his recommendations in the beginning about a couple of things, like helium or sodium cooling.

Wigner was a smart nuclear physicist. I remember taking him around once when we were under construction. I took him through the concrete batching (mixing) plant we had set up and showed him how it all worked, the automatic features. Now it would be considered an antique freak. He ended up that tour by saying, "You know, I can't understand how you can handle anything as complicated as a concrete mixing plant system." He was kind of a funny character. He was responsible to approve all of the Du Pont design plans relative to the operation requirements. I used to talk to him quite a lot because he was often a little delaying factor. We weren't looking for any delays of any kind.

As far as my working relationship with Du Pont was concerned, of course, we had differences from day one. I was fortunate that Gil Church and Walt Simon (Du Pont's project construction manager and operations manager) were people I could deal with and respect, and we had a very good working relationship. I remember one time Granville Read (Du Pont's assistant chief engineer) called up Groves and said Matthias and Church were having a big argument about something and what should we do? Groves replied, "Well, if those two guys don't have some arguments, then neither of them are worth a damn."

Some amusing things happened. I had a letter one time that came to me, through probably 20 different places in the War Department, from a congressman who had a letter from a guy that worked at Hanford. He told this congressman that it wasn't bad out there, they had good food and they were getting good pay and working hard but he said the big problem is that all the women in the area were behind fences and it was pretty hard to do it through a fence. I sent the letter back and all I said was, "Imagine that?"

I suppose there were brothels in Pasco, I'm sure there were, and I'm sure a lot of those shacks along the river between Richland and Pasco functioned that way. Those were problems to us, mainly because of health. We didn't want any big, tough health problems to surface. It never happened. Du Pont had quite a group for industrial medicine. We kept them running around looking at all these places. We did some thoroughly illegal inspections, I'm sure.

It's true the women lived behind barb wire, and we tried to control access. We know we didn't succeed 100 percent. They would get the gals and go out in the sage brush, occasionally. And they were free enough, except they lived in these barracks.

We made up our minds when we first started that we would put people in barracks regardless of what they looked like. It wasn't more than a few weeks after we started getting people in our camp that I had a visit from a whole bunch of black guys led by a black minister who said they would rather have their own barracks. They hadn't had any real trouble, but they figured they would.

I dealt with the unions, and Du Pont and I did a good job of batting problems back and forth and confusing the labor leaders. I did that also with the colonel in Washington, D.C. who was head of labor relations. We kicked problems back and forth. I would say, that bastard in Washington doesn't know what he's doing. He would do the same thing, and blame me for all the problems. It worked great. We kept kicking them around until they disappeared.

We had a one-day work stoppage, by the pipefitters and plumbers. We didn't have much trouble. Joe Keenan, secretary-treasurer of the Building Trades Council, came out from Washington to help us when there were potential problems. He was a great help to us. When I talked to Keenan, I had to guard against making dirty cracks about unions. You got the feeling he was one of you.

We didn't try to keep organizers away, we accepted the idea of union organization. We did not have a project contract. We agreed at the beginning with the labor leaders in the region that we would follow standard union practices. We set the basic labor rate at $1.05, the average between Seattle and Spokane. That was for common labor. Electricians and pipefitters got more. We had a fuss with them once, but we settled it, and I think gave them a little increase.

A lot of local people would ask us what was going on at Hanford. We rigged up a cover story right at the beginning. There was a new explosive developed just before the war that I think was called RDX. It was much stronger than gun powder, and dynamite, or nitroglycerin. When we started out, we spent some time thinking about what we ought to call it and what we ought to get together on when we were pressed. we ended up calling Hanford a place to make RDX. Nobody questioned it. Du Pont was known as an explosives maker.

I handled the newspapers early. I got to Spokane, for instance, to talk with the Spokesman-Review and others up there the day the order came from federal court to start acquiring land. That must have been in January, 1943.

I went there, and I went to Seattle and Portland. Another man on my staff, Bob Nissen, covered all the little towns along the Columbia all the way up. I went to Yakima and Walla Walla. I told people I needed their help in keeping this project quiet. I told them it was a big important war project, and that's all I could tell them. We had very few problems after that.

When I was given this job, I went to the war censorship department. One of the real high-ranking people in that organization was a guy who was a fraternity brother of mine at Wisconsin and we were very close friends. I went to see him and told him we needed all the help we could to keep Hanford from being publicized. He told me you know we can't censor anything. I said I was asking for his help because he must have quite a lot of influence among the newspapers. He gave me a hot line telephone number and told me any time I had problems, I should call and they would try to intercede.

I told them, all the papers, any time there was news they could use, I would see that they had it. When this thing breaks open, I will see you get the word. I managed to keep that promise the day the first bomb was dropped.

We had one incident where Truman committee investigators turned up, and tried to get into Hanford to see what was going on. We had a deal with (Senator) Harry Truman that his special committee (to investigate national defense construction) would not bug us, an agreement between Truman and the secretary of war. I called Groves, and they were gone the next day.

One of the things I am most proud of is that I didn't let a British scientific delegation get into the reactor areas and the other closed areas. They had a guy named Klaus Fuchs (the British scientist, later convicted of spying for the Soviet Union) with them. It was after the first reactor was operating, later '44 or early '45. They didn't have proper credentials.

There was never any indication of espionage or sabotage that we knew of, never any Russian or German activity. We had a few things happen. One guy wrote me a letter from Oklahoma and said he owned a radioactive spring, and would we be interested? We thought here was somebody who suspected something, but he turned out to be a mountaineer who wanted to sell water from a spring. I did have a military counter-intelligence group of 10 or 12 very carefully selected people, most of them with FBI experience.

There were some Indians at Priest Rapids, 30 to 50 of them, and they wanted to fish for salmon at White Bluffs, one of their traditional fishing places. White Bluffs was about 15 miles from their village, which was farther north. I had a number of visits with the Indians and was invited to one of their tribal festivals. They didn't like the idea of having to get a pass. I had a formal meeting with Johnny Buck, their chief, and explained to him that if you don't let us give you passes, and you are admitted through our gates, somebody in this big work force might do some damage and accuse the Indians since we gave you free run. I'll arrange to take your people up to the White Bluffs island every morning by truck and you can do your fishing and bring you back by night or in some cases maybe let you stay there overnight.

I called them Priest Rapids Indians, but I think Wanapum was their right name. The first time I met Johnny Buck he produced a little weatherbeaten treaty which gave them the fishing rights. I liked him. That guy ruled the tribe. He chased them into the river once a week in the summer.

Hanford was a lot different from my later career. It was very much different in that I had ways of getting things done that put tremendous pressures on people because of the war effort. I had a senior officer in the Army, Navy and Air Force I could appeal to if I ran into problems. That was great. We did everything in record time. We had the authority. We didn't wait for anybody.

FRANK MACKIE

Born in 1903 in Baltimore, Mackie studied civil engineering at Union College in Schenectady, New York. In 1934 he went to work for Du Pont in construction and retired in 1968 as manager of construction. "They called me manager, now they call them directors. They give them a big title, but they gave me more money," he said. After the war, Mackie was construction manager at Savannah River, the plant in South Carolina built by Du Pont in the early 1950s to produce material for hydrogen bombs. Slim and handsome, Mackie resembled actor Richard Widmark. He also was self assured, a trait of Du Pont executives. Mackie was interviewed at his residence, a luxurious retirement center near Wilmington.

I was manager of the war construction division of the Du Pont Company, and I handled the construction of Hanford from the Nemours Building in Wilmington. I was manager of all construction for quite a while, but at that particular time we had more going for the government than we did for anything else.

Hanford was quite the largest plant Du Pont ever built up to then, and other than dams and things of that sort in faraway places, I guess it was the largest thing anybody had ever built. Right away I was aware of the plant's

One of the many billboards at Hanford Engineer Works.

U.S. Department of Energy

purpose. They took us down to the eighth floor of the Du Pont Building here in Wilmington, put us in a room and gave us a book to read, even before we got started. The book was one our design division and our engineering group had prepared with certain of the men who been working on the problem.

Very frankly, some of the physics in there was a mile and a half over my head. I spent a few sleepless nights. We weren't a company to fail on doing anything. I wasn't too damn sure that with the lack of knowledge ahead of us, that we would be able to do it. Du Pont said it would not take any of the atomic work unless we operated it. Unless we built it, we wouldn't run it.

They were building the Alcan Highway at the time and people were coming and going to that. We even put recruiters on the boats that brought the men back from Alcan. We knew we had to build a camp, and find ways to keep the people reasonably satisfied out in the boondocks. I don't recall the turnover rate, but my recollection is that it wasn't a good deal worse than jobs where we had 14-15,000 men.

In construction we were doing things people hadn't done before, that's for sure. There were extremely close tolerances and we were working with certain materials we had never worked with before. We had something in our favor. We not only did the construction, we also did the designing. We had our design division in Wilmington, with a nucleus of a design group at Hanford. If we got into a problem one night, we'd try to have it solved by our construction and design groups by the next morning. We had quite a few design men at Hanford, and they were only a telephone away from the big group in Wilmington. Now, a job of that sort, one that had never been done before, gave an opportunity for it to be a job that was in continuous change. Fortunately, and I say fortunately because I built some plants for Du Pont that we never got done changing for two or three years after they were put in operation. Fortunately, we were able to hold design changes to a minimum at Hanford. I can't say enough for the designers of that plant. People like Crawford Greenewalt, that ilk, who really burned the midnight oil to make sure we weren't getting something in today we had to take out tomorrow.

As far as materials were concerned, Hanford had the highest priority for government work and we could almost pick and choose what we wanted and when we wanted it. Worker quality, in general, was high. We had very good supervision, all Du Pont employes, who knew standards for safety and putting things together properly and not letting things slip. The men were a little older than average on construction jobs. I don't mean in their fifties and sixties, but they were a bit older than on jobs earlier in the war because the draft had taken quite a few of the younger men.

We had some accidents, you don't do a job of that size without having some accidents. We had a contractor who was building some underground tanks for storage of toxic materials who had some fatalities, but it was a very safe job, and well recognized as such. We used to have difficulties with certain contractors who didn't want to do certain things of a safety nature but either they did it our way or we got rid of them.

I would say I visited the site an average of once every two months and I would stay two or three weeks. I found out early that unless you got out on the job and saw for yourself what was going on you weren't supervising very well.

Building the piles and separations plants, putting these things together wasn't easy, and we trained men for weeks or whatever was necessary to get them able to do it right. We had inspectors always on the job. You see, we didn't know if this thing was going to work, and some of our vice presidents weren't too damn sure about it either. I don't think there was any appreciable difference between the separation plants or the piles when it came to building them. We tried not to shift men from one to the other, both from the standpoint of secrecy and also from standpoint of once they had learned to do one thing properly, it is better to let them do it. We never experienced any serious labor problems. None. Union men were hired but there never was a contract with a union and no union organizing activity occurred at the job. I knew all the national officers of the building trades by their first names, and if anything was brewing I called them and got it straightened out.

I had the greatest respect for General Groves. He was quite a man in my estimation. Especially, I liked his choice of officers to run the Corps of Engineers at Hanford. I asked Groves how he managed to have such good judgment. "That's my trade secret," he said.

I found out about the first bomb on the plane from Hanford to Wilmington. I got off the plane in Denver and there it was. I wasn't surprised when the second bomb was dropped. I learned early in life never to be surprised at anything anybody does.

ROGER W. FULLING

Roger Fulling and his wife Isabel lived in a penthouse near West Palm Beach. Scattered through their comfortable study were New England landscapes by Mrs. Fulling, as well as photographs and other mementoes that reflected Fulling's 38 years with Du Pont and his friendships with company executives and members of the Du Pont family.

When Fulling consented to be interviewed, he said something was on his mind. "The missing link," he said, "in the Manhattan Project story is that the atomic bomb was a product of American industry. This story has not been told. I want people to understand, before I go, the importance of industry to this project."

During several days of talk in his study, the 78-year-old Fulling, a mechanical engineering graduate of the University of Delaware, remembered fondly his long association with Manhattan Project boss General Leslie Groves.

Fulling began with Du Pont in 1934, and during World War II, he was a division superintendent in Du Pont's war construction program. During the Eisenhower Administration, in the mid-1950s, he was an acting assistant secretary of defense.

At the West Palm Beach Airport, Fulling shouted a final admonition from his Cadillac Seville. "Remember, the Du Pont effort was based on team work, and don't forget the absolutely vital role of American industry in the bomb-building effort!"

During the early days, before the Manhattan Project, when Du Pont was building smokeless powder plants, TNT and other plants for the war effort, I had contacts with then Colonel Leslie Groves, who was helping to operate the military construction program for the U.S. Army Corps of Engineers.

My personal analysis of Groves was that he was a qualified engineer as well as an outstanding military officer. At all times in my many years of contact, I found him to be very understanding, and at all times a gentleman. He was stern, he was demanding, and like many other great leaders, he was egotistical, to the point of being overbearing to some people. People were in awe of him, for several reasons. He had a good solid engineering background. He was a handsome man, tall, very solidly built, and was an impressive personality.

But, to identify myself and my Manhattan Project work, I reported to the assistant chief engineer, and I was responsible for procurement from the design, getting the orders placed, the inspection and the expediting of all materials for the Du Pont war plants, including Hanford. At one time, I had 500 engineers throughout the United States expediting and inspecting equipment. In addition to that, I was the major liaison with General Groves for all the logistics concerned with Hanford, on materials, priorities, and allocations of materials.

For instance, we had to take equipment away from utilities in order to build Hanford. We couldn't get copper for the electrical stations, for the transmission stations, for transferring power from one voltage to another. Following General Groves' arrangements, we borrowed ingots (mostly silver) from Fort Knox to use as conductor substitutes at Hanford. The electrical capacities were different from copper, but it worked.

Initially, we had a hell of a time getting the graphite block program through Union Carbide. I had to go up to the Union Carbide New York offices and present the program to their senior executives as to how important this was, and why we had to have it in large quantity and on schedule.

The graphite blocks were laminated with a very special composition of fiber board. The machining was very, very interesting and requiring very high precision. And the only people who could do this was Vermont Marble in Rutland.

The aluminum tubing and canning programs were the most difficult. Extrusion is an art. You would start with a stock and you would extrude at the right temperature, cooling atmospheric conditions had to be just right. Alcoa did a tremendous job.

The welding of the (uranium) fuel cans (containers) was intricate. You had to have the right alloy, you had to have the right temperature and atmosphere, the right welding techniques and equipment. The welders working on the aluminum cans to contain the uranium fuel were not like you would see welding a steel plate to a steel beam or two steel beams together. These men were artists. They were the top of the craft, like the old goldsmiths.

I remember we had difficulties obtaining the required delivery of switch gear for electrical equipment. At that time, the major producer of switch gear mechanisms was Westinghouse. They made the best and we had their major capacity, and we had to jog them to improve delivery dates, that was a real problem, but Westinghouse met the challenge. Structural steel was terrible. Steel was needed also for steel plate for ships and for making tanks.

Military logistics leading to an objective are exactly the same as an industrial engineering construction program leading to an objective, namely a plant that will produce a product. Much has been said about the scientific and the technical factors of the atomic program. To my knowledge, very little has been said about the importance of logistics and the great part American industry played.

It was very necessary that we establish specifications, availability, quality and quantity on a time schedule of all the major equipment for the construction site. There were times when we didn't have the quality or the quantity, and we had to substitute. Materials of construction were extremely important because we were handling reactions and processes that had never been handled before outside of the laboratory. We had needs for new materials, new alloys, and for great quantities that people could not understand. They couldn't understand why we would require miles and miles of concrete pipe, miles of transmission cable, why we would need such quantities of special alloy steel, why so many valves, the type of valves used in boiler plants, chemical plants and shipbuilding, especially submarines.

This brings up the point of some of the conflicts we had with other defense programs. We were at the height of the shipbuilding effort. Kaiser was building ships on the West Coast, there were shipyards on the Gulf Coast, the East Coast. Landing vessels to battleships. This required labor, we were competitive for skilled labor, we were competitive for the materials, particularly steel piping and tubing, steel plate. All were used in shipbuilding and we needed them for the atomic program. At times, we ran head to head in conflict with shipbuilding, Army tank and projectile programs.

We were looking for skilled labor. Welders, electricians, pipefitters, steel workers, carpenters, masonry people. These people were in demand. Many in their trade were in the armed services. The Kaiser Corporation was building ships on a production basis and they had a great demand for the same type of labor we wanted. We ran head to head in recruiting. Kaiser had recruiters throughout the United States and so did we.

Here's a little sidelight, hearsay only. Baseball was a great source of relaxation and at Hanford each craft, like carpenters, fitters and so forth, had its own team and there was an organized league between the crafts. One craft in particular was not doing too well. The head of the craft, the superintendent, said he wanted some changes in the league standings. He instructed recruiters in that craft to do some screening in the selection of candidates for hiring. This craft superintendent, unnamed but known to me, told his recruiters to concentrate on the Pacific Coast League baseball players. As a result, the craft went from the bottom to the top of the league. Du Pont corrected this method of recruiting labor.

In aluminum, we were asking the manufacturers, mostly Aluminum Company of America, to extrude aluminum tubing that they had never extruded in quantity before. We were running in competition with shipbuilding and aircraft builders. Aircraft builders needed aluminum tubing for struts and wings and aluminum sheeting for the fuselage. In no time, Hanford had exceeded the aluminum company's capacity in this tug of war for war materials.

If we weren't getting what we thought we should, we would raise strong voices. Calls would come into Wilmington and sometimes I had to contact General Groves in Washington, D.C. In many cases, Groves personally would have to call the president of a company. Groves would quiz me about the problem, if we had tried alternatives, if we had done everything we could to get a particular item. You might say I made the snowballs and Groves threw them. But I had to make sure the snowball was well packed and we knew why it was necessary for him to throw it.

After he was convinced of the need, he would get on the phone with the company, not rant and rave but calmly point out to the executive what was going on, that Hanford was an important job that had the personal endorsement of the president of the United States and that it was the highest priority in the country. Groves would ask that the president of the company look into the matter personally. We had to do this a few times and never did we have any resentment or have anybody complain about undue pressure. And, it worked.

Occasionally, a company president or industry group would meet with Groves in Washington. I recall once there was disagreement and Groves asked his secretary, Mrs. O'Leary, to go to the office safe and take out President Roosevelt's letter which gave the atomic work presidential priority, which Groves read to the group. These situations did not come about because of lack of integrity or lack of planning. It happened because the industries were over-taxed.

Remember, at Hanford we were embarking into an area where there was no experience. We were plowing new fields. We couldn't take chances. I remember when Groves first came to Du Pont in 1942, he challenged us and told us we not only had to do the job on time but we had to do a quality job. He recalled when he was a company commander the barracks toilets were always clogged because of over-use of toilet paper. He said if you needed to put larger lines in to prevent this, do it. Get it right the first time.

I think I should talk a little bit about General Groves and Du Pont. He wanted the Du Pont Company to participate in the Manhattan Project because of the company's capability and integrity, its history in the explosives program and because of his direct connection with Du Pont through his position in military construction. Groves recognized not only the construction requirements for the atomic program, but he was a very strong advocate of on-site construction safety, and in that Du Pont was proud of its record.

Another thing, General Groves never, to me, expressed any misgivings about the atomic bombs. To his death, I believe he felt it was the humanitarian thing to do. It certainly saved American lives, the casualties to the Japanese, although not desirable, and there was great grief to the Japanese people, you had to equate that to the casualties on the battlefield if there had been an invasion. That very definitely also is my view. I guess I'm still a hard-nosed patriot, but I think the bombs were necessary, a humanitarian thing to do. A bit on the vindictive side, but the Japanese played damn dirty to us.

LEON OVERSTREET

Oklahoma-born Leon Overstreet went into construction in 1941 after he learned a little pipefitting with American Can in Kansas City. He retired in 1979 after helping build the Fast Flux Test Facility and Washington Public Power Supply System No. 2, both at Hanford. During the interview at his Richland residence, he was especially amused by his recollection of an outhouse scrawl he read at Hanford in 1944. "Come on you Okies/Let's take Japan/We took California/And never lost a man."

I was the ninth fitter hired on the Du Pont construction job and my brother Paul was the tenth. We came in together. I was working at the Sunflower Ordnance Works in Kansas, near Kansas City. I was a steamfitter. On a day in May, 1943, I happened to be in the can and I heard two laborers talking. They said, "Boy, there's a big job out at Walla Walla, Washington." I called after work that day, to the union business manager at Walla Walla, Washington, and he happened to be a barber. He said to come on out and bring all of them who are willing to work. He said he heard it was the largest construction job in the world. I got my brother and a welder I was working with interested and we got all our coupons for gasoline and tires and came on out.

Why did I want to leave Kansas? Because when I was a kid in Oklahoma in my geography classes they had these big pictures of snow-capped mountains and clear running streams. In Oklahoma and all the water you fished in there smelled, and so did the fish. Man, I could just visualize that Northwest out there. I had always heard of it and I thought man this is my chance to get out there. So we did.

We came on out. It took us several days. The welder pulled a trailer and him and his wife would cook our meals. My brother and I, they only had one bed in that trailer, we slept in the car. We got out here and landed in Prosser and stayed in a hotel. The morning when we went out to go to work, this fella we rode out there with, a carpenter or somebody, he said it was the largest construction job in the world. When we came over the hill and looked down on this Hanford site, all we saw were eight or ten buildings, frame buildings, under construction. It didn't look very big to us. That was the 7th day of May, 1943.

Our union was the United Association of Journeymen Plumbers and Steamfitters. All the crafts people were unionized. I'm sure Leslie Groves had foresight enough to know, well, he was in a hurry to build that, and he didn't want any labor problems. If he had had mixed people, some non-union, there would have been delays on the job. I knew of no labor troubles. Oh, we protested over the firing of a boss one time. Jack Dimmler got fired and everybody working for him went into the superintendent's place and protested, more or less of a shutdown for a little while, and the guy was hired back. I remember it was terribly hot, and no shade. There was always ice water. At first the lids on the ice barrels were open but they had to lock them after some guy was caught washing his false teeth.

Working conditions were good. They wanted to get on with the job. If you had a problem, they would try to deal with it. Du Pont made an impression on me, probably the best company I ever worked for. They know how to build a job, I'll tell you that much. Of all the places I've been since then, around Hanford, nobody comes close to Du Pont. They knew how to organize and build a job. I worked in the Hanford Camp for about a year. They came around with a Q clearance, and told us we had been selected to be Q-cleared to go out in the areas to work. A lot of people that were not selected because they had criminal records.

We went out to 100-B (the first reactor) in May, 1944, we were among the first steamfitters on the job. I was, I guess, amazed. I couldn't figure it out. I looked at that thing we were working on, this reactor. It had all kinds of tubes and pipes running through it, and graphite blocks that the other crafts were laying around the pipes. Nobody could understand what kind of a contraption it was. They had never seen anything like it. You can usually understand what you're doing. But boy that one floored us.

I had never heard of anybody splitting an atom. I had studied atoms, being the smallest particles, in school, you know. But I had never heard of anyone splitting one of them. When I first saw B, it was just coming out of the ground. They had the base of the thing already down. Other crafts had done that. A lot of the preliminary work had been done, but we came in on the piping end of it. And boy they was really ganging that thing. You could hardly take a step without running over somebody. We swarmed over that thing, like flies. When I first got to 100-B I was running three-quarter inch stainless steel pipe through the graphite blocks. I never did know what these were for.

The aluminum tubes that held the uranium were about an inch and a half or three-quarters in diameter. Later I was put on the aluminum tubes. We had to anneal them on the end and make a flange on each end. The annealing was to soften them so they wouldn't split when we flanged it. The flange was to make a seal against another flange which would be put on the face. Then the pigtails would come off the threadalets on the cross sections. The pigtails supplied water to go through the aluminum tubes and also to take it away.

I never lived in the barracks. My family was in Prosser. I went back and forth every day. We worked overtime nearly all the time, probably 10 hours a day. In a week, I'm pretty sure I worked 10 hours a day, sometimes 50. Most of the time we worked six days, they were in a hurry. Sometimes we worked on Sunday. I was making $1.65 an hour, but that was high wages then.

I remember Colonel Matthias called a mass meeting, outside at White Bluffs, the spring of 1944. Thousands came. He wanted to get it across to everybody how important it was. Some people didn't seem as dedicated as they could have been. He made a pretty good speech. It gave us all a shot in the arm. When we left there we were ready to build a plant. He did say that it was impossible to tell us what we were doing because the enemy would like to know. We were not allowed, he said, to discuss it with each other, just like our foreman had told us. But he said I can tell you this much, that it's important and the enemy, Germany, is attempting to do the same thing we are, to build a plant like this. And whoever gets there first will win the war. And that was enough said. We didn't ask any further questions.

Most of the construction workers were older than me. I was one of the youngest, I was 30. I wasn't drafted. When I was in Kansas, I told my draft board I had a chance to go to Washington to work in a war plant and they said that would be all right as long as I kept in touch, because they expected to be a-calling me before too long. I fully expected to be out here about a month or two and get called. But as it so happens Du Pont was getting us deferments. I had two kids, but they wouldn't have kept me out forever.

When we heard about the bombs, it was a great feeling. I felt that my effort had been worthwhile. Everybody I worked with was glad to be able to talk about it, and we were all pretty glad we had been a part of it. That ended the war, and saved a lot of lives. When I heard about the bombs, I was in Richland maintaining swamp coolers.

ROBERT E. BUBENZER

Bob Bubenzer was supervisor of Hanford plant protection for Du Pont from 1943 until early 1945. He was interviewed by telephone at his home in Indianapolis.

At the peak, in July, 1944, we had 1,395 patrolmen, which were the same as police, but Du Pont called it patrol. That was plant patrol, boats on the river and perimeter patrol. There was military intelligence out there, and from time to time FBI men. We never had any serious attempts at sabotage. All of the espionage cases, as I recall, were crackpots. We had some doozies.

In one particular accident, we had a steam locomotive run into a diesel engine. If I remember correctly, all four of the men in the cabs, two in each cab, were killed. I think there was another accident where seven people were killed in the collapse of a tank. The railroad accident was about halfway between Hanford and White Bluffs. I remember it very specifically. It was a very foggy morning and somehow they got their signals crossed and they ran headon into each other. It looked like a scene from a silent movie, bodies hanging out. It was really a morbid scene.

We had our own kangaroo court, and our own jail. Every morning we would screen them and unless it was awfully serious, a pat on the back and "Don't do it anymore" was our theory. Fights and drunks. We had some homicides. Usually they occurred in or around the barracks. Motivation was usually little or none, a crap game or stickup, a couple of arguments got out of control. We had very little racial problem, the blacks were in separate barracks.

We tried to control gambling. We wouldn't let any professional gambling set up. We had to let the poker and the dice games, you know, a group of guys wanted to shoot craps, we permitted it. We knew bootlegging was going on, and we knew where it was going on, but at that time booze was rationed, I think we got one fifth of bourbon every two weeks at the liquor store. A lot of these boys got legitimate liquor out of Chicago and they would bootleg it on the premises. I think it was common knowledge with the management and the military. They mainly wanted it kept under control.

I remember one particular fellow came in and laid $10,000 in bills in front of me and said he wanted protection for a game, he was going to run a card game. He happened to be a fellow I knew out of St. Paul. There was no way we would let him run it. I believe he would have run a very honest game.

Another of the morale-building war effort billboards.

U.S. Department of Energy

Due to the fact the women were in separate barracks, and you had to sign in, and the men and women both lived in dormitories, there was some prostitution but not too much. Most of the rapes occurred because a customer didn't want to pay. We had quite a bit of homosexual problems, among certain blacks who came out there. After a while, military intelligence told us we had more important things to do. It was confined almost entirely to certain barracks and these guys would all try to get in the same barracks.

In some cases, we would terminate lawbreakers, but in most cases it was important that we got them back to work. We needed workers.

Drunkenness was prevalent. And depression was quite a deal, and this was a big reason for people leaving there. Homesickness too, it was a depressing sort of a place. It was almost like being in prison. Wired in, barb wire. Men separated from the women, even husbands and wives were separated sometimes. We had a number of nervous breakdowns of personnel. It was loneliness and depression and they hit the booze very hard.

We had some crackpots that kept harassing us. They were amateur detectives. I remember one particularly, a woman from Tennessee, who came in the office one day and said "I am the black widow, and I will attack the Germans." We had a number of these and they were strictly uncategorized. They would come in to report a guy had a radio, and were sure it was a two-way radio. These incidents had to be put somewhere, so we put them under "Un-Americanism."

Un-Americanism also might be criticism or protest against Roosevelt. They would be gradually eased out, or told to shut up. They would make stump speeches in the messhalls. They would stand up, half drunk, and put on a little bit of a show. We had to quiet them down quite often in the messhalls. A lot of times I would go down myself and talk to them. One day I got beaned by a coffee pot.

We had a woman, Olive Coldiron, she was one of the people in a Western Union stickup. Stoppelmoor, a blond kid, shot a rigger in a crap game, a guy named McDonald. Stoppelmoor went and shot him four or five times. He had lost money in a crap game. When we arrested Stoppelmoor, no problem at all, and brought him in, he agreed, he said "The big boy took the bullets like a man and I can take whatever's coming to me like a man." The big guy recovered and refused to prosecute. Stoppelmoor was held for murder, but the man he shot didn't want to prosecute. He said, "Ah, he's a good kid."

D.W. Lindsey, a woman, was tied in with another fella on a murder. She was picked up originally on theft charges at a barracks and when we took her in the first thing she said was "I've got syphilis, so they'll throw the book at me." It turned out she was wanted in Missouri for murder. She was in with C.K. Melton. They were wanted for murder, and were suspected of killing somebody on the reservation. Tolliver was with them. He was a tough nut.

The homicides generally resulted from little female problems, and hold-ups of crap games or muggings that turned into homicides. There were very few murders in fights but people did get badly injured. Everyone who came on the reservation were searched. They checked in their firearms and one time we must have had 5,000 guns at patrol headquarters. Some of the most beautiful guns I ever saw in my life.

Most suicides were caused by mental collapse. One little girl she lived across the yard from us in Richland. Here again, she was despondent. She put a bullet in her head. I recall another fella who slashed his throat. I think he was homesick and he was wanted by the police back home.

We had to bring cash in every pay day for the bank. We had an armored car, and we had two cars in front of it and two cars behind it and an airplane overhead. We would bring it from the railroad station at Pasco. My guess the cash came from Spokane. It was cash for cashing checks and we took it to the bank in Hanford Camp. I think we thought we were transporting between one and two million dollars. In mail sacks. This was on a Friday, and every Friday we would have 12 armed guards at the bank.

We had several fatal automobile accidents. I remember the first one, it was out on the back road from Hanford to White Bluffs to Yakima. A couple of people were killed. We had no ambulances so we put my bed in the back of a panel truck and put this woman on it, and as we were going over a hill here were six or seven wild horses. We took the ditch and when we got to Yakima she was certainly dead.

They had a Navy training station at Pasco, and a bomber base at Walla Walla. These fliers from Pasco would come over the area and shoot coyotes. I can remember three or four crashes of the training planes. They would swoop down over the river, and when they would try to go over at White Bluffs evidently there was a turbulence right there and two or three crashed right across the river from Hanford. All that would be left of the pilots would be the torso enclosed in the pilot suit. We also had these bombers, they were cutting up, they would fly real low and if you know the road between Hanford and Richland was sort of up and down. You'd be coming up a ridge and all of a sudden a bomber would come over the top of you, right in your face. They were four motor jobs, B-17s I think.

Has anybody told you the story of Willie Stokes, the black boy from New Orleans? He was probably retarded, and for years he sold newspapers on the streets of New Orleans. Somehow he was recruited for Hanford, and he came out on the train. He didn't eat for three or four days and was probably abused on the way. Well, he ran into the Columbia and tried to swim across and he died. That caused quite a stir out there because the lad had been mistreated. I know Frank Mackie and the top echelon raised a barrel of hell about sending out a man like that. He arrived horribly frightened and wrecked a messhall. We had to put him in a cell for his own protection. We had a fellow named Jim Salisbury from Tennessee, a southerner, a real southerner, who talked to Willie and we thought had him straightened out. We promised he could work in the orchards. This seemed to please him. The next day when the police officers unlocked his cell, out Willie went and nobody could stop him. He ran to the river and tried to swim across. He was tremendously strong. Six foot one, 230 pounds, terrific strength, probably about 30 years old. We had power boats, and four or five men tried to get him into a boat. He fought us. I am sure he died of a heart attack.

You know, when we first went out there, the fishing was terrific at that fish ladder on the Yakima. It was wonderful, with the orchards, and you could shoot all the geese and ducks and pheasants that you could haul.

But, I got no pleasure in putting people in prison. You know, I wasn't cut out for a police officer and the misery that went with it. Trips to Walla Walla and a few other places and seeing these people in jail, it started to turn me against it. I thought it was an interesting part of my life but I wouldn't want to do it again. After the war I went into building materials out of Cincinnati.

Summary of incidents dealt with by police during peak construction period from March 15, 1943 through August 28, 1944

Intoxication 3,156	Burglary 1,124
Petty larceny 593	Assaults 522
Public nuisance 478	Grand larceny 450
Wanted elsewhere 217	Vagrancy 197
Robbery 177	Gambling 161
Trespassing 144	Drunken driving 123
Missing persons 108	Auto theft 105
Juvenile delinquency 97	Mental cases 89
Bootlegging 88	Sex cases 69
Draft evasion 50	Un-Americanism 44
Natural death 25	Mob demonstration 19
Accidental death 19	Violent death 5
Suicide 4	

Data from R.E. Bubenzer

LESTER BOWLS

Lester Bowls was retired from Boeing. He lived in Seattle's North End and ran a saw sharpening shop at his residence to make a little spending money. He called himself "a guy with a fourth-grade Arkansas education who raised seven kids, and five went to college."

I'm from Arkansas. Little Rock. I went to work for Du Pont, war plants in Tennessee, then Alabama, then Tennessee again, Oak Ridge. Du Pont built a mockup of Hanford at Oak Ridge. Well, I worked on that as a carpenter. At the end of the job at Oak Ridge, they classified me as a millwright. A millwright is kind of a mechanical carpenter. At one time millwrights and carpenters was in the same local, but millwrights went more for setting machinery.

We kind of nicknamed the Oak Ridge plant the chewing gum plant or something of that nature, Hanford too, we didn't what we were working on. I came out here to Hanford in July, '43.

I worked a week or such a matter at the construction camp, then I got sent out to 2-West. They sent me up to be an expediter, furnish materials for the crafts. You know, run materials down for the crafts. A person would have to be there to really understand the madhouse that was going on. They was hiring everybody that was loose, and they got here and there was nothing you might say for them to do or nowhere to put 'em. Some of the people wouldn't stay three days before they would be gone again.

I worked primarily a lot with millwrights and machinists. A lot of our stuff come through the machine shop. For instance, somebody would give an order for so many hundred tie rods, a certain length, or something like that. That was my job. I would collect my information of what the craft foremen or general foreman would want, and then I would supply that to him, from the millwrights, or the machine shop or the lumber yard. I had around 140 foremen at one time ordering through me. That went on for quite a long while, I don't know, six or eight months. Eight months is a long time in a construction crew.

After I worked at the reactor areas for a few months then the job was winding down and we were given a chance to go on maintenance or into operations. I went into operations, at the 300 Area, processing uranium to get ready for the reactors. That was in the latter part of '44. My job was primarily to run a turret lathe. We were cutting the slugs. The uranium looked like, as best as I can explain it, a piece of cold-rolled iron. It came in billets, then it was hot and extruded out into smaller rods and then the smaller rods is what we turned. It was precise work, I think we had about five or sixth-thousandths of an inch tolerance. A slug was about eight inches long and an inch and five-eighths in diameter, but in fact I'm not gonna tell you those things. They were canned in aluminum, but the exact measurements I'm not gonna tell you.

I had no big complaint living in the barracks. They were two men to a room. Of course it was like batching anyplace, or living anyplace, you really had no privacy. I just wanted a place to sleep. They furnished good bedding. The messhall was very good, I would say it was exceptionally good food there. The variety was good, and plentiful. It was sanitary, I got no complaints about it.

The bombs wasn't a big surprise. Oh, cause really I was one of those type of people that as far as the secrecy and all was concerned I didn't let it bug me, I didn't care in the least, the less I thought about it the better off I figured I was and so consequently if they said we was making chewing gum it was all right with me. But they dropped the bomb, it all fell in place.

HARRY PETCHER

Harry Petcher was the box lunch king. He and his late wife, Maxine, worked in Hanford's food service almost from the beginning. Interviewed at his apartment in Bellevue, Washington, Harry played a couple of swing tunes on his living room jukebox and cracked some beers before telling his story.

Let me start from the beginning. My wife and I we got married in May, 1943, and I was managing a night club in Chicago at that time, and during the day I was working for the Army Signal Corps on Pershing Road in Chicago as a nomenclature clerk. The reason I was doing this work is the fact I had flat feet, and they eliminated you from the draft if you had flat feet. I became a 4-F with the stipulation that I do war work, so I took this job with the Signal Corps, and the reason, General Carver, a good friend of my dad's, he was in charge of the Signal Corps and my dad was in the meat packing industry. He said to my dad, he says he could get me into the service and I would be a major before I knew it. My dad said, "Naw, I don't think he wants to go into the service. He's got flat feet."

Workers jam one of the eight mess halls which had a total capacity of 19,500 diners. Millions of meals were served, with few complaints about quality or quantity.   *U.S. Department of Energy*

The night club I managed was across from the Morrison Hotel, and it was called The Talk of the Town. One day my wife called me up at the Signal Corps. Well, basically we were looking for some other work. One of the reasons was I had a real fantastic Jewish mother. She would call us up at 8 o'clock in the morning. My wife worked at the Latin Quarter, as a cocktail waitress. And my mother, God bless her soul, would call us at 8 o'clock and say, "How are you kids?"

"Fine mom, how are you?"

"Are you getting ready to go to work?"

One day my wife told me we were getting the hell out of Chicago.

My wife was from Iowa, and had worked in New York. So anyway she called me at work one day and said, "Honey, I just took a job for both of us at a place called Hanford, Washington." I said you gotta be kidding. What are we going to do there? She told me I would be a waiter and she would be a waitress. What's it going to pay? She told me 55 cents an hour. I said you gotta be kidding. They promised a 12-hour day, seven days a week, time and a half after eight hours. That was 85 cents an hour, room and board, big wages.

Nobody complained about lack of food during the Hanford Camp era, or about the cost. A week's mess hall grub cost $12.98: Breakfast: dry cereal, grapefruit, oatmeal, eggs, minced ham, fried potatoes, toast, butter substitute, coffee cake, coffee and fresh milk…Dinner: ham and beans, gravy, parsley, buttered potatoes, spinach, mixed green salad, cottage cheese, jelly, bread, peanut butter, black cherries, cookies, coffee…Supper: fried chicken, country gravy, mashed potatoes, corn, asparagus, celery, raw carrot strips, cottage cheese, bread, butter substitute, cream pie, coffee. The first meals were served April 21, 1943, and the last mess hall closed February 20, 1945, when construction ended. The eight mess halls had a capacity for 19,500 diners. Total meals served from April 27, 1943 until January 1, 1945, were 20,950,181. Box lunches totaled 3,088,480.

The company that had advertised was called the B.F. Brown Company, which owned the Olympic Commissary which is what the Hanford operation was called. B.F. himself, and young Jim Brown, kind of looked at me when I came up to the office. I'm wearing a gabardine suit, a Borsalino hat, and this is in July, '43 when I was 27. He asked if we had experience, and we said we had. So he got us tickets for the Chicago, Northwestern, we connected with the Great Northern in Minneapolis. A fellow named Frank Palordi picked us up in Minneapolis and we stayed overnight.

Basically, it was a troop train, it was endless, just endless hours to get where we were going. And July 3rd, we arrived in Pasco, Washington. And let me tell you something, being raised in the big city of Chicago and eating in some of the finest restaurants in Chicago, we got off that train and I looked around and I said, "Honey, I don't know if we're going to make this or not. She was a pretty sturdy girl, and she said, "No, we're going to do it, we're going to do it."

They took us to a barracks to sleep that night, separate. The next day was July 4th, and we spent it in Pasco. They had a six or seven horse parade, drums, maybe six drummers, up and down, flags, and we spent the day in Pasco. It was 105 degrees. The next day we went to the personnel office and the guy looked at Maxine, and said to her, "I'm sure you can do more than waitress work." Maxine said she was the head waitress at the Latin Quarter for a couple of years. He looked at me, and said I must know more than being a waiter. I explained I had had experience in the meat packing industry and immediately we got a raise from 55 cents an hour to 75 cents. My wife would go to work as a mess hall supervisor and I would be a butcher.

The next day they put us in these buses that ran in the 1933 World's Fair in Chicago, long open buses towed by a truck. Let me tell you, we ate more sand in the 40 miles to Hanford, it was endless. We got off the bus and we sank in sand a foot deep. There was no such thing as a sidewalk. They took us to the Grange Hall and that's where we had our first meal.

The way the food was prepared was all family style. The waitresses or waiters would run with these big carts up to the front where the cooks were dishing this stuff into family pans, like fried chicken. They would heap these big pans with fried chicken and run down the aisle and scoot it on these tables where all these guys were sitting, banging their hands. It looked like a prison camp to me.

We had what we called a center kitchen, and we did our own baking. It was a very good camp operation. We would lay butcher paper over the table after the tables were set with silverware and napkins. The reason for that was that at four o'clock every afternoon, the wind would come up and blow that sand. I mean that sand would sit anywhere from a quarter of an inch to an inch on all this. All we would do is pull the paper off and the sand went on the floor. We didn't bother sweeping the floor except to pick up food.

Working in the meat shop, I was more or less assistant to the butcher, John Dickey. He took off one day. He left me in charge of the meat market for the messhall. Dickey told me not to forget the meatballs, get the meat ground up for the meatballs. Don't forget the seasoning. Meantime, a couple of supervisors showed up. Jack Maline came into the messhall and said Dan Shea and I want to talk to you. I went to the guy under me and said don't forget the seasoning in the meatballs. He was a real fat comical guy, I don't know if he is still alive. Instead of putting salt into the meat, he put sugar in. The next day when all this meat was sent to the messhall kitchen to be made into meatballs and cooked and simmered, everything was fine. until we got a police call. There was a riot in the messhall. Everybody was standing on their benches, picking these meatballs up and throwing them at the cooks. Getting hit by one of them was like getting hit by a golf ball. We had to call the riot squad. That was called the meatball riot.

Anyway, one of the reasons Shea and Maline called me, they wondered if I knew anything about making sandwiches. I said I did. They gave me a new job, they called me the nosebag. We were making sandwiches for box lunches, putting them in a paper bag. The first day I made something like 500. That went on, then we got the second messhall, and the third messhall, and the fourth messhall, and the box lunch orders were getting bigger and bigger and bigger, til finally Bob Burton, one of the Du Pont project managers, said we need a space for manufacturing these box lunches. They built a complete unit in about six days. I mean, these people, you would get up in the morning and walk through your barracks and there's about 20 more barracks that weren't there last night.

I moved into the unit, and I had my own kitchen, my own cutting rooms, and my peak we were making anywhere from 50,000 to 55,000 box lunches a day. I was in charge of the box lunch department, a 24-hour operation. I had about 370 some odd people, mostly women who were wives of construction workers.

The messhalls were not segregated by race or sex. We did have a lot of people from Arkansas, Texas, Oklahoma, people that today we call Arkies and Okies. They came with mattresses on top of their cars and trucks. Really, I thought it was the "Grapes of Wrath" to be honest with you. There was not any great segregation, that I could detect. I never heard of any racial trouble. If there were any incidents, it was basically a personal matter.

Coming back to the box lunches. We had what we called field messes. A lot of the box lunches were distributed out to the field messes for people who were way way out. I had from 20-30 refrigerated trucks running out into the areas delivering these box lunches. Most of them were picked up in the mess hall after breakfast. The mess halls made the coffee to go with them. Some messhalls made anywhere from 150 to 350 gallons of coffee a day. Everybody had a Thermos bottle. The bread was manufactured on the premises. We built another bake shop. They did pies and lots of different pastries, like dough-nuts and muffins. The food was very, very good.

Bascially, we had scrambled eggs, eggs up, pancakes, roast beef, chicken, fish. Most of our fish was fresh, it came out of Seattle. Salmon steaks, baked salmon. We had mashed potatoes, fresh because we were close to Moses Lake and Ephrata, the potato belt. We served a lot of beets from Utah. Most of the beef came from the Chicago-Omaha area. We served steak, not a lot of it, but we served it.

It took them 10 minutes to eat a meal. The way it worked was, all this food was dished up by the cooks in great big bowls and platters. A table took care of 12 people. Two bowls of potatoes, two bowls of chicken, two bowls of whatever was served. The waiters came along pushing carts of food. As fast as one was emptied, there was another. You couldn't sit anywhere you wanted. You were sent to the first empty table. And there was no lingering over a second cup of coffee. We did have a little alcove at the ends of the mess halls where there were containers of coffee where a guy could fill his Thermos and take it to his barracks.

The box lunch was like this, about 1,500 calories. We had three sandwiches with three ounces of food in each sandwich. Cheese, beef, or ham or chicken. There was fresh fruit, every once in a while we had salad. We used to give them a cold baked potato. A potato is a good vitamin source. Another thing, we dropped in two salt tablets in the box lunch. Toward the end, we started putting in candy bars, chewing gum and cigarettes, a sample pack of four. Our lunch cost was about 38 cents. We charged 55 cents.

We did have one problem. One of the girl's husbands solved it. Jessie Green, her husband Jimmy Green solved it. The way we made our sandwiches, we would put 12 to 18 pieces of bread on a tray and one girl would put margarine on them, another would put meat on and another would put the top on and another would put it in the wrapping machine. We were having a terrific slow job spreading the margarine. It was a bottle neck. But Jimmy Green came up with a good idea. He took a paint spray gun and he filled it with margarine and then he put two cathodes with electric heat and put those down into the margarine. Then after the margarine got hot and liquid he would take the spray gun and spray the bread. Necessity is the mother of invention.

After a while, my wife and I found a little house in White Bluffs. We had been living in the barracks and then a trailer for a while. Then, I found a place over toward Connell, about 12 miles from Hanford, across the river, for $20 a month. It had been a sheep ranch, and there were fruit trees, peaches, cherries, apricots, nectarines, fruit they called a yakamine, a cross between a nectarine and a peach. Alfalfa grew like it was going out of style. There was a creek running through it, and asparagus and rattlesnakes. Lots of rattlesnakes. And, we were allowed to have horses.

We used to go up to a place called Priest Rapids where there were Indians. The Indian chief was Johnny Buck. In order to get the horses, we had maybe six or seven gallons of wine with us, and we would say to Johnny Buck, we want to buy horses. He'd get the braves together and say we wanted horses, and everybody was having a good time with the wine, and two or three hours later here would come a load of horses, wild mustangs. You picked any you wanted for $2 a head. We promised Johnny Buck more wine. He died 12-14 years ago and they buried him at Priest Rapids. I went to the funeral. It's gorgeous there.

The social life was fantastic. We had a lot of married people we knew. Carpenters, electricians, plumbers, truck drivers, secretaries for the Army and the Du Pont Company. We had people over to our ranch, I hate to say I was a rancher because I'm not, I'm a nice boy from Chicago. I don't think I wore any boots until I came out. I didn't know what a cowboy was, except for Hoot Gibson and Yakima Canute, they're the only people I ever knew who had boots. We had potluck barbeques at my place. I bought an old Model A Ford convertible for the 12-mile drive to Hanford Camp.

As hard as those guys worked, on Saturday nights they drank a lot of beer and had a lot of fun. They used to grab one of the dump trucks that belonged to the company they worked for. They would pull mattresses out of the barracks, throw them into the dump truck, load the dump truck with people and everybody had beer or booze and head for the desert.

When it came to women, well a lot of fellows were able to get away for a while and go to Sunnyside, Yakima, Spokane, Prosser, Moses Lake. Moses Lake had a lot of sporting houses. A lot of guys would go to Spokane. Spokane had a red light district.

My wife and I would work six straight weeks and go to Yakima for a little vacation. We stayed in the Chinook Hotel, a couple of blocks up from the bus depot. We would hitch hike through Moxie and drop beer in the creek, to get cool.

The life was good. We did have the advantage of saving an awful lot of money. When I left I was getting close to $1,150 a month, my wife was getting about the same. At that time in the '40s, it was great money. We were able to save because we had nothing to spend it on. After the bomb went, there was nothing much to do. We became surplus employees. When the bombs were dropped my recollection was, "God, is that what we were doing here? Did we get poisoned?"

MONSIGNOR WILLIAM J. SWEENEY

Monsignor Sweeney, a folksy talkative man in clerical garb, was inter-
viewed at his residence, the rectory of Christ the King Catholic Church in
Richland. Although slowed somewhat by age and heart surgery, Sweeney
was clear in his recollections. He studied for the priesthood in Worcester,
Massachusetts, and came to Washington state in 1938. He had kept his
New England, slightly Irish, accent.

After I left Massachusetts, I was stationed in Spokane and after that I went to
Republic, up in the mines. In July, 1943, then, I was sent down here by the
bishop when Hanford was just starting. Like he said at the time, I don't know
what they're doing down there but you go down and take care of us.

On Holy Days during the week, I said Mass in a private home. There
would be only a few women there. This project was only just starting, so
there was no grass, and there was a lot of dirt and dust. When I finished
saying Mass, I had brought a vacuum cleaner from Kennewick, I would vacuum
the floor.

I went to Hanford. I was trying to find a church up there, at the construction camp. I have to back up a little. We started at White Bluffs. There was a
church at White Bluffs, it was a Catholic church, an old dance hall originally,
evidently. There was a ticket window in front. On my way driving up there, I
would pick up the workers who were walking from Hanford to White Bluffs
to go to church.

After that, they gave us a tent, in Hanford. A small tent, maybe a hundred
feet long and just so wide. They put a confessional for us in there, a closet
actually. The tent roof leaked. I said Mass there one Sunday when it was
pouring rain. No lights. I used to light two candles on the altar so the people
could know where the aisle was. That seated about a hundred at the most.
One Sunday it rained and my housekeeper was there with her mother, and
they had to sit between the puddles on the seats. I was giving communion and
water was coming down on my bald spot and running right down my face.

That tent was absolutely inadequate. That's when they told me I could
use the circus tent. It was already up, it was a big one, a regular three-ring
circus tent. It was so big you couldn't see the people sitting in the back. It was
a movie theater during the week.

Circus tent that was used for church services and movies at Hanford Camp,
"a regular three-ring circus tent."   *U.S. Department of Energy*

They gave me a room at the front, with a live steam pipe running through
it. The room had two doors, one going into the theater and one to the
outside. No windows. I would hear confessions on Saturday night and there
would be two lines, everything had a line out there, one line going into the
theater and the other line going to confession. The sound box was right in
back of my chair and I would be giving instructions or hearing confessions,
and I could hear the movie sound. Sweet music, sometimes machine guns.

Before the circus tent, I would give instructions in my car in front of
Mess Hall No. 1. I would park my car in front and after they would finish
dinner a couple who wanted to get married would come and I would give
them instructions in my car. The windows would fog up, it was cold weather
then.

The altar for the circus tent came from a church in Hanford, the town. It
was one of those plaster altars, very decorative, and it made the tent look like
a church. It was put on a platform, with wheels and everything. On Sundays it
would be moved out of a storage room, and they made a little altar rail for me
and a few kneeling benches. When I got the tent, I hadn't really wanted it, I
wanted a church, but it was a good thing. One of the officials, told me if you
ever fill this tent, I'll quit. Well, the next Easter, in '44, I filled it.

Sometimes, I was so busy I wouldn't eat breakfast until 4 in the afternoon. I had a private room in the barracks and would sleep there sometimes. You never knew who you were going to meet in the hallways, but they were always kind, very kind. Those people up there were extraordinarily kind.

We filled that tent Sunday after Sunday. The tent got ragged. One of the women at the service told me you know the people here are really obnoxious. They whistle all during Mass. What she heard was ripping canvas and the wind whistling through the guy wires.

There was a big accident, later in '44. I was on that. I had another priest living with me in Kennewick. I went home to Kennewick that day and the other priest came out white as a sheet, and said the Red Cross is trying to get ahold of you. The Red Cross wanted me to get out to the project because something had happened. I started out from Kennewick, and I got to George Washington Way, at the bridge.

There was a patrol car with two patrolmen. I said I've got to get through to Hanford, something has happened. They said we'll take you and they started blowing their siren. You had to drive in the ditch then because they were building the street. The patrolmen started speeding, and from there on, that police car kept ahead of me in my little Chevrolet and I tried to keep up.

The speed limit was 35, I don't think in all my life I had gone over 40. My dad had an old car back home and when you got to 40 miles an hour it would vibrate. I tailed the patrolmen and we went by the 200 Area and they said we were going 80 miles an hour. All the guard stations waved us through. We got to Hanford and another police car took us to the hospital.

There was almost panic up there, with women from the trailer camp coming into the construction camp hospital to see if their husbands were hurt. The men had been working on a big tank and the tank fell. One fellow was on the operating table and I went in to him. Then they took me in to where the dead men were. They were black as coal, I thought they had been burnt. Peg, the head nurse, had gone through the pockets of these fellows and she found some Columbus medals or something on one of them, or two, so I took them first and anointed them. Then I went to the others.

When I left, I thanked the patrolmen for taking me up and you know what they told me? If our car had been up to snuff we would have got you up there in a hurry. I heard their car blew two tires the next day. I would have been killed because I was driving so close.

Yes, I was surprised at the bombs. I was in Spokane, in a store. I looked at the paper, and there was the story. That's when I found out. I don't recall my feelings then. But it was a terrible tragedy, and much worse than we knew. I object to nuclear weapons in war, but I don't object to nuclear energy used for peaceful purposes.

I remember a man in Spokane asked me how I could work out here, he didn't know how I could work in a place like this. I told him I am here because there are Catholics here.

MARGARET HOFFARTH

A woman in her mid-eighties, Mrs. Hoffarth was born in Colorado and came with her parents farther west, to Idaho, in a wagon train. She lost a son in the Pacific during World War II. Mrs. Hoffarth had some faded papers, which she brought out during a conversation at her kitchen table. One was a certificate which said she owned one share in a Boeing B-17, named "Day's Pay," which the Hanford workers bought and donated to the war effort.

I was living in Yakima, and they were advertising for help at Hanford. So a friend and I decided to go over. We went to Pasco, and signed in. They took our fingerprints and family history and then we went by bus to Hanford. I was a widow at that time, 43 years old and had three kids. That was in the spring of '43. Hanford Camp was just opening, and at first we stayed in the school house, but they could put up a barracks in two or three days, and I lived in the first women's barracks. I worked in a mess hall, waiting tables. There were lots of nice people there. I recall one man gave me $5, and said you have always been nice to me and helped when I needed some food. I didn't want to take it, I felt so dumb.

One time the men started screaming and yelling about some bad fish, it smelled terrible, oh, they got mad, they screamed and they yelled. One man threw his fish on the floor. That made me mad, and when the same man wanted more butter I told him I wouldn't give him more butter even if they had it. He looked at me, and said, "I'm awful sorry." Some of the cooks were greenhorns. One put a 100-pound sack of potatoes in the steamer, sack and all.

The barracks life, well, that was real nice. There were an awful lot of rough people there and they came from Chicago and everywhere. But I made a lot of friends and had a good time. They had a big high fence around the

**In 1944, Hanford workers contributed a day's pay to donate a Boeing B-17
bomber to the Army Air Forces.**   *U.S. Department of Energy*

women's barracks, way way high, and at the top they had barbed wire. So the
men couldn't climb over, you couldn't trust those guys. They had a man always
at the gate, and he always questioned you if any men were coming in. Check-
in, check-out.

We used to hear about people being killed, maybe somebody was killed
and their body was in a garbage can. I think that actually happened. One
time, at the recreation hall a bunch of us were sitting out and drinking pop
and we saw the guards taking a man out, and he had one of those old long
butcher knives. They took it away from him, so what he was trying to do, I
don't know. There was lots of nice people and some not so nice.

On entertainment nights, I always told the girls not to go by themselves,
never go alone with anybody. I had a little Indian girl friend, my roommate,

my partner, she called me mom. She was from North Dakota. She worked in the mess hall. She would bring some of these men over to meet me, and of course I had red hair and was real light-complected and she was so dark. They would wonder why she was calling me mom, and I would tell them, well, you know her dad could have been dark.

If anyone ever talked about his work, he was canned. We never knew what we were doing out there. All we were ever told was we were doing something to win the war.

Once, I was away from Hanford for two days, and when I came back I didn't know where I was, they used to put up a building in two days. Everything out there was sheer hurrying. When we packed up and left it was like a funeral. All those mobs of people, then nothing. I went to Richland then and worked in the mimeograph room and at a post office. I didn't stay long. I left and come back to Yakima.

ROBLEY L. JOHNSON

Rob Johnson arrived May 2, 1943, at the age of 35, one of the first Du Pont people on the scene. He came from Gopher Ordnance Works near St. Paul, a powder plant. At Hanford, Johnson supervised Du Pont's photo crew. The War Department photographs of Hanford released after Hiroshima and Nagasaki were his, although he got no credit, by name.

White Bluffs was a little bitty town of maybe 150 people. It was an orchard town, a ferry crossed the Columbia there. White Bluffs had a drug store that sold the best milkshakes I ever had, and an ice house, a train station. It was strictly a fruit-staging area, and a lot of orchards around there were just coming into their own when the government came in. I remember when I first came, we had a picnic at White Bluffs, near the ferry landing, on a Sunday and the next day I went to work.

We operated at first out of Pasco, until we opened the employment office at Hanford. I got here the second day of May in '43, and it couldn't have been more than a week later we started hiring and shipping people out to Hanford. We had recruiters all over the country. It was kind of scraping the bottom of the barrel you know, the war was on and a lot of people were gobbled up by the Army.

Robley L. Johnson, Du Pont's chief Hanford photographer, with his 4x5 Speed Graphic camera. *U.S. Department of Energy*

The people were met at the train, fed and put up temporarily and sent out to Hanford by bus. A lot of them would get off the bus, stand around for a while, see a dust storm coming and get on the next bus back to Pasco. They never even stayed overnight, a lot of them.

People, including me, came out here thinking Washington was the Evergreen State, and got dumped in a desert. I remember my boss came in one day and he said, "Well, Rob, we got two people on the rolls today. We hired 650 and 648 quit." The reasons for quitting were isolation, dust and no place to live. For a while, we couldn't hire enough carpenters to build barracks. We got over that hurdle and made progress, and eventually I made 145,000 ID photos. We used to have a saying, if you quit Hanford and joined the Army, you were a coward.

I had a Q clearance, the highest they were issuing at the time. It allowed me access to most any place. My people and I did everything. There were 50 to 60 of us, working three shifts. We used 4x5 Speed Graphics. If there was an accident we rushed out. I took some pictures of the face of the pile and the loading, but that was getting close to operations, when I was at the end of my tenure.

During the construction time, we had murders, we had rapes, it was a microcosm of society. I have pictures of stabbings, suicides, robberies, auto wrecks, a collision of two steam locomotives, on their sides, belching steam. One after a train engine hit a car and killed two occupants, Christmas gifts all over the place.

I went into operations for a while, as an operator at the 200 Areas, but I hated the goddamn work, it was so repetitious and boring, so when Colonel Matthias asked me if I wanted to do some publicity picture work for him, I jumped at the chance.

You know, it was a most unusual situation back then. You couldn't repeat it to save your life, not even if you had unlimited funds, because you had a world situation that affected it. It was just the experience of a lifetime. I enjoyed every minute of it.

F. J. McHALE

Francis McHale was a security and safety man, a civilian, with the Corps of Engineers. He came to Hanford from the Pennsylvania Ordnance Works to set up fire and safety and police protection for the Manhattan Engineer District. McHale retired in 1972 as director of security for the Atomic Energy Commission at Hanford.

I arrived in Pasco on the train around 1:30 in the morning, May 1, 1943. The wind was blowing like hell, and if a train had been going back East I would have been on it. I went to Hanford the next day, a Sunday, and nothing was there. No barracks or anything else. I was on per diem and was told to stick around. I was told this was Washington, the Evergreen State, and after a month and a half nobody could have gotten me away. It was an adventure.

I lived in a Pasco hotel for three or four weeks, then in a trailer camp near the river in Pasco for a month. After that I moved to a house in White Bluffs and stayed there until construction was done. Lots of housing was left in White Bluffs and wasn't torn down until construction was complete. Buildings in the town of Hanford were torn down right away so they could build the construction camp.

At White Bluffs, nearby, was a marshaling yard for the railroad, and warehouses. Also, the ice house was used for the project, as well as an old drug store, hotel, a saloon. They did business until construction was finished, and then most were torn down. Now, all that's left is what had been the bank and the ice house. There also was a red wooden railroad station, with green trim.

My title then was safety engineer and fire marshal. We had some major fires, and lost a fourth of one barracks. We had some trouble with water on that one because the water lines were just being put in. The fire was caused by a smoker on night shift. Nobody was killed. We did have some fatalities in construction. But accidents weren't common. This job had the lowest fire loss and lowest accident rate of any Corps of Engineers job.

I also worked on patrol security. The worst crime we ever had was when the Western Union was held up. They were caught in Yakima. Mostly, it was picking up drunks, and stopping fights. When you have construction workers, you have fights.

Remember a big percentage were Okies and Arkies. They were family people. They came here because they had nothing at home. They were damn good workers. That's what General Groves said. "It was the Okies and Arkies who built this job. The ideas may have come from the scientists but these people built it."

Groves was a rough, tough construction man, fair and honest. If he gave you a job to do, you damn well better do it. I used to see him periodically because he was an old fire buff and when he came out to Hanford he liked to visit the fire stations. Groves liked to have a meal and sit with the fellows and talk.

WILLIE DANIELS

A lively and talkative man in his early 80s, looking crisp in his seersucker coveralls, Daniels sat on his front porch in Pasco and talked of his Hanford years. He laughed a lot, his gold teeth flashing. Daniels was one of thousands of blacks who left low-paying jobs at home for high pay at wartime Hanford.

My home was in Kildare, Texas. I grew up there, went to high school in Jefferson, to college in Prairie View, a segregated school.

I took general education, and taught school for about four years in Texas. That was during the Depression, and man when you came out of school you had to scuffle and scuffle hard to get a job. Trouble was you only got paid for six or seven months teaching school in those days but you got to live 12 months a year. I worked anywhere I could.

I went to Texarkana and worked at the creosote plant and from there I worked up and down the railroad, loading ties. At Texarkana, I was working at a concrete plant, making $33.33 a week, that was good money then, working as a common laborer. I worked there a couple of years, and when I left there I heard about this job in McAlester, Oklahoma, in about '42, a naval air station. That job kinda went down, and we heard about this job in Washington state.

I had an uncle who come out here, and he wrote back and said they was paying a dollar a hour. I say, "What?" My brother say "A dollar an hour?" I say to my brother, "You going?" My brother was working on the railroad. He say, "I don't know. Them jobs don't last long." I say, "Man, I'm going, you do what you want. I got enough money for you to go." We got together, my brother, Vanis, myself and another boy. We came out to Hanford, in the late summer of '43. We went to work on Labor Day.

We came by bus, we paid our way. Du Pont was shipping some people, but we paid our way. Oh man, that bus broke down in the desert somewhere, and we sat a long while. We finally got to Umatilla, and we was looking at the country and we come around that road to Pasco alongside the river and that bus was leaning and it looked like that bus was going to jump over into that Columbia River. I know that man driving was looking at us back there, I imagine he was having fun looking as us so frightened.

I was so glad when we got to Pasco. We got off the bus at the station and looked around. I asked "Where that job is?" and nobody told us anything, so I went back to the bus station and said, "Lady, where's that big job going up around here." She say, "It's out at Hanford." I say, "Where's Hanford?" She says, "Sixty miles out. You go on the bus. One just left and the next one goes after midnight." I asked "Where do the colored people live around here?" She said, "Over across the track." We went across the track, and looked down the main street. We saw one or two houses. I said "Let's go back."

I went back to the station and said, "Lady, when people come in, going out to Hanford, where do they usually stay until the bus runs?" She said, "Well, Du Pont's got a place up there by the railroad station." We went up to the place, and an old colored gentleman was in there. I said we wanted to stay

The pay day view for Hanford workers. *U.S. Department of Energy*

the night until the bus goes. He said, "Did Du Pont send you?" I said, "No," and he said, "Well, I can't let you stay."

"Look," he said, "If you stay here and Du Pont didn't send you, that gets my job, if they find out. I'll let you stay, but be quiet about it." We lay down because we was tired. Along about two o'clock in the morning, this train came in from Chicago, loaded with fellows. The next morning, we got with those men and went to breakfast and didn't have to pay. We followed them around, and signed up to go out to Hanford on the bus. We went on out, no charges, and we got there and there was an old boy from home. I knew him from when I sold men's clothing. He says, "Hey, boy, did you bring your samples?" I say, "Yeah, I got 'em." "Well," he say, "Make me a suit."

They told us we would have to stay in tents that night. But I saw some barracks was finished but nobody was living in them. We got a blanket and slept in the new barracks in beds. The next morning there was so much wind and so much dust, everything was plowed up, you could write your name on our luggage.

We got signed up, and went to work for E.I. Du Pont. Our first day of work, we made $19.20, my brother and I together. They sent us to work on postholes, and we got some overtime. "Gee," my brother said, "$19.20 is more than I bring home in a month." I say to him, "I told you to come off that railroad."

The barracks were segregated. Lots of black people were out there, in construction, and lots more were just out there, not doing nothing. We would go to work and come back and some guy had been there ransacking our room. Once we came back to the barracks, and there were some guys in there scuffling. This guy had another one down, beating him, kicking him with steel-toe shoes, stomping him. He said, "I'll teach you to go in a room and take stuff, I'll bet you won't go in another one." In the barracks, there was drinking and fighting, and carrying on. Oh, man. There'd be gambling in the washrooms, and playing cards. Some of them were professional gamblers, out there to get all the money. I didn't mingle with that bunch, not at all.

No. 5 mess hall was where most of the colored people ate. Some whites ate there and some coloreds ate up in No. 2 mess hall. Generally, they ate separately. The food was good, and plenty of it. Long as you raise your hand up, they would bring you more.

I remember at Christmas, '43, some guys got to fighting in the messhall. Some guy with big ol' dark shades on, he was jumping on this little guy, and another guy was running from him, and this guy jumped up on a table and stepping from one table to another, trying to hit people, and everybody was running. He got close to where my uncle and I were, and I said I'm going to get that guy off that table, he don't have no business there. He got to the table next to us and threw a cup at the wall and almost hit my wife. I said I know I am going to get him off now, if he hits that little woman over there, I know what will happen to him. They'll take him to the cemetery and me to Walla Walla, cause I'm gonna eat him up. I had a jackknife, I still have it. It was sharp enough to shave a cat running. I used to trim carpet with it before I got into construction. You weren't supposed to carry a jack knife in your pocket, but I said this is a tool. In a few minutes, the security guards came and got him.

In those days, we worked about 12 hours a day, sometimes we worked more. Besides that, I was selling stuff, like toilet goods and I was working at that for Lucky Heart, cosmetics, perfume, hair dressing, powders. I was doing that on the side, some weeks I made as much at that as I did on the job. I was getting about $50 a week on the job, sometimes as much as $70 a week, with overtime. I was also selling men's clothing for Stonefield Corp. out of Chicago, and for W. Z. Gibson clothing company. I was selling men's shirts and ladies clothes, those Fashion Frocks. At night, when we come in for dinner, I'd get my little bag and go to the mess hall and recreation rooms and get some sales. Oh, yeah.

Where I was working was up at various places, pouring concrete flooring where they stored the trucks. We pushed wheel barrows through there and put matting down. Some of those guys didn't know how to push a wheel barrow. Boy, they was in trouble. That was hard work, yes, it was. I worked common labor when I wasn't in concrete. We worked at 2-East. My brother and I poured the first mud [concrete] there, and spread it out of the mixer truck. I also worked at the 100 Areas, all three of the reactors. My brother helped haul and unload the bricks that built that smokestack at 300 Area.

I knew what I was doing when it came to spreading mud. I spread the first load of mud at 100-F. They call concrete mud because it looks like mud. They hauled the mud in trucks, from a mixing plant at Hanford. When the buildings got high, they pumped mud through steel pipes. I worked high up, sometimes. They called that "pump-crete."

I thought working conditions was fair. We didn't have no cruel supervisors. I remember two of the guys in our crew, they'd get to telling tales, and everybody in our crew, including the supervisors, would stand there laughing. The supervisors would say, "Okay, boys, stop lying, and let's go to work." I remember Wyatt Durette, a white fella who was Du Pont's concrete supervisor. He used to get on a big box, one of those big ol' shipping boxes, and say, "All right, boys, I want you to go out and do a good job. Say, if you see a nail sticking up somewhere, take your time and bend it down because we don't want nobody hurt here. You got all your hands, fingers and toes, and we want you to keep 'em that way," I remember he would get on that big crate on a Monday morning. We got friends and brothers over yonder fighting and we want to do a good job here, he'd say. Sure, I remember Durette.

Only one time I remember any racial problem at Hanford. We was working on postholes and drains at the trailer camp. We had to pull a water line. I forgot his name now, but this white carpenter called one of our boys by name and the boy said "Yes."

And this carpenter said if you was back in Mississippi now, you would say "Yes, sir!" The boy said back to him, "But you ain't IN Mississippi now."

A lot of blacks worked in concrete. They didn't mind getting in that mud. We wore rubber boots, hard hats, slicker pants, gloves, to keep the concrete from messin' your clothes. We wore those steel-toed shoes. Durette always said "Be safe."

In the barracks, when I wasn't working, we'd play whist or dominoes. I didn't have a lot of spare time. I went to Kennewick once, Pasco once, I would go to Yakima because that was where my wife was when she first came. I was a church member, but out at Hanford they had one little house for a colored church, an old farmhouse. I understand some of the preachers got to fightin' and squabblin' over something. I never went to church while I was out there, unless I would go when I was in Yakima.

On Sundays, during the summer sometimes I watched baseball games. Whites and blacks played on the same teams. Some of the guys would go swimming. I never attempted to go swimming because they said that Columbia River don't give up the dead. No, sir.

None of us knew what we was doing. Durette tell us if anyone ask what you are doing, tell 'em you working. It was way along in the game when they told us we was building that bomb that was dropped on wherever it was, Nagasaki. I say "Is that right?" If we all would have known what we was doing, some of us would have been frightened and left. I would have stayed. I figured if it was safe for somebody else, it was safe for me.

I left Hanford the latter part of '44, when the job was kinda playing light. I went home to Texas, and I had more money than I ever had in my life. I was down there in Texas in '44, for Thanksgiving, and I took out my friends and told them to get what they want, this was my bill. I was spending money with both hands. At Christmas we went to see my wife's people in Alabama. After we stayed home for a while, I bought some hogs, some cows, put some wire around our pasture at Kildare. Said, well, I guess we'll be here a while. But I got to thinking and told my wife, why don't we go back where we can make some money. It's all going out, none coming in. She ask, "Where we goin'?" I say, "Well, there's a shipyard in Vancouver, Washington."

JOE HOLT

They called him "Honey Joe" because of his bee business, which he went into after he left Hanford. Holt lived with his wife Lois in a large and handsome brown house on the side of a hill above the Yakima River on the west edge of Richland. Behind the house were jack rabbits, sagebrush and an Indian cemetery. His other big construction job was the Golden Gate Bridge. He quit the bridge in 1937 before completion because he didn't like the foggy, cold weather and he got nervous after 10 bridge workers died when a scaffold collapsed and they fell into the Golden Gate. The interview took place at the kitchen table.

I'm Joe Holt and I was born and raised in Kentucky. In 1939 I started to work for the Du Pont Company in Charleston, Indiana, on construction. I worked there, it was a powder plant, as a carpenter on maintenance for four years and then in 1943, they started Hanford. And they asked me to transfer out here to Hanford. They were asking every craftsman in the whole plant at Charleston, probably 800 people.

I got to Hanford by train. When we left Louisville it was practically a carload of guys coming to Hanford who had worked at Charleston. A lot of us knowed each other. We got to Pasco after dark. They said they would pick us up, and they did with some stretch-out buses and they hauled us to North Richland, to stay in tents. Well, I came out in October, 1943. There was hardly anybody here. Within a week's time we moved out to what they called Hanford, about 30 miles north. Nobody knowed how big a camp it would be, so we started out building the camp like an army camp. Two men to a room, four wings to a barracks. We started building mess halls. I would say, within two weeks, they was a thousand men a day coming in.

Most everybody worked 10 hours a day. They was building facilities to entice people there, a big theater, a grocery store, a trailer camp. Living in the barracks was good. The food was good. A lot of people griped. It was better than the Army.

We were the first carpenter crew out there at the first reactor, and everybody worked with the engineers driving stakes, and then they started bringing in equipment. Heavy equipment, cranes, there was a trainload a day. Some of those cranes were so big they sat right on the track, all kinds of heavy equipment. Everything they asked for, I guess they got.

Then they started digging this hole for the reactor building, and it was like going down to China. They put in three different concrete mixers to pump the concrete. I don't know how deep that hole was, just for the base, before they started with the forms.

The concrete was made right there, they had the gravel and sand, all they hauled in was the cement. They started pouring this concrete, and it got below zero, so they brought in steam locomotives. They must have had, I don't know, 10 or 15. They built the railroad, and run the steam locomotives in there. They were coal fed, and they took all the steam the engines could produce and they had the concrete covered with tarps and these steam locomotives was furnishing steam underneath to keep the wet concrete from freezing before it set. Steam was flying every place. They estimated, I remember very plainly, there was better than 5,000 men on this one area at 100-B.

I was working setting forms. After they started setting the forms up, there was a lot to it. Most of them metal forms, tie rods. It was a big job. I had never worked on a job that big. Working conditions were good. I worked there 27 weeks, seven days a week, anywheres from 10 to 12 hours a day. I was paid $1.40 an hour, that was top wages for carpenters, anything over 40 hours was time and a half. You didn't hardly get time to go to sleep. I sent the money home to Kentucky.

I didn't have any time for fun. All we done was work. I made some friends. I knew four or five of the guys who come out with me. It didn't matter what, if a man had only one arm or one leg, if he wanted to come to Hanford he had a job. I saw a lot of men there with a stick with a nail in it, picking up paper. Most of the men were older than me, a lot of them were in their 60s. They needed help so bad. They were determined to build a plant at all costs.

One thing I always will feel bad about. There were a lot of fine orchards out there before the government came in, a lot of young orchards that had just started in production. They had put in irrigation systems, and the government gave them little or almost nothing. There were some bitter farmers, really bitter. They felt bitter towards us coming in here, not all of them, but some of them. They felt like we overrun them.

Well, they got the first reactor building up and then started laying the graphite. I helped on that. It was wonderful, very precise work. The blocks were different lengths, but all had to be fitted to tolerances in the thousandths. We had to wear protective clothing, shoe coverings, so there wouldn't be any contamination of the graphite. There were guys running a vacuum cleaner all the time to keep anything loose off the graphite. You wondered then what you were doing. I got acquainted with one of the engineers and he said "Instead of killing Japs by the hundreds, we are going to get them by the thousands." He had an idea what we were making but he didn't tell me. To tell you the truth, I had no idea. Some guys had theories, but most of them said we were making sand paper. All you had to do was hold it up and sand would gather on the paper.

I was in Richland when they announced the bombs. I think I was at the laundry. It come over the radio. The next two or three days reporters from every place all over flocked in here, trying to stop you and ask you questions. I never will forget one stopped me and he asked me what I had done. I said, "Well, a carpenter." Did you see any of the stuff? No, I told him, I didn't see nothing. He says, "Well, I don't see how they ever made anything because I ain't found anybody who ever done anything."

I thought the bombs were a good deal. In fact, I don't like it because the Japanese murdered them so in Hawaii, then here these newspapers and politicians say how cruel we was to drop the atomic bomb. Well, you get killed you get killed, I don't care if it was from an atomic bomb or a bow and arrow. They had no mercy on the Americans when they bombed Pearl Harbor. I think it was a good deal.

JERRY SAUCIER

Saucier was mowing his backyard on Basswood Avenue in Richland on a warm morning in May, and he turned off the engine and we sat in deck chairs under a sycamore tree. Speaking of his years in Richland, he said, "It's part of me now, I've been here half my life. We planted these trees. This is a sycamore, and we got cherry trees, including Bings. They'll be ready before long. It's a good town, I love it."

I came in November of '43. I started out in the Hanford Camp, in maintenance. I was an inspector. The barracks, you know, they had to be kept up, roofs, steps, doors, toilet facilities, general upkeep. We had lots of that, due to the number of people. People get a little rough sometimes, tear things up, we had a lot of that, especially on weekends when there was lots of heavy drinking and gambling.

I came from Lowell. Lowell, Massachusetts. I was working for Remington Arms at the time, a subsidiary of Du Pont. A fella came back there, and he was looking for people out here and I decided, well, it took me a while to make up my mind, of course, I had never been out West before and all my good friends were in the service, you know. It was a good chance to see the West. They paid my way out. I had never been away from home before. I was 26 or so.

When I came out, I lived in the barracks at Hanford for two years. It was rough, different than I ever experienced. Two men to a room. It was hard, a lot of dust and dirt. I worked as many hours as I wanted to work, sometimes 52 hours a week or more, time and a half after 40 hours. We always had lots of problems, like leaks in the steam lines. The living conditions were good, for a barracks, the same as if you were in the service, like any army camp. They were built to standards, rough, but ample. Food was good, mass produced, but plenty of it, cheap. And clean, everything was clean, kept disinfected.

Weekends were not much to do. You had to go to Yakima to get out, to get a change of life, and see some green grass, to get rejuvenated, and come back and fight the mass. That was when Yakima had trolley cars, we would ride the trolley cars way out to the far end of the town. We got there by the Hanford stage, that was a bus. No air conditioning, hotter than Hades, and I tell you, perspiration, you name it.

Yeah, a lot of trouble, on weekends. They would do a lot of damage, break up a lot of doors and windows and dry walls. They would get drunk, I suppose, and let their macho out. Pull urinals out of the wall, probably they would had have lost in a game. They had some big games, down in the shower rooms, on the cement floor down there. They'd put their week's check down, and boy, that was their fun.

And the beer hall. It was pretty good-sized, a long bar, about the longest I had seen. They had a special crew to take care of the beer and the ice. It was a popular place, all during the day people working different hours. It got pretty rough some nights. I don't know what happened one night, I was in there and all of a sudden all hell broke loose. They had a riot squad, with trucks and they backed it up to the door and a guy gets up there with a bullhorn and tells them to break it up, and they weren't about to break it up. They were breaking chairs and raising hell. Finally, the cops started using clubs and throwing guys in the wagon. And things got back to normal again. It was like an old western town where Marshal Dillon came in and had to straighten things out.

When I got here in '43, everything was torn up, Richland was torn up real bad. They were building every place, the houses, the roads, putting in all the different systems, the church was done, the Catholic church, a couple of the other churches were about finished. And the old Kadlec hospital was about finished. The streets weren't completed yet. We had a cafeteria across from where the federal building is now, and that's where we all ate. If you didn't want to eat there, you could go to Kennewick and eat at some cafe.

Kennewick was still small. They had a tent city down there for people to live in, trailer camps, it was still a little town. People still kinda resented us. One instance, I went to a drug store to pick up a few odds and ends and the

The Western Union office on pay day was a busy place as construction workers sent money orders home to their families.   *U.S. Department of Energy*

old man owner, I gave him a check and he didn't know how good it was, I said it's good, I just made a deposit. He picked everything up and told me to get out, that's the way it was.

We had no liquor store in Richland, I don't think there was one in Kennewick at the time, we had to go to Pasco for a bottle. You had to buy a permit and stand in line over there. In order to get a fifth of whiskey you had to take a fifth of rum. The state really had something going. I never drank such rotgut, paint remover I called it. Then you could bring it back if you didn't drink. When I lived in the barracks out there you could sell a fifth for $50-60.

Sleep and eat, that was about it, or play cards. They had dances, finally when we got the big auditorium completed. Lots of name bands came out there, to keep the people vitalized.

Wages were better than average, they had to be, to try to hold them. That was the only incentive. Living was cheap. People came from every place. There were people out there who were illiterate, they couldn't read, they couldn't write. I can remember one old codger, I met him on the main street in Hanford. He didn't have any money, so I asked him if he ever got any checks. He said, "No, all I get are these slips," and he had bib overalls on and he had all his checks in his bib. I said that's your money. He was used to cash, he was from the Ozarks. I took him to a friend of mine, a major. It got straightened out, they reissued his checks.

Most of the fellows were older, most everybody else was in the service. They always called me the kid. And most of them left after construction. Some went into operations, but after they found out what they made, they got scared off. Even people who had worked on TNT and nitro all their life, even they after they found out what was made, decided to leave this place.

I don't think anyone was too upset about the bombs, the way it was put out at the time, we would save so many lives by doing this, and what the Japs did to us, I still have never gotten over that, Bataan, all those islands, my feeling was they did the right thing, Harry did the right thing. He saved a lot of lives, we had been in that thing so long, my God, what we could lose. Really, just like fodder going over there. And they were prepared for us. Look at Guadalcanal.

Well, it was all new to me, I had a good time. See, I came out here, you notice I got one arm, I thought it would be good to get away and do for myself. If I was going to make it, I had to get away. You see I was a printer before, an offset printer, which was top of the line. It was just coming out, and I worked in some pretty good-sized places back there in Lowell, and had a good job and was making good money. I started as an apprentice and got up to pressman. Of course the war came and I would have gone into the service, I was 1-A. In the meantime, my arm goes through the press, went through the cylinders, flattened it out like tissue paper. So, that was that.

After that, everybody was telling me what to do. And I said to myself, you know a good way to get away from everything would be to get on my own. I had a good home. My father wanted me to stay.

You know I think I found myself, by coming out here. I really did. I think I probably would have ended up being a drunk if I had stayed back there. I was getting depressed, everybody was doing for me. The priest talking to me. It was beginning to get me down so bad. But out here, living in the barracks, you were on your own. You had to do for yourself, or else. I got so I was independent.

SAM CAMPBELL

Sam Campbell, native Oklahoman and an avid golfer, talked in the living room of his Richland home. Before he came to Hanford he had a varied work history, including service with the coast artillery in the Philippines and pipeline construction in South America.

I was working for Du Pont in Pryor, Oklahoma, a powder plant. At Pryor I was chief of security patrol. The work was similar to work at Hanford, protecting classified areas, life and property. I was transferred to Hanford in November of '43.

In November '43 we were building up the force. We hadn't completed the fences around the areas. When I first came I was area commander of 100-B, the first reactor and the first one they put the fence around and tightened security. Prior to that, you had to go through a barricade. The primary problem was during construction. They ran buses from Kennewick and Pasco to Hanford and we had lots of people who would come out there who were not employed.

Olympic Commissary had the contract to operate the messhalls and sleeping quarters. They shipped people out here, gave them meal tickets and paid their transportation. They got them out of Kansas City, Chicago, Detroit and in fact I think they might have combed Skid Row. I would say quite a few of those didn't come out to work. They came out to fleece those who were working.

They claimed one of the better jobs was to be in charge of a barracks. I forget what they called this fella, but he would reserve one room for gambling. They would set up this room for gambling, sell drinks for a dollar a shot, perhaps watered down a little bit. They would cut a percentage of the crap games, poker games. There would be a regular percentage cut of each pot, or each roll of the dice of each pass. Patrol was raiding these places as soon as we were aware of it, and they would start somewhere else.

Some of the women were prostitutes, or making a little side money. There was quite a bit of that. I have heard of cases of intercourse done through the fences around the womens barracks. I do think we had some bush business along the river.

Your beer halls and barracks were segregated. You had a beer hall for blacks and a beer hall for whites. We had an 11 o'clock closing time, and a lot of them didn't want to leave. There was a certain amount of tear gas used to

Christmas, 1944, at one of the women's barracks. Security was tight, with barbed wire and gate guards. *U.S. Department of Energy*

get them out, a lot of rock throwing after they got out. I can understand how at 11 o'clock, after working hard all day they were just going good.

Most violence was fists and knives, but we picked up lots of guns. I know some of the knives were like ones made in the penitentiary. Shivs. We had quite a bit of robbery, because of all the people with cash in their pockets.

We closed up Hanford Camp in February of '45, which was my responsibility. I was shipped into Richland as a captain. About then a captain at 200 East was drafted and I was sent out there. We were manning the towers by then, which was operations time. I am trying to recall, we had 225 patrolmen in that one fenced area, where they did the plutonium separation work.

We had so many because we were manning the towers. They were wooden structures, right on the fence, with lights. We had .38-caliber sidearms, and then in our arsenal at that time 12-gauge shotguns, and later on we had .30-caliber machine guns and .50-caliber machine guns. In a short while, we discontinued manning the towers. Instead we had inner road patrols by cars, on the asphalt roads that went inside the fence. We felt this would be as sufficient as having somebody in a tower, perhaps asleep, in the wee hours in the morning. No way to check these guys in the towers without without climbing the stairs and by that time he's awake.

My recollections of when I got to Hanford, in November of '43, was that it was chaotic. As best as I can recall, we had 400 patrolmen, working around the clock. One of our busiest periods was keeping people from being run over there at shift change, primarily 4-6 in the afternoon.

OPAL DRUM

Mrs. Drum, a frail widow in her mid-70s, lived in a white ranch-style house across the street from a golf course in West Richland, not far from the Yakima River. A few days after arriving in late 1943, the Drums and their two girls moved into the Hanford Trailer Camp, an orderly community of more than 4,000 trailers and 12,000 residents. The Drum family lived in the desert camp for about 10 months. Her late husband, Frank, was one of the first three men chosen to operate the overhead cranes inside the separations plants, one of the most difficult tasks in the plutonium-making process.

We came from Oklahoma. Frank worked on construction, at Tulsa on a bomber plant, at Oklahoma City, Dodge City, Yuma, all defense jobs. He was a scraper hand, earth moving, then he became a crane operator.

I believe we heard about Hanford first while were in Dodge City, and later in Yuma, I think it was in the papers, and we went back to Oklahoma and some friends, he was a carpenter, decided to come out here and we went with them, with our 1940 Studebaker and our trailer. That was in 1943, in December. We got out here the 23rd of December, and he went to work for Du Pont, I believe, after Christmas, at 2-West, helping to build the separations plants. He ran a backhoe for a while, then outside cranes, then late in 1944 he went inside to run the overhead cranes after operations started.

When we first got out here, we were put in a temporary trailer camp for a few days, then we came out to the big trailer camp at Hanford. I think we moved in the 27th or so of December. The Hanford trailer camp was wonderful. It was the biggest trailer camp in the world, at that time. It was policed, it was kept clean, they had great big bath houses. Back then, very few trailers were modern. The bath houses were kept clean, the school was good, I have no complaints, it was a marvelous place to live. One thing I liked was that around the trailers it was kept clean. There wasn't any tacky trailers. They weren't big mobile homes, but they were neat and clean. The people in the trailers were family people. No riff raff out there. The barracks people were completely different. I felt a lot safer out there in 1944 than I do today living in this house in town.

Domestic scene on patio at workers' trailer camp, 1944. The camp was the largest in the world at the time with 4,000 trailers and some 12,000 residents.
U.S. Department of Energy

Our trailer was 27 foot, inside, by 8 foot wide, I guess. The girls were 10 and 12, and they went to school at the camp. My day was just about the same as anywhere. Lot of visiting. You got acquainted. Everybody was away from home. Nobody tried to impress anyone else. The kids got along , the people got along. They were all interested in each other, it was very enjoyable. I was terribly homesick, but outside of that I liked it.

My husband put in awfully long hours on construction. The first time he had a day off where we could go anywhere, was months after we started. We went to Boise, Idaho, to see some relatives. Land, we thought we had gone clear around the world. He worked seven days a week, sometimes 12-hour days.

It was so hot out there. No trees, no air conditioning. We all had little porches, little canopies, we were all young, nobody suffered much. Our trailer didn't have a toilet or shower but we did our cooking in it, on a little stove with an oven. We had a divan at one end, and a stationary bed at the other end, with clothes closets on the sides. It was like being on a vacation. The kids went to matinees on Saturday in the camp auditorium.

We stood in line a lot, at grocery stores, the post office, service stations. That was part of life. We played cards. There wasn't a heck of a lot to do, to tell the truth. We did play bridge with our neighbors. I did a lot of sewing, for my girls. I read a lot. Books, magazines, anything. We never went to the bars.

Frank never talked during the war about his work inside at the separations plants. Not much later either. The kids never knew what their daddy was doing. He told me he didn't know and he couldn't tell me if he knew. He told the kids he was making Pepsi-Cola. They told everybody that's what they were doing. Even in the church circles or card clubs, the women were not allowed to discuss anything about it. We were told not to talk about it. It was a no-no. And, nobody did talk about it.

When the bombs were announced, we were on our way to Longview to visit some friends. We heard the news on the car radio. After they heard the news, Glenda, our youngest, she was 12, said, "Daddy, you told us all along they was making Pepsi-Cola." She was about half-mad. My husband had told them he would bring them the first carton and they were looking forward to that.

I had a brother killed at Normandy in '44. He was a tank commander and he lost contact with the infantry and my brother opened the hatch on his tank and he was shot right through the heart. He's buried over there, in France. You know, it's so funny to me on these anniversaries of the bombs, on television they show those pictures of how awful it was but you know they don't show a thing about Pearl Harbor. That's the darndest thing I ever heard of. Everybody here thought the bombs were justified, I still think it was justified, you bet. It took lives, it took innocent lives, but it saved a lot of lives.

JESS BRINKERHOFF

Round-faced and friendly, Brinkerhoff lived with his little dog in one of the original Richland prefabs, his home since late 1944. He and his late wife, Elva, had six children. In 1943, he was working at Du Pont's Remington Arms ammunition plant in Salt Lake City as a warehouse and shipping foreman. The plant was shut down and he transferred to Hanford as a fireman.

I lived in the barracks from December '43 until March. To me, it was fine. Lots of people, they gambled and stayed out all night and things like that, but that wasn't my cup of tea, as you might say. I enjoyed the barracks life. I had a roommate, a very congenial young man, and I enjoyed eating in the messhalls. Quite a few of the construction workers were kind of a rough bunch. Quite a lot of drinking although I didn't see too much personally, but I heard about it, and they had fights and ruckuses. I suppose I was sort of naive, and I called myself a good church member.

My family came up in March of '44 and we got a three bedroom farm house. They had a few houses in real nice shape out on the perimeter of the Hanford Camp and we rented one of those. We lived in the farmhouse for about six months. The house was about half a mile south and east of the camp, and I got to live in it because I bugged the housing authority. I was just a fireman, but I had four children, two boys and two girls, from age 1 to 10. They finally said if I would sign a contract that I would move with five days notice if they wanted to tear the house down, I could have a house.

As soon as operations started in July of '44, I transferred to the power department in 100-B Area. The power department had responsibility for furnishing all of the cooling water for the reactor, purifying the water and running the settling basins and filters. Also, we had the power house, to generate electricity in case of a power failure, it was coal-fired and was always on ready standby. It was always going, we always were generating some power, but it was put back in the Bonneville power system.

I stayed at B for six weeks, then I transferred to D, and stayed there for about 15 years, until D shut down. I was there when the boiler in the power house started up, and I was there the day they shut it down. My job was cleaning the grates and making sure everything was monitored. We had boiler feed pumps to feed water to the boiler and we had to clean the grates, they were stationary, old ones that had to be cleaned twice a day.

But, to get back to the farm house we lived in that summer. When we were there, there were lots of orchards left. Anyone could pick all they wanted. Where we lived, we had everything, apples, apricots, peaches, pears, plums, cherries, all around our house. We had a little irrigation ditch so we raised a real nice garden.

There was no electricity out there, no inside facilities, an outside toilet. Our water was brought to us each day in a barrel with ice in it. We lighted with coal oil lamps. My wife washed clothes on the washboard. We used wood and coal for fuel in a stove. The rent on our farm house was exorbitant. If I

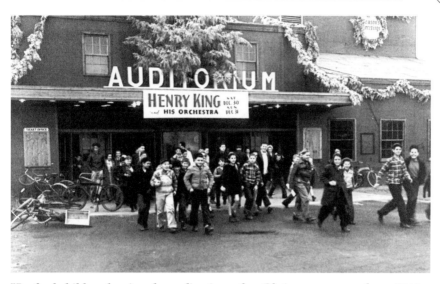

Hanford children leaving the auditorium after Christmas season show, 1944.

U.S. Department of Energy

told you how much it was, you wouldn't believe me. Seven dollars a month for the rent and a dollar extra for the furniture.

The bus rides were all free, our kids could go wherever they wanted. Whenever I got a day off, we would take the bus up to the river and take the ferry across and walk on the north side of the river. We would go on a Sunday. I'll tell you what my wife said then, and she said it all these years. That she enjoyed that summer at Hanford in '44 more than any summer she put in during her married life, and we lived together more than 52 years before she passed away. It was so peaceful and quiet out there. Nobody come to bother us, and we had acres of orchards, a garden spot, and we could walk down along the river.

LUZELL JOHNSON

Mr. Johnson was slim and courtly, soft-spoken, somewhat taciturn. We talked in his front yard, under shade trees, on a warm morning, not far from the Pasco rail yard and passenger station. Like Willie Daniels, he was a southern black man attracted to Hanford by higher pay.

I was working in Mobile, Alabama, at a creosote plant, 35 cents an hour. I heard about the job out at Hanford, you could get tires and gas to come out here, from Du Pont. I was classified 1-A in the draft. By the time I got to Hanford in the spring of '44, I had my draft call, and I went to the office and they got me a deferment.

I knew something about concrete work, and I became a cement finisher. After the laborers poured it, we finished it. Before that, the laborers had dug it out and leveled, the next crew was the pouring crew, next was us. We worked with trowels, 12-inch trowels and 18-inch trowels. I made $1.75 an hour, six days a week, eight hours.

I lived in the barracks, they was segregated, blacks from whites. There were quite a few blacks working out there, laborers, lots of them in the concrete department, and quite a few in the mess halls, cooks and waitresses. The barracks was kinda exciting. I didn't drink. My room mate drank, and he gambled. I was disturbed all through the night.

And, every weekend, there was somebody coming through with goods, through the barracks, you understand that? Prostitutes. They would start at the head of the barracks, put a girl in a room. They would come through and ask, room by room if we was interested. They got $10. Since we worked six days, usually they come through on Sundays.

There weren't no restriction on gambling. Shooting craps was the main thing. Professionals ran the games. I imagine they had card games too, but they was kinda private. With craps, anyone could come in. My room mate would run a game some night, and I would go somewhere else.

I didn't run into much racism at Hanford. Everybody was working together, and everybody was eating together at the mess halls. White and colored could go in together and eat. I didn't go to the beer halls, I didn't drink beer, so I didn't have no experience with that.

Everybody played baseball together, the teams was black and white. I played baseball, there was pretty good ball players from all over the country. Like on Memorial Day some big team from back East would come out and play the best Hanford players. The professionals usually won. I played center field, not regularly. The manager would play maybe me this week and somebody else next week. The catchers and the pitchers and the first baseman and shortstop were regular, all the others traded off.

When my wife come out, she lived in a room in one of the old farmhouses on the reservation. I had saved $700, and we drove around and found a trailer at the trailer camp for $600 and some dollars. We bought it, and moved in. Hanford was a big town, like. Everything was there. Banks, drug stores, grocery stores. We went to the stores and went back to the trailer and my wife cooked. After she started cooking, I hardly ate in the mess halls.

I was a little surprised when the bombs were dropped. When I got back to Alabama, they knew more about Hanford than I did. That's what you all was making, they said, something to kill people. That shocked me.

They laid us off after construction was finished, and give us certificates for tires and stamps for gas so we could go back where we come from. I went back to Alabama. I didn't do anything there because the pay scale was what it was when I left, 35 cents an hour. The same as I was making when I left Mobile. They said I could have my old job back at the creosote plant, but I decided to come back out here, where I was getting $1.75.

CPL. HOPE SLOAN AMACKER

Hope Sloan was 25 in 1944, a dark-haired WAC corporal and secretary in military intelligence. In July, she joined the construction camp's morale-building effort by entering a beauty contest, part of an "exposition" promoting safety on and off the job. Miss Sloan, already Sweetheart of the Hanford Engineer Works, won the exposition's Queen of Safety title. Exposition entertainment included a jitterbug contest, the Hanford Engineer Works' Railroad Quartet, a concert band, an appearance by Jan Garber's band, and an amateur show featuring men dressed in women's underwear. Mrs. Amacker, still blessed with beauty queen good looks, lived in Kennewick in a house with a sweeping view of a golf course and the Horse Heaven Hills.

I was on a train on New Year's 1943 coming to Hanford, traveling with another gal, a WAC. We had stopped in Oak Ridge for a little indoctrination, and then came out here. Mr. Carpenter, the president of Du Pont, was on the same train, on his way to Hanford. He knew we were on the train, and he asked if we could come into his compartment and have a New Year's Eve drink. I guess the train was somewhere in Montana, west of Glendive. We left his compartment door open and the military police kind of hung around, and we had a drink with him. He was a real gentleman. He was lonely, and he had pictures of his family and we told about our families. That was kind of a highlight of my Army career.

I came from Middletown, Ohio, between Dayton and Cincinnati. I enlisted in the Army because I was lonesome. Everybody was gone or married, and I

The Auditorium played an important role in maintaining morale. One of the many touring acts—The Esquire Girls—perform at the 1944 Christmas Show.

U.S. Department of Energy

was living with my mother. I left basic training at Daytona Beach early to come to Hanford with the Army Corps of Engineers. In those days, coming to Washington was like going overseas.

When I first came I was in military intelligence, as a secretary. After that I went with public relations, working with Milt Cydell who was head of that for the Corps of Engineers. Milt wrote the news releases for the project, and called on all the newspapers and kind of kept them happy so they didn't get too inquisitive. He was a Seattle native and he knew all the people in the newspaper business in the area. He talked with reporters who called. He talked at length but he never said anything.

There was not much to do until they built the rec hall, and big name bands starting playing at Hanford. We worked nine hours a day, and that was pretty much it. Weekends, if we got a pass, we went to Yakima or Seattle or Portland. Usually four or five of us would get together and drive. After we moved from Hanford Camp to Richland, it was better because the married couples had houses and they entertained a lot. And, we had parties in our dorms.

At one time when I was in military intelligence I monitored phone calls. As far as I was concerned that was really cloak and dagger. I was supposed to find out if anyone said anything that sounded wrong. I didn't know what I was listening for, except for anything that sounded covert or to find out if anyone were speculating about what was going on at the plant. I probably wouldn't have known what they were talking about if they were talking about the bomb.

I remember when I won the beauty contest. I don't remember how I was chosen, but there were 40 or more girls in it. I got $100 and an engraved loving cup. The cup fell apart. It was silver-plated and I suppose tin or something that didn't hold up very well.

In 1944, everyone was young here, and it was heavenly. The experience was once in a lifetime. You knew you were doing something important, but you didn't know what.

DEWITT "BILL" BAILEY

A raw-boned man, originally from New Albany, Mississippi, Bill Bailey and his wife Phyllis lived in Kennewick in a cluttered comfortable house filled with furniture and books and two dogs. Bailey had been a construction worker most of his life, including jobs like the hydrogen bomb plant in South Carolina, the Alaska Pipeline, and Washington Public Power Supply System plants.

I was working in a Mobile shipyard when a friend told me "Go to Hanford, boy, everybody's there." I quit the shipyard and headed out here, I was 34, and about ready to be drafted if I hadn't come to Hanford. I got here Jan. 6, 19 and 44, about 8:30 a.m. I got in line with two or three hundred other people. A fella asked if anyone had worked for Du Pont before. I raised my hand, and he said, "Come on in, you are already on the payroll." They made me what they called a special material handler. That meant I was handling classified stuff, setting machinery, millwright work, lining up shafts, stuff like that.

When they transferred us in to 100-B they didn't even have the outside walls done. They were just starting the reactors. That thing was so secret, maybe a person would be cleared for only one side of it. Four sides square, and maybe a guy would be cleared for the intake side but he wouldn't be cleared for the exhaust side. And everybody was not cleared to go up in it. You get about halfway up, going up a stair before you come over into the thing, and they'd be an armed guard, and he would check you out and if your name was on a list you could go by. If it wasn't that was as far as you went. That was every day. Maybe you could go up Monday and you couldn't go Tuesday.

We were running three shifts. They had electricians, pipefitters, millwrights, and those people were working all around the thing. That was where I met Joe Holt. Everything was being done at practically the same time. And it was so engineered that when one phase finished out, all of it was about finished and it was ready to pull the switch. We would repeat the work on the other reactors.

Hanford construction was well organized. There were coordinators, there were no problems between the crafts. Expediters handled equipment. There was no reason to run out of anything because they could tap into anything in the United States. It was much better organized than the pipeline in Alaska.

WPPSS construction (Washington Public Power Supply System) was organized confusion.

No way did I have a notion of what we were doing during the war. I don't think anybody else did. They only had one guy who could look at the blueprints, and would give you a pencil sketch. A general foreman or superintendent would have a question about some phase and he would go in and there would be a guy who would get him a pencil sketch off of the main blueprint and only one man saw those.

You didn't talk about it. I heard a guy ask a question about a certain object he was working on, and a fella told him, you ask that question one more time and you'll go.

The reason I say no one knew what they were doing was, for instance an electrician would put a piece of wire through a hole and he'd talk over a wall or through a hole to somebody. He'd say you handle it from that side, everything is okay here. He would never know who he was talking to on the other side.

I went to the beer hall occasionally but I was not much of a drinker. I preferred for the roommate and I to have a bottle in our room. There was too much noise in that beer hall, and when I was growing up I was told to stay away from big crowds and avoid problems. It was a fairly wild place. They used tear gas in there several times to quieten somebody. There would be eight or ten people at a table with their mug beer and a couple of them would start in arguing and somebody would start hissing them on, and yelling "Go get him! Go get him boy! Get him! Get him!" First thing you know they would start swinging. The patrolmen would come in and would use tear gas.

They started serving beer at 5:30 in the evenings and quit at 11. One waitress would have two rows of tables. She'd come down with three pitchers in each hand, set them down on the table, go back and get six more and set them down and she would go right on down the row and come back later and collect. One gal there, they said she had cleared $25,000 and was going back to Minneapolis and put her in a restaurant. Some guy would throw a $5 bill down and maybe the beer was only $3 and would say "Keep the change." I think beer was 50 cents a pitcher. I think so anyway, it's been a long time.

I worked seven days a week at times, sometimes three or four hours in the evening after everyone else was gone, a small group of us would keep working. Working conditions were real good. No one rushed you, but they didn't like people missing time. If people who missed a lot of time were young they went into the armed services. I knew one guy who went into the Navy because he missing too much time. He was never there on Saturday. They took his draft deferment away.

I was making $1.40 an hour plus overtime. Maybe $125 a week, it was good money then, equal to a $1,000 a week now. It was a safe job, Du Pont set national standards for safety. If someone got hurt, it was just cotton-picking carelessness, it was no fault of the company. I never saw anyone hurt when I was there. I heard of a guy got hurt on another shift. He was working on a crane, and he was going to come down on a choker and his feet slipped and he fell on some reinforcing rods and they stuck through him.

Yeah, I heard of the waste tank accident. This subcontractor had these tanks setting up on blocks. They assumed these guys working chipping hammers was all working the same way, but they weren't and six or seven was killed when the tank fell off the blocks. A chipping hammer is a cold chisel operated with an air hammer to smooth welds or check them. Nothing to do with Du Pont. They wouldn't have been killed if it was a Du Pont job.

I was surprised about the bombs. I was going to work and somebody had a bulletin, a paper, and I hadn't even heard it over the radio. The paper was telling about the bomb dropped on Hiroshima or Nagasaki, I don't know which came first. Everybody was saying, "My, didn't you know what was going on there?" They were lying, they didn't know no more than I did. I thought maybe we were making poison gas or nerve gas. We felt real good about the bombs. I got a silver pin for working on the bombs and I had it made into a tie clasp.

VINCENT AND CLARE WHITEHEAD

Vincent "Bud" Whitehead met his wife, Clarebel ("like the cow"), in 1944 when they were sergeants in military intelligence. Both were from Portland, Oregon. Bud, a civil engineering graduate, was working for the U.S. Army Corps of Engineers when he was drafted in 1942. A boisterous couple, the Whiteheads were eager to recall their wartime days in the desert.

BUD: I was a counter-intelligence agent at Hanford. Everybody was suspicious but mostly it was unwarranted. Everybody was spied on. I had my own network worked up, mostly women. They liked to play cops and robbers. Some of them were stenographers, or women who worked at the hotel. If I were curious about somebody at the hotel, I would ask the girl on the desk what she knew.

I never ran across a spy at Hanford. One German showed up. I pitied him. He was a craftsman and we had a tank that had to go up. It was stainless steel, which was like using gold in those days. It was about 80 feet high, and it had to be exactly plumb. They looked all over the United States for someone who could make stainless steel wedges that could make this thing plumb. And the guy turned out to be this German. He went to his work one morning, then he was on a plane and he was at Hanford. He had been in this country long before the war, but he still spoke with an accent. My orders were to see that he wasn't fooled with. I was to shoot anybody who made any motion toward him. I had that damn Tommy gun cocked and ready to go. People thought I was pointing a gun at the German, but actually I was there to protect him. He was a nervous wreck.

CLARE: I went into the Army training center in May, 1943. That was down in Georgia, Fort Oglethorpe. I was in the WAAC (Womens' Army Auxiliary Corps) at the time. After that they sent us to New York. They wanted us in the Manhattan Engineer District. I learned a little bit there, and then they sent three of us to Tennessee. We worked there, at Oak Ridge, in classified files, and at the last of October, they talked about sending some of us to Hanford. I wanted that, because it was close to Portland, my home. They said no. But I wouldn't sign up for the regular Army unless they sent me to Hanford. Guess where I ended up? We were the only WACs at Hanford for a while.

The head of intelligence came to me and said he needed a receptionist and somebody who could type. I was tickled to death. It was a new experience, so I moved to his office at Hanford Camp. I was a secretary for safeguarding military information. After that, I worked at the military intelligence office in Richland. I was the first WAC there, and they treated me nice. Bud and I worked in the same office, and that's how we met. I didn't know what he did, because nobody asked anybody what they did.

BUD: I got calls at all times of day and night from informants. I told them they were working for the U.S. government, in a highly-classified job. And not to tell anybody what they did because it might get them killed. I had two old ladies there in their 60s who were especially active.

CLARE: DON'T YOU CALL THEM OLD!

BUD: They were dears, I'll tell you that, and they gave me some awfully good information. I would just ask them and they would check it out. They knew a lot of people. They lived in a little house just outside the project. They belonged to every knitting society and blanket society. They were busy. If they came across any little thing, they told me. One story they picked up was that we were making rockets, anti-personnel rockets. They told me who had said it. I told my office this person was starting rumors and they took care of it. The guy was young, and unmarried, and he got drafted real quick.

CLARE: When I was in files, I didn't know what was going on. But there was a job in intelligence, where each of us was assigned so many periodicals and newspapers and we had to watch for words. One of the words was "atom."

BUD: That reminds me. I got a lot of information from files. They put me in charge of headquarters, everybody had to take their turn, answering the phones, a 24-hour service. I went through all the files. Of course, they were under lock but I could pick the locks. I found out from reading the files that they didn't fancy me much as an agent. Once, soon after I first hit the project, I was not invited to a party. But I put bugs in the house where the party was and I got some very enlightening information. They all hated the officers in intelligence, and they said some very uncomplimentary things about these officers. I got the agents together and I played this thing for them. I was included in every party after that.

CLARE: I didn't know what Bud did. I thought he was the office photographer.

BUD: The regular photographer went to another base, and I had to pick up his job. Being a photographer was part of my cover. I carried a detective special pistol. I would rather have a brick. In my car was a carbine, a Tommy gun and a gas gun. I was an arsenal. I had an intercept car, a Ford, that thing would do 102 miles an hour.

We had a little plane. An artillery spotter plane. The pilot had been in Europe, and he was wounded and lost an eye. I used to fly with him every morning, to check the fence all around. It took about an hour and a half. We were looking for tracks. We never found any.

CLARE: Has anybody ever told you about the milk shakes at White Bluffs? It was just a little drug store, these people were still there and hadn't been moved out. The officer of the day would stop at the WACS barracks and take two or three of us up there for milk shakes. I have never tasted a better shake.

BUD: We did spot checks on telephone conversations. Not everybody, but there were some trunk lines we listened to. Maybe some colonel's wife talking to another wife. The purpose was to find who was breaking security.

CLARE: I took my turn listening to conversations. The room was right across from the military intelligence office.

BUD: I would record a violation, and the man would be charged or scolded. For instance, there was a code name given to each piece of apparatus, and some of those professors for Christ's sake would just in the clear say the description. We had a mechanical hand that was used to pick up objects in the separation facility. They spent a lot on that, and that damn fool used the name and mentioned delivery dates. We didn't have conversation scramblers in those days.

CLARE: But after the Smythe Report was out, secrecy was out. (Henry DeWolf Smythe, a Princeton physicist, wrote the official government publication on the bomb, and described the project in detail. The book was published in 1945, soon after the war ended.)

BUD: Have you ever tried to get an egg back in a hen?

One thing I recall, before the bombs were dropped. I remember a Du Pont guy got up to give a speech and he said, "Folks, I can finally tell you what we are making here. We are making horses' asses and they go back to Washington, D.C. for final fitting." You could hear a pin drop, and then that whole crowd fell over. Everybody got drunk after the bombs were dropped on Japan. They finally found out what they were making.

CLARE: Do you remember that wild party? That was a shameful affair.

JANE JONES HUTCHINS

After a cup of coffee in her dining room in Yakima, Mrs. Hutchins, a smiling and assertive woman, brought out newspaper clippings and old photographs and told her story.

Sis and I got on a bus in Coffeyville, Kansas, in August of '43 and we landed in Pasco. The bus depot was right in the center of this teeny-weeny little town and these wierd-looking men were sitting around. She was 17 and I was 22, and how we had the guts to go any farther I don't know. We weren't recruited, we heard about these fabulous salaries they were paying out here. They said secretaries were making $60 a week. In Coffeyville, I was making $20. Sis was just out of high school and doing nothing. We started off, two dumb kids tired of living in Kansas.

Sagebrush Christmas tree, 1944.   *U.S. Department of Energy*

We caught a bus from Pasco out to Hanford and went through employment and both got jobs immediately. I went to work in the training relations department which handled the Sage Sentinel, which was the company newspaper, and also the library, the entertainment.

Sis went to work for Rob Johnson, he was the chief Du Pont photographer. I was a secretary for the manager of training relations, and head cashier at the entertainment hall. There was entertainment every night of the week. I think Monday was boxing, and Thursday, Friday and Saturday were name bands. But something every night. The theory being, you had those termination winds and people would quit by the thousands, something was needed to keep them. You were 70 miles from anything.

Those nights out there were wild and woolly, for a 22-year-old kid who had lived in Kansas all her life. They were an eye opener. Liquor was rationed but they always seemed to have it. The guys would pick up a can of Coke and go out to their car for a bottle. You drank it straight, and washed it down with Coke. Some of the bands were Henry King, Kay Kyser, and one not so well known, Tiny Hill. We also had Ted Weems and Jan Garber. They would play three nights and get paid off. Thousands would show up, at the auditorium, a huge building, which I recall was built in 10 days.

The women's barracks had a house mother. A lot of men were family men, and they weren't interested in what you would call dating. And if you did have a date there was no place to go except Yakima for dinner and that was 70 miles away. At the women's barracks, a guy would have to go in the gate, say who it was he wanted to see and the woman would be escorted down. At midnight or 1 o'clock, whenever the curfew was, they would scratch off names of men leaving the barracks, and if some names weren't scratched off, they would come looking for them.

I look back now and realize this was a free country but we were living behind barbed wire at Hanford, all to protect womanhood. I know that where women were concerned, Hanford could either make you or break you. Gals who had never had male attention before were, you know, popular. You could either become a slut, I suppose, if you wanted to, or you could become very strong, and be able to say "No."

The rooms were nice. Two beds, two dressers and four walls. The food was pretty good. No one starved. You ate all you wanted. When the bowl was empty, you held it up and it was refilled. Once, I did that in a Yakima restaurant and I was so embarrassed. They served the biggest chicken legs at the messhalls I have ever seen.

Our first Christmas, in '43, was rough, being away from home. I remember we planned a great big office party but there were no such things as Christmas trees, so some of us went out into the desert and got a big hunk of sagebrush.

We all got along pretty good. Maybe it was a different attitude. No inkling what we were doing, and I had no reason to be curious. I was busy with my job. I came from a little town. Believe it or not I had an inferiority complex, and at Hanford I knew the only way I could make friends was to be a friend myself. I came out of my shell.

When they dropped the bombs, that was an exciting time. I had never heard of such a thing as atomic power. Right after that, the war ended. Well, I fought the war at Hanford. It seemed as if we were doing our bit. It was a lark, it was exciting.

After they dropped the bombs and the war ended, I was out at the old Hanford Camp, it had closed in February, '45, with Colonel Matthias. We watched some half-wild goats walking in front of the movie theater. The colonel turned to me and said, "You know, Jane, this is like going to your mother's funeral. This was a living, breathing place with a personality." It was hard then, really hard, for anyone looking at that place, sagebrush and sand, a few goats, to visualize the 51,000 people who had lived there at the peak of it.

View of construction camp, with barrack hutments in foreground. There were 131 larger H-shaped barracks units and 880 hutments of varying sizes housing a total of some 40,000 workers. The trailer camp was home to another 12,000 residents, including dependents. The camp also included steam and power plants, theaters, banks, a hospital, mess halls, commissaries, recreation halls, churches, a huge tavern seating 530, and an airfield.

The trailer camp had names of streets such as Attu, Bataan, and Corregidor. In the main camp the streets were named for famous military figures such as Eisenhower, Doolittle, and Patton.   *U.S. Department of Energy*

Front face of the B Reactor, showing the movable scaffolding used for loading the 70,000 uranium fuel slugs into 2,004 fuel tubes. After sufficient neutron bombardment to form plutonium the fuel slugs were pushed to the discharge or rear face. Cooling water inlet pipes may be seen on both sides of the front face.   *National Atomic Museum*

OPERATIONS

C aptain Frank Valente, a chemist and the Army's liaison with Du Pont at the reactor areas, often escorted important visitors on tours after plutonium production began. Some he labeled "the 25-cent variety" because he was not allowed to answer important questions. When someone did ask what was being manufactured, Valente would reply: "We are dehydrating the Columbia River for shipment overseas."

In a Hanford reminiscence, Valente said many visitors probably did get the impression Hanford was "a gigantic water works" because of the hundreds of pumps, the tanks holding millions of gallons of water, the chemical treatment facilities and the pump houses along the river."

The real reason for Hanford's existence was less fanciful, but not less fantastic. In simplest terms, Hanford's job was to make plutonium inside the nuclear reactors by bombarding uranium fuel with neutrons, and to separate the plutonium from the irradiated uranium. The first step was nuclear; the second was chemical.

During the late afternoon of September 13, 1944, Enrico Fermi inserted the first uranium fuel slug into the face of the B Reactor to begin the plutonium-manufacturing cycle. Two weeks later, early on September 27, the initial power run began. By late that afternoon, however, the reactor had shut itself down because, as learned later, xenon-135 was created and poisoned the reaction by absorbing too many neutrons. Thanks to Du Pont's conservative design, extra fuel tubes were available, and more uranium fuel was added to overcome the poisoning effect.

B Reactor discharged its first plutonium-bearing irradiated uranium in November. On Christmas Day, several more tons of irradiated uranium were pushed out of B. D Reactor had been running since mid-December, and F was manufacturing plutonium in February.

By February, 1945, Hanford was humming like a factory assembly line. A more poetic view of plutonium and its manufacture was expressed by physicist John Wheeler during a speech in 1982:

> An observer from afar, looking upon the scene in 1944, would have been convinced that he was looking at one alchemist's dream inside another. It was preposterous enough to think that dead uranium, put into regularly-spaced crannies in tons of dead black graphite, would come alive. It was still more preposterous to imagine this life, this silent darting back and forth of invisible neutrons, as producing in the course of time not merely a few atoms of plutonium, but billions upon billions of them, the philosopher's dream of synthesizing a new element achieved in kilogram amounts.

Glenn Seaborg, a co-discoverer of plutonium and the scientist in charge of developing the chemical separation process, visited Hanford in December, 1944. One of his stops was the B Reactor and he wrote in his Met Lab Journal that "slugs coming out of the pile glow red from photons shooting out. They are dropped into a deep waste channel and caught in big buckets which carry them to large lead coffins, after which they are hauled out into the desert five or ten miles to cool." He saw 221-T Building, and wrote that he saw nothing but 860 feet of control boards, valves, meters, indicators, "a fantastic sight."

The first 100 chemical separation operators arrived at Hanford in October to begin their duties in what became known as "the separations area." On December 26, the first run using uranium fuel rods from B Reactor began and the production runs were completed by early January, 1945, Before the end of the month, plutonium was readied for the journey to Los Alamos, where the thick liquid solution would be transformed into plutonium metal for use in the New Mexico test bomb.

Manhattan Project records on file in federal archives describe the production process, from the manufacture of the aluminum-clad uranium fuel slugs to the final product—the plutonium nitrate solution that was sent to Los Alamos. Uranium metal, which was refined natural uranium, was received at the fabrication area in the form of short thick slabs called billets. These were extruded into rods and then machined into shorter slugs. Slugs were encased in aluminum cans and tested before being used in a reactor. Inside

The 100-B reactor area was the first to operate of the three reactor areas built at Hanford. The reactor building, looking something like a giant wedding cake, is at the right, between the water tower and the smokestack. The large structure at left held cooling water for emergencies.

U.S. Department of Energy

the piles, the U-238 atoms in the uranium fuel (about 200 tons in each reactor) were bombarded by neutrons originating from the fission of U-235. A tiny portion of the U-238 was transmuted into plutonium 239.

After discharge from the reactors, the plutonium-bearing fuel slugs were transported by rail car, in lead-lined casks, to the chemical separation areas. The first stop was short-term storage so that part of the radioactivity could diminish, followed by transferral to a "canyon" building where the fuel slugs were dissolved and plutonium was separated from the uranium and most of the highly-radioactive substances, called fission products, that resulted from the fission process inside the reactors. Scheduling of the time when a particular batch of uranium fuel slugs was dissolved was guided by meteorological forecasts of wind direction and other atmospheric conditions. Some gaseous by-products were so toxic that one cubic foot of gas required one cubic mile of air for safe dilution.

Next, the solution was decontaminated further at the concentration building. By this stage, the original solution had been reduced in volume by a factor of 1,300 and in radioactivity by a factor of 10 million. Near the end of the separation process, a ton of uranium slugs had been reduced to about eight gallons of solution weighing 79 pounds.

Radioactive waste was stored in underground tanks of steel-lined concrete. To reduce the formation of plutonium-240, an unwanted and troublesome isotope, each metric ton of uranium was left in the reactor long enough to form 200 grams of plutonium-239. At the last processing stop, the isolation building, the plutonium was refined and prepared for delivery to Los Alamos, known as the consumer or customer.

This official description was of an industrial process, not unlike other chemical plants except for the radiation dangers. Thomas L. Hankins, a professor of the history of science at the University of Washington said, during an interview:

> I try to emphasize that the real achievement of the Manhattan Project was the organization of it. After the war there was this problem of espionage and the popular press seemed to indicate there was a secret to the bomb and these scientists had discovered a profound equation somewhere. That wasn't the case. What was needed was an enormous industrial effort. At Oak Ridge, at Hanford, and at Los Alamos. And, it was a very large industrial effort, a major effort that required a lot of very skilled engineering and designing.
>
> Hanford hasn't received very much attention, and there are several reasons for that. It was a production site, not a major research site. The other reason is it was run by Du Pont; it was an engineering operation, although some physicists were involved. But the engineers are the ones who have not got enough credit in the Manhattan Project.

Physicists such as Fermi, Wigner and Wheeler were big names on the Hanford scene until early in 1945. The role of physicists diminished after March, 1945, when full-scale production began. Before then, physicists had been on hand to act either as theoreticians or consultants, as in the xenon poisoning, or as babysitters who guided the reactors into production. After March the show was turned over to engineers, chemists, and technicians who did the shift work at the reactor and separation areas. Most of these people had been trained at the University of Chicago or at the Oak Ridge semi-works. Others came directly from other Du Pont munition or chemical plants and learned the new atomic trade on the job.

Thomas B. Cochran, senior scientist for the Natural Resources Defense Council and a co-author of the Nuclear Weapons Databook series, said that during calendar years 1944 and 1945, "the U.S. probably recovered about 209 kilograms" (460 pounds) of plutonium from the Hanford reactors. This total would have been enough for 34 Fat Man Nagasaki-type bombs.

WALTER O. SIMON

Walt Simon, a chemist, was Hanford's first operations manager. In 1943, before joining the Manhattan Project, he was plant manager at Wabash River Ordnance Works, a Du Pont plant near Terre Haute, Indiana. He was interviewed at his home in Wilmington, Delaware, not far from Du Pont's original black powder mills along the Brandywine.

When I was called to Wilmington from Terre Haute in 1943 and told what we were getting into, I was flabbergasted. I couldn't sleep that night and the next day I thought, "Well, I better find out more about this." Atomic energy wasn't my field. I went down to a bookstore and I picked up a book on the subject that had all the current information. It was "Applied Nuclear Physics" by Ernest Pollard and William Davidson, published in 1942. I still have it. There was quite a debate about withdrawing that book from the market, but it was decided that would be a sure sign of what was going on. I was asked if I wanted to take part, and I knew it was an atomic weapon. They were pretty sure I would say yes because I was already involved in war work and there was nothing else to do until the war was over.

In the summer of 1944, I moved to Richland from Wilmington as the plant manager-designate. We had groups of men training at Oak Ridge and Chicago, others were scattered around in small numbers at other Du Pont plants, small enough not to attract attention. They were learning everything they could about uranium and plutonium.

One error in some accounts is that Hanford was chosen because of the availability of Columbia River water. When Hanford was chosen, the concept of a water-cooled reactor had not been developed completely.* Later, when this was decided upon, the presence of a good water supply was a matter of unbelievable good fortune. So many things like this fell into place in the life of the project that it seemed to have been blessed with a special element of luck.

The night B Reactor went critical we had a lot of high-ranking technical people watching this startup, and when it went critical and then shut itself down, the silence was deafening. It was complete consternation. As background to this, the scientific people, the Chicago people, the Nobel Prize winners, Wigner and Fermi and Szilard, were all much more on the risk-taking side than Du Pont was. Du Pont was a conservative organization. For instance, if someone asked for a two-story building, Du Pont design would put enough steel in it for four stories, being convinced that sooner or later someone would add an extra floor or two. Du Pont conservatism paid off on the reactors. Enough extra fuel tubes had been added to overcome the fission product poisoning.

There was a great deal of team effort in this whole thing. There were no autocrats who could say, you know, take the cigar out of his mouth and say, "Do this or do that." Things were pretty much decided in a consensus of judgment. The whole project was like a three-legged stool. The military, the scientific community and the commercial corporations were built on different philosophies. Spurred by a common fear of Nazi Germany, the three groups got along reasonably well as the results indicated, but this did not eliminate their fundamental differences. Each one needed the other two.

There was friction between the scientists and Du Pont, honest differences of opinion on how to get the job done in the quickest way. Friction may be too harsh a word because we were all on speaking terms. They were annoyed, let's say, that Du Pont people were exercising some degree of judgment, but on the other hand people in the Corps of Engineers had encouraged Du Pont to exercise judgment. They often said that is what we hired you for. At one point, we weren't too keen on technical dissension. We had to go.

At the beginning, looking at it frontways, the reactor looked more formidable than the separation process, which was a chemical process. The main problem with separation was it had so much radiation, it had to be manipu-

---

* Helium and heavy water had been considered leading possibilities for cooling the reactors, but by February, 1943, the design of cooling with ordinary water took precedence.

lated with various automated equipment, but as a process it was understandable to our chemists. Protecting people from radiation added a dimension that made it a little more difficult. The scientists were absolutely astounded at our ability to design arms and devices that could do these tasks. They stood a little bit in awe of how it all worked out. It was technically very good.

Another thing that worked out. There was a discussion in the scientific group as to whether you should build a reactor with a solid material like carbon or a liquid like heavy water. The Germans were making a great point about making heavy water in Norway and shipping it to Germany. Of course at that time everything the Germans did was considered very smart. So, the design problems of a heavy water plant looked insurmountable. Keeping it from leaking, the corrosion, all sorts of things. A solid material, carbon, looked like a practical solution. The heavy water advocates, of course, always thought we were going down the wrong path.

Fermi was very discreet about disagreements. He was a very pleasant person. He had a mind that raced all the time. For instance, if there was a little time to kill while they were loading the reactor, he would do equations in his head, with someone next to him with a calculator. You know, multiply 999 by 62 and divide by this and that, and he did that for amusement. His mind raced so much the only way he could relax was to walk on the desert. They would try to take him to a movie, and he would sit there and in five minutes he would have the whole plot figured out. He had a tremendous intellectual capacity, absolutely. Fermi was interested in chess and one or two of the men who were run of the mill technical people had spent a lot of time playing chess. Boy, when he found a good chess player, he tied him up. One boy was not particularly intellectual but he was a supremely good chess player. Fermi would come around calling for him, "Where's so and so?"

In early '43, there was quite a bit of discussion on how the government was going to operate Hanford. There was some thought you might put everybody in the military. After all, they would not be any worse off than if they went to Europe or the Pacific. Groves reacted very violently to this possibility and, I think, wisely. He wanted it run as a civilian operation, to get the maximum output from a voluntary force.

Now, one of the most difficult problems we had before plutonium production began was making the uranium fuel slugs. The uranium was held in an aluminum can, a slug, about eight inches long and an inch and five-eighths in diameter. The can had to fit very tightly with no air space or bubbles. They couldn't leak because if water got into the uranium it destroyed the ability to react. So the concept was that the scientific people would find out how to do this and give us instruction. They found out how to design it but they never made a slug in the laboratory that didn't leak.

Well, the summer of '44 was coming along and the reactor was shaping up and there would be nothing to put into it. We had a production superintendent at Hanford named Earl Swensson, who was a real dyed-in-the-wool production man. This was a case where one man did sell an idea. He said you know they'll never make one of these in the lab, even if they work on it for 10 years. It's a statistical matter. Why don't we make a thousand a day, we'll examine each one and test them all, and the poor ones we'll strip the aluminum can off and save the uranium and the next day we'll make another thousand. The first day a thousand failed, but there were maybe 10 better than the others and we tried to figure out why these 10 were better. The next day maybe they had 18 that were better. And they kept doing this and lo and behold after about three weeks there was one perfect can. Purely statistical. If you made a thousand a day for three weeks, you had made 20,000 until you got one good one. They made five good ones the next day, and 10 the next and after a while out of a thousand they were making 500 and then 600 a day that were all right. That's how they did it. It was a little terrifying because if we didn't have them it would stop the whole thing. The reactor would be ready on September 15 and we would have nothing to put into it.

I do want to say that the director of Du Pont's plutonium effort, the TNX Division, was Roger Williams, and the success of the project was due to his skill and guidance. He was a genius. The books to date on the Manhattan Project rarely mention him. He was a modest man and avoided the limelight.

After the first reactor started, there was extreme pressure to produce a certain specified number of grams of plutonium which in retrospect must have been enough for a test bomb and the Nagasaki bomb. Several deliveries were made, the first one on February 2, 1945, and the final (wartime) portion was June 15, 1945. After this, the pressure decreased markedly, both because the Germans surrendered on May 8 and the achievement of the required quantity. I don't know how much plutonium we shipped. We were strictly forbidden to keep notes or diaries.

We shipped it in a solution. I remember I wasn't very excited when they showed me some. It looked like brown molasses. We shipped enough by June that we were cleaned out. We had the goal, we accomplished it. After June things began to settle down. We had already shipped enough. We wanted to avoid accidents. There was an air that things were winding down. It was only five weeks until Hiroshima. I took a week's vacation in late June with my family, to visit Seattle and Victoria, British Columbia. So the pressure was really off.

After that we began returning surplus Du Pont personnel to the company and planned for the end of the war. The Du Pont contract expired nine months after cessation of hostilities and we fully expected the plant would shut down by that time. The Du Pont Company was dead serious about withdrawing when the war was over.

I want to mention something else, the Japanese balloon bombs [see Mikesh reference in bibliography]. They were a real worry. Everybody at the plant was always looking up because of the statistical chance of one falling. I remember seeing 40 at one time going over. The Navy planes at Pasco chased them regularly but they had poor luck. Matthias and I went over to prod them about getting better protection. They never managed to shoot one down, although a number came down on the project, but away from the buildings. The bombs never went off, but the balloons blew around and the military were a great sight trying to round these up without being blown up themselves. The only balloon that caused any damage to Hanford was the one that landed on the power line from Grand Coulee Dam, and it knocked out the reactors very briefly, the only American war plant shut down by enemy action during the whole course of the war. We mentioned that to Groves and he said, "I suppose all you fellows will apply for the Purple Heart."*

Something else is radioactive releases. We put very high stacks on the separation plants. We did worry about gas emissions when the uranium from the reactor was dissolved to separate the plutonium. We monitored them very carefully, and in that period up to June, 1945, if there was a good velocity of wind to distribute them, we might have taken some chances. Naturally, all of these things were being done for the first time and time was of the essence. Forty balloons in the air reminded us time was of the essence. I do remember that at the beginning some of the first batches of uranium being dissolved left off a little more gas than we would have liked, but we learned to control it. But, up until June when the amounts they wanted at Los Alamos had been delivered, the pressure was tremendous.

---

*   On March 10, 1945, a falling balloon bomb brushed against a Bonneville Power electric transmission line 15 miles south of Toppenish, Washington, causing a power outage at Hanford which shut down three reactors for a brief period.

We watched everything that went into the river. We had a whole building where the effluents were monitored. We had big tanks with fish in them. The effect on the fish was watched. I don't recall any problem with anything going into the river.

Now, a great number of idealistic technical people hoped the chain reaction would not work, that it would be impossible to have a nuclear explosion. The ones who visualized what nuclear weapons would be were sober about the whole thing. The outburst of enthusiasm when they were used came from knowing the job was done and that the war would be over. After five years, the people in this country were getting tired of war, tired of shortages, tired of people being killed. It was a subconscious weariness. But something that suggested the war was going to end was really something. There would be no invasion of Japan. After the experience of Okinawa anybody who had relatives in the Far East was scared. The death toll on Okinawa was beyond all expectations. One man said the bombs cost a lot of lives but also saved a lot of lives, including his. The apprehension among people who would be going into Japan was tremendous. They knew there would be a lot of criticism about dropping the bombs, but at the time it was the biggest relief they had ever experienced.

JOHN A. WHEELER

John Wheeler was the leading physicist in residence at Hanford. He solved the riddle of the B Reactor going dead a few hours after it started, an event that threatened to delay seriously the first production of plutonium. Early in his career at Princeton, in 1939, Wheeler and Danish physicist Niels Bohr collaborated to develop the first general theory of the mechanism of fission, which included identifying the nuclei most susceptible to fission, a landmark accomplishment that helped make Wheeler, at age 28, world famous among nuclear physicists. After the war, at Los Alamos, he directed the group which produced the conceptual design for the first family of thermonuclear weapons. He became interested in astrophysics and coined the term "black holes." In 1976, Wheeler joined the department of physics at the University of Texas at Austin, where he was interviewed.

One of his regrets was that the Manhattan Project got off to a slow start. Another was that he had waited so long, until February 1, 1942, to work fulltime on the bomb. No one, he said, up to then had a more central position in nuclear physics than he did. He felt that every month the war was shortened would have saved many lives, including that of his brother, Joe Wheeler, killed in Italy in 1944.

John Wheeler, shown in recent years teaching at the University of Texas in Austin. *University of Texas*

I was at Hanford in residence from July, 1944, until September, 1945, and before that I made a roundtrip from Pasco to Wilmington once a month on the train. Arthur Compton assigned me to be what you might call a know-how transferer from the Met Lab to Du Pont. My first experience was Thanksgiving Day 1942. We were meeting in Wilmington to decide where the plant should be. It was my function to bring in all kinds of factors that otherwise might be overlooked. As for example, the highest number of thunderstorms per year, or obvious ones like security or water purity, you name it, I had to think of it. You might call me father confessor to the project. Somebody who looked under the bed for things.

I never thought of Hanford in terms of being a factory. There was a sense of adventure about it. I associate it with pioneering. I would think it was like the first steamship, that must have been exciting. The first airplane was exciting, the first locomotive was exciting. I feel these comparisons are the right comparisons.

Hanford is a song that hasn't been sung properly. There was a great romance about it. The way to get the feel of that romance is to put yourself back at that meeting in Wilmington, when we had a map of the United States spread out in front of us, and different possibilities there for where this plant might be sited. Great expanses of land, it was almost as if you were Columbus deciding where you would go exploring, or as if you were setting up a new republic.

Then, to pick that particular place, a most fantastic place. Whoever thinks of that northern state of Washington having a hot desert in its middle. That's a story one person in a hundred knows. And that beautiful, bright blue, ice cold Columbia River coming down through it, from the ice fields of Canada.

Then, the history of the place, the pioneer settlers who had desperately tried to irrigate it, and had irrigated it. Then pouring in, all this caravan, all different ways of getting there during the war. Railroad, airplanes, cars. The variety of people there, that too was romantic. Those Okies and Arkies coming in, several hundred a night, being unloaded there at Pasco. Those beer joints with windows close to ground level so that tear gas could be squirted in. The immense mess halls, accommodating those thousands of people. To see all those tables, table after table of people. Gobble, gobble, gobble.

As far as me getting the credit for solving the poisoning riddle, let no man be his own judge, but I can say I have seen no objection to that position. When the reaction died, the mood was excitement and puzzlement. It took the fact that it regained its activity to give the clue. Of course I had been working on fission product poisoning for a long time. My friends at Wilmington, especially George Graves, were always asking me questions that gave a chance to stimulate my imagination to dream up things I otherwise might not have thought about.

Fermi. He was a marvelous person with a tremendous drive. We would go out on a Sunday morning hike, and we would be moving along at a reasonable pace that didn't kill anybody but certainly was not an old ladies' tea party. When the last quarter mile was approached, Fermi would speed up. He was going to be there ahead of anybody else. One Sunday afternoon, John Marshall, myself, and George Weil and Leona Marshall were at this concrete irrigation canal, with sloping sides, maybe 45 degrees, with three feet of water going down at some clip. Should we go in swimming? How would we ever get out? Some of us stretched a rope across so we could grab it. But Fermi, he thought that was sissy, he was going to see how you would get out if you didn't have a rope. So here he was being carried downstream, trying desperately to clamber up, and sliding back down, trying again, sliding down, finally he made it, his shins were bleeding. He was in quite a shape but he made it. That was Fermi. That's how he got things done.

I lived in Richland with my wife and three children. They went to Sacajawea School, a romantic name. We worked six-day weeks, and I can recall going out on a Sunday with the children in the direction of the Horse Heaven Hills and the youngest child, maybe three, climbing a hill, the sun behind her golden hair. It was an absolute halo of color. I realized how the painters of old got the idea of painting halos. It was not an invention of man but a consequence of nature.

By the way, have you ever held a piece of plutonium in your hand? Well, you want to do that because there is something it does for you. People at Los Alamos gave me a piece to hold. It was shaped like a half of a hollow sphere. It was nickel-plated so that the alpha particles from it would not reach the skin. But the marvelous thing about it was the temperature of it. Here, day in day out, producing enough heat to keep itself quite warm, not for 10 years, not for a hundred years, but for thousands of years. It gives you an immediate sense of energy capacity.

At any rate, in the end it was indeed the plutonium that turned out to be the proper fuel, although of course there were backup propositions, such as the electromagnetic separation method for uranium. But there was nothing like the productive capacity of Hanford. Plutonium is like, what is the best grade of gasoline, super? Plutonium is the super-premium of fissile material.

JOHN MARSHALL

The Marshalls, physicists John and Leona and their baby boy, arrived at Hanford in July, 1944.

We came by train from Chicago. We had a car but the tires were not fit to go that distance. We were assigned a house, right off. I started in the 300 Area, a technical and laboratory area, and we worried about startup procedures, getting geared up for starting the reactors. There was a bunch of us known as babysitters. Our job was to be on hand 24 hours a day, some of us, during startup and sort of monitor what was going on, and assist the chief operator in checking things out. We also were there when the reactor was loaded. Somebody was making a joke once, probably John Miles, a Du Pont physicist who headed our technical group. He said we should be called proctologists because we were specialists in piles.

I was there for the poisoning. That's an amusing story. What happened was that the brass was out there for the startup day, I was on the four to midnight shift. The thing was started without a hitch, then everybody went home, Fermi, Crawford Greenewalt, John Wheeler and various others. I wasn't there during that time. I came on just as the reactor died. They had started pulling the control rods out and out and out, finally they couldn't come out any farther and it turned off. Well, of course, there was consternation. The chief operator and I were trying to figure out what in hell had gone wrong, and chased around looking for what seemed probable to us. For instance, a water leak in the reactor, or a loss of helium and a replacement with air. There was something like a percent of reactivity that came from getting rid of the air and putting in helium. The reactors were slightly pressurized with helium, so we checked for helium leaks. There weren't any.

The shift ended and I went home. It was still dead. Somebody came on, I think it was George Weil. He decided he would find out how far below critical the reactor was. He put in a foil that measured the radioactivity and told what level of neutrons there was if all the control rods were pulled out. By that you could tell how far below critical it was. He put the foil in and had the rods pulled out and the thing started. Of course, it shut down again by the time the next shift came on. During one shift it killed itself, then started again. Then it shut itself down again.

The next day Fermi and Leona and John Wheeler and somebody working with him, a Du Pont theoretical type with an Irish name [Dale Babcock], decided something radioactive was doing the job. Both teams were analyzing reactivity as a function of time, as given by the control rod position, and from that deriving the radioactive periods that were involved. Then, all they had to do was look in Seaborg's table of fission products and they could pinpoint that it was iodine and xenon-135. By that afternoon Fermi had worked out a set of formulas so you could predict the reactivity as a function of time. Shortly thereafter, the fuel load in the reactor was increased. The reactor had been taken just barely over critical in the initial loading.

At Hanford there wasn't any organized opposition to the use of the bomb. We were concerned, and hoped it wouldn't be used against cities. There were relatively few people there who knew there was a bomb, just the scientific staff and some management. There was discussion among a few of us about what would be done with the bomb but we didn't try to exert any pressure on anybody. Since most people there didn't know what we were doing, all sorts of stories popped up. I remember one was that we were making the front end of horses to send to Washington, D.C. to assemble with the other end.

We didn't have much time for a social life, except some with the other physicists. Once we went by bus to Seaside, Oregon, and another time to Chelan and took a boat up Lake Chelan. Recreation was hiking or working around the house figuring out ways to get a swamp cooler to work or putting up a fence to keep the baby from wandering. The only thing rigorous about the weather was the dust storms. They were spectacular. Richland is laid on river pebbles, which come in any size from microscopic to the size of your head. They bulldozed the place flat, got rid of whatever top soil there was and brought in silt from the Yakima River flats. They put six inches of this stuff over the town. There's all of, I think, six inches of rain there a year and when the wind blew you wouldn't be able to see across the street. Every morning there was a sand dune under the front door, a crescent dune.

LEONA MARSHALL LIBBY

Leona Woods was 23 in 1942, the only woman present when Enrico Fermi's nuclear pile at the University of Chicago went critical and into the history books. In a 1946 photograph of the Chicago reactor group, Mrs. Libby looked strong, robust and almost girlish, standing among the older men in their white shirts and ties and business suits. Mrs. Libby was one of the few women scientists in the Manhattan Project and probably the most well known. Even so, during an interview she laughed off questions about what it was like to be so distinctive. She did mention Du Pont had been thoughtful enough to provide her with a private bathroom at the reactor buildings.

Leona Marshall Libby, photographed as a young woman when she was one of the few women scientists taking part in the Manhattan Project.

U.S. Department of Energy

After Mrs. Libby's death in 1986 her former husband, John Marshall, remarked that she "was an active scientist, quite apart from being a woman. I think perhaps that is why she didn't want that stressed. There were other women in the project, Jane Hamilton Hall and Kay Way were two of them, but Leona probably was known to more people" because of her association with Fermi, which began in 1942 at Chicago and lasted until Fermi died in 1954. Mrs. Libby was interviewed in her office at UCLA.

I worked with John Wheeler and I helped solve the riddle of the Hanford xenon poisoning. Remember, this was the first big reactor in the world. Here were all these bigshots, lining the walls, to watch the startup. The operators were all coached. They had manuals. They had been through the routine X-Y-Z times. So here comes startup. You can see the water getting hot, the readings going up on the Brown recorders, you could hear it rushing in the tubes, you could see the control rods coming out and out and out. Later, something happened, and there was no more reactivity. The reactor went dead, just plain dead. People stood around and stared at each other. Wheeler had been at Oak Ridge, so he knew about the Oak Ridge reactor, which had showed signs of misbehavior, which could have been interpreted as poison, but you couldn't prove it. At Hanford, we had the time period, the time it took for the reactor to go up to power, die and come back on. I would say Wheeler solved it, no doubt.

Before the xenon trouble, there was the problem of putting jackets on the fuel slugs. We walked around, and looked and walked around, we were supposed to figure it out. The guys who dipped the slugs in the molten flux solved it. They called it underwater canning. Well, nothing was going to work if the slugs didn't work. One of the technicians, as I recall, solved the slug canning problem. I must say they never got enough credit. It was a clever person, whoever it was, and I hope he got a bonus but I doubt it.

We wanted to get out of Hanford as fast as we could but we couldn't since we were babysitting the reactors. I remember John was on the night shift and I was on the afternoon. My mother was there to care for our child. For recreation we looked at the desert a little bit, but have you ever been to Hanford? Yes, Hanford was a factory, a plutonium factory. That was why it was built, exactly right.

Yes, I knew Szilard. He had a very special place in the world. He developed a group of fresh Ph.Ds who formed a clique. They brought their minds to bear on problems that would become important after the war. Nobody else did that. Already, he had given over more or less the physics problems to Fermi and Wigner and concerned himself instead with these in part philosophical, but also exceedingly practical, questions. A really amazing man, really an amazing man. Fermi was very steady by comparison.

I think everyone was terrified that we were wrong (in our way of developing the bomb) and the Germans were ahead of us. That was a persistent and ever-present fear, fed, of course, by the fact that our leaders knew those people in Germany. They went to school with them. Our leaders were terrified, and that terror fed to us. If the Germans had got it before we did, I don't know what would have happened to the world. Something different. Germany led in the field of physics, in every respect, at the time war set in, when Hitler lowered the boom. It was a very frightening time.

I certainly do recall how I felt when the atomic bombs were used. My brother-in-law was captain of the first minesweeper scheduled into Sasebo Harbor. My brother was a Marine, with a flame thrower, on Okinawa. I'm sure these people would not have lasted in an invasion. It was pretty clear the war would continue, with half a million of our fighting men dead not to say how many Japanese. You know and I know that General (Curtis) LeMay firebombed Tokyo and nobody even mentions the slaughter that happened then. They think Nagasaki and Hiroshima were something compared to the firebombing.

THEY'RE WRONG!

I have no regrets. I think we did right, and we couldn't have done it differently. Yeah, I know it has been suggested the second bomb, Nagasaki, was not necessary. The guys who cry on shoulders. When you are in a war, to the death, I don't think you stand around and ask, "Is it right?"

DAVID HALL

David Hall and his wife, the late Jane Hamilton, went as a team to Hanford. Also a physicist, she worked in the medical-safety division. In later years, he became head of the reactor division at Los Alamos and Jane Hamilton was the assistant director at Los Alamos. Hall was interviewed at his home near Santa Fe.

We stayed at Chicago until early in 1944, and then we went out to Hanford to babysit the construction of three reactors. We reached Hanford in June or July. I remember when we first got there the houses weren't ready and we stayed in dormitories. Blast! Those bedsheets were hot. You touched them and they were hot. I had never experienced that dry heat before. Our front lawn, after we got a house, had wild asparagus coming up. The only remarkable thing about our house was that the contractor apparently had not been able to get regular bathtubs and so the bathtubs were poured concrete. Kind of gritty on your bottom.

The perception of Hanford by the people at Chicago was that Hanford was going to gin out the plutonium from the irradiated uranium. The real question was how pure they could make it, because to maximize production the quality goes down. It's a tradeoff. I really don't know how much I can talk about that. The more that was turned out the less pure it was isotopically.

I worked with John Wheeler and George Weil, checking the quality of the graphite for B Reactor. They were pouring the reactor foundations, putting in the shielding, a massive building. Part of my job was to see if anything was in trouble, if anything was wrong, if the workmen were performing their jobs, and generally overseeing.

The Du Pont people say their foresight provided for the unexpected, as in the case of the xenon poisoning. In fairness, and I am not criticizing Du Pont, I think they may not have done what they had done if they had been in a competitive position. They were running at cost, and they did not get a profit, but there was no expense to them. For example, my wife and I, both with Ph.Ds, were hired to do really quite menial tasks, jobs that could have been done by people without training. It was over-kill, and it paid off.

Our social life was very good. There were three shifts, headed by senior people, whom I knew quite well. Henry Newson was in charge of one. It was a congenial group, we used to party together. The most tedious and monotonous thing was the long bus ride from Richland to the reactors. All the people I knew were married and they had their wives with them. Meta Newson, Dot Hughes. I think it must have been kind of cliquey, with not much intermingling with Du Pont. I hadn't known Henry Newson before, but we kept up a friendship for many years after that. My friends were mostly academics, and the Du Pont engineers also tended to stick together socially. We worked 44 to 48 hours a week. For fun, we would go to Pasco, that was the source of liquor. We had weekend parties, but the weekend might be a working day. We played cards. Nothing wild. We heard stories of violence at the taverns in the construction camp, but that was to be expected since many of the workers were displaced and without their families.

We got used to the weather. I was fascinated by that long finger of temperate climate that extends up the Columbia River from the coast. You see an isothermal up the coast line, then it goes shooting in along the river and comes back. We were interested in the Horse Heaven Hills , and dry farming. I stayed until April, 1945, and went back to Chicago.

META NEWSON

Meta Newson, a homemaker at Hanford during WWII, was married to the late Henry W. Newson, a Manhattan Project physicist at Chicago, Oak Ridge, Hanford and Los Alamos, and later a professor at Duke University. Interviewed at her Chapel Hill residence, Mrs. Newson had among her memorabilia a lease agreement, dated Aug. 19, 1944, for a house at "a manufacturing plant, at or near Pasco, Washington, owned by the federal government and operated by Du Pont."

The first two years after we were married, from 1934 until 1936, we were in California with Ernest Lawrence, at the cyclotron at Berkeley. When the Manhattan Project started, my husband was at Stagg Field, at the first chain reaction. When I went to Stagg Field to pick him up in the evenings, I couldn't go in, he would have to come out. He came out one day with little blocks of graphite. I thought, "That idiot, he is starting to play with blocks."

We went to Hanford in August, 1944, and stayed until about February, 1945. We had a three-year-old daughter, Meta Mary. My first recollection of Hanford was that people told us to guard our dog because the coyotes would come and either lead the dog into the pack or kill it. The second thing was the mosquitoes. And, the sandstorms. Once, Henry told me he was reading a book during a sandstorm. He must have been six feet from the windows. He had rags and newspapers stuffed around them and he said every time he was ready to turn a page he had to blow the sand off.

The housing in Richland was very nice. We had a house with three bed-rooms, one bath, a large L-shaped living room-dining room, a very adequate kitchen, a full basement and we paid $50 a month, including utilities, stove and refrigerator. Those were the good old days.

A typical day. Well, I was a typical housewife. They didn't have a nursery school, so I kept my daughter at home. There were very few children to play with because so few people had children. The ones who did were probably Du Ponters. The Du Ponters were in the Establishment there. The Du Ponters were a little snooty. If someone wasn't a Du Ponter, you were the lowest of the low. There was a family across the way, and they were Du Ponters, with five or six children. One next door neighbor was an FBI man. He said the best information he got was by going to the brothels down in Kennewick and Pasco. And his wife would go along, and sit in the car and wait for him and time him. She was a beautiful woman. I don't know why she was worried.

Shopping was marvelous. You could get everything there you couldn't get in other parts of the country. When we left, we took 15 cartons of cigarettes and I don't know how many cases of Cokes. Meat was plentiful. It was rationed but you could get anything you wanted. I think they were trying to keep us happy. It sure was out in the sticks. We had loads of mice. When the land was cleared all the mice decided to move indoors. I would catch one, and as soon as the trap was reset, click. I would catch four or five a day. We had lots of black widow spiders. I called the health department and the hospital to ask what to do about my child if she's bitten. "Well, if she goes into convulsions, bring her into the hospital."

I had no idea what was going on. My husband always told me I wasn't interested in physics, so why should he try to explain. I wouldn't have known what an A-bomb was anyway, if they had told me. I think the scientists were pleased the bombs were successful. But, they were so successful I think later they had negative feelings. Too powerful. I was also glad they were successful. The propaganda was that we were going to send so many troops to invade Japan and how many would have been killed then. You know, take your druthers, which would you rather do? Yours or theirs?

WARREN E. NYER

Warren Nyer was 19, a physics student at Chicago, when he was hired as a research assistant with the Office of Scientific Research and Development, an early part of the bomb-building program. Nyer, although he did not have an undergraduate degree, traveled the circuit of the Plutonium Project: Chicago, Oak Ridge, Hanford, Los Alamos, Trinity. He became a management consultant to electric utility firms, and was interviewed by telephone at his residence in Idaho Falls, Idaho.

I stayed at Hanford until February of 1945. After the reactor started up, I was still young enough that I didn't understand much about organizations. I wasn't too happy with the Du Pont organization, it wasn't as exciting as laboratory work, and I didn't foresee that it would be very exciting from then on, so I went to Arthur Compton who had made it possible for me to go the University of Chicago originally and told him I wanted to go to Los Alamos. So he called Oppenheimer and arranged it. I met Oppenheimer several times but I didn't move in those circles at all. Except weekly, at our colloquium, he usually came and filled us in. He was the world's best, greatest, laboratory director.

As far as my feelings on the bombs were concerned, you have to remember a couple of things. One is the feelings of people toward the Nazis and, later, the Japanese after the Bataan Death March, and people with longer memories remembered the Japanese and the rape of Nanking. That's one aspect. Another is that it was my age group that was out there dying. All of my friends were either in Germany or the Pacific. I would certainly have had no hesitation to sacrificing any number of the enemy to save even a small number of my contemporaries.

C. N. GROSS

A native of the West Virginia mountains, C. N. Gross came to Hanford in January, 1944, from Wilmington, to be a reactor consultant. He and his wife decided to stay after 1946 when Du Pont left and General Electric took over. They liked the atomic energy business as well as the Eastern Washington sunshine, and GE offered a good job at a time when Du Pont management people were stacked four deep on the East Coast. He was interviewed at his house in Richland, with a wide view of the Columbia and the flat farming country to the east. His house, with its fine furniture and art and crystal and air of good taste, epitomized the refined residence of an old-line Du Pont executive..

When I came I was working as contact man, liaison, between operations and construction. I think I was called construction consultant for operations at all three reactors. I made sure construction followed the blueprints. The teletype between Hanford and Wilmington was going 24 hours a day on design changes. You have to give credit for a lot of the original ideas on construction of the reactors to the Met Lab. They did a whale of a good job, and Du Pont picked it up and it is almost unbelievable to me today that Du Pont did what they did in two years.

I was aware of what was going on. I was told in Wilmington in '43. I spent about nine months there working with the design people. I looked at blueprints and suggested ideas on how best to build a plant we could operate. I remember helping with the design of the control rods, that moved in and out on racks, and were water-cooled. The control rods were horizontal and controlled the reaction. The vertical rods, the safety rods, were used if we had an electrical outage. The safety rods would automatically drop. The safety rods were not used to control the reaction because they would not withstand the heat. They were not water cooled. The nine control rods had tubes inside them, connected with water. When the rods were pulled out of the reactor they were radioactive so there had to be a shielded control rod room.

We had fuel elements that ruptured. After a fuel rupture, the reactor may or may not shut down automatically. But you would know you had a rupture. The fuel tube itself would overheat and each tube was monitored. That was a main reason for shutdown, except for shutdown for unloading of fuel elements.

Unloading was done with computers, although they weren't like the ones we have nowadays. You would figure that certain tubes at certain temperatures that had been operating so long had produced so much plutonium and they were ready for discharge. The tubes on the fringe would take a year or so to get ready. The ones in the center might take only three months because of greater neutron availability.

The design level for plutonium production per reactor was 250 grams a day, when the power level was 250 megawatts. Each megawatt was supposed to produce a gram of plutonium per day. But that was ideal, and the reactors did not produce that much a day in operation. What came out of the separations area was far less than that a day.

The bombs, well, I more or less took the news as what is to be will be. I felt like, when they were dropped, that the war was effectively over. I don't know it was really necessary to drop them on cities, but they did what they were supposed to do, end the war.

BETSY STUART

Mrs. Stuart was married to Charles F. "Stud" Stuart, a personnel troubleshooter for Du Pont at Hanford. A resident of Charleston, West Virginia. she was interviewed at her daughter's residence in Kirkland, Washington.

We went down to dinner the first night at the Transient Quarters and the salad dressing was so wonderful. We pigged out on the salad, and we had diarrhea for days. They were making the salad dressing with pure mineral oil, you couldn't get regular salad oil. Everybody got a good case of diarrhea when they came to Richland.

I went right to work as a secretary at the 300 area, for C.O. Malley, an electrical engineer. You can believe this or not, I don't think you will. When I was typing, one of the Army engineers might come in. They were insufferable. They thought they knew it all, they had a high disregard for civilians. One man, he was a pompous ass, he would come in and say something like I don't care what you are doing, this has to get out.

So I would have to take something else out of my typewriter, and this is the part hard to believe. The paper I took out of my typewriter I would have to put in a flat box and lock it. I would put the flat box in an inner tray and lock that. You locked the file drawer, then you locked your typewriter, and when I left, I locked the door to my office. That was five keys. You also had to do all that to go to the bathroom. I didn't go to the bathroom very often.

We were young, most of us, and used to doing what we wanted to do. We were a stratified group. Most of us were from the same social background. We had been to college. Most of us were from the East. Few of us had cars. We used public transportation, we walked everywhere. There was one movie for 15,000 people, which ran every day, three times a day. There were lines all the way down to the TQ.

I had been in the 300 Area for three weeks and all of a sudden Mr. Malley came in and said you have to go into Richland. They sent a special car for me and I went to the hospital. No explanation. Something had registered on my pencil (radiation detector) that they didn't like. To be hauled in like that, here were these grim-faced people, nobody would answer a question. The second time it happened, I had walked down a hallway to the main building in the 300 Area, a long hall lined with tiles, like bathroom tiles. I stumbled as I was walking along the narrow hallway. I hit the wall. I went on and delivered whatever it was. After I got back to the office, they called me into Richland again. I had set something off when I hit the wall. I could hear a buzzing sound but I didn't ask any questions. I don't know if there was something built into that wall that was a monitor or what. At Richland, they did a blood test. I never had a report. It's made me angry so many times. I know they were trying to protect us from radiation but not to be told anything was upsetting.

We were sort of like social directors. Somebody would call and say so-and-so is in town and needs to take a break. Sometimes they wouldn't stay more than an hour. They would talk about anything but what they were doing.

We would talk about the newest shows in New York, and sometimes about the shows in London. We talked about the newest books. I remember Alexander Woollcott was really big then. We read both Seattle papers, always. We got The New York Times for a while. You could buy it at the drug store, it was a week old by the time it got there. The book review columns were always the first thing everybody fought over, and all the theater news.

Seattle was like a dream. We would get a gang together, find anybody who had an automobile. We would all save all our points, to get the gas. I'll never forget. We saw "Voice of the Turtle." A wonderful time. We would come on Friday evening, and everybody would try to get off early, and that wasn't easy. I remember we got out at Snoqualmie Pass and threw snowballs at each other. Not far from Seattle, we came around a hill on one trip and it seemed like everything was covered with deep blue flowers and I'll never forget how wonderful it looked, and we saw boats on the water with their sails and I thought I had never seen anything so beautiful, and I never have since.

General Leslie Groves, I can't remember anything good to say about that man. He was at my home one night, for a cocktail party. I don't believe he used an alias. But he was strictly Army. He had little regard for civilians. Enrico Fermi brought a young woman scientist with him, an Italian. She was a physicist, a brain. She was extremely shy and so unhappy. They wanted to keep her, so they asked me to talk to her, and try to break through. I knew a little Spanish and a lot of Latin. Little by little I was able to communicate with her. One thing that was difficult. They were all there under assumed names, and I would forget. And they would ask me to please try to remember. Fermi was called Mr. Farmer.

I remember so plainly, we all knew and all suspected what we were doing, but we didn't call it the atom bomb. We called it degeneration. These people were very intelligent, and most of them were engineers. I think they put 2 and 2 together. I remember I was hanging up some clothes one day and I was talking with a neighbor. Her husband was a mechanic of some kind. She asked me, "What does your husband do?" I said, "I'm sorry, I don't know." She said, "You don't know what your husband does?" She talked to her other neighbor, and she said something she shouldn't have, and she disappeared overnight. Believe me, when we got together we didn't talk about what we were doing. You had this constant "somebody is listening" business. It was an exciting time. It also was a boring time.

We had a crowd of people, all with children that needed babysitting. There was no domestic help to clean your house. Most of us were used to having at least once a month, having somebody come in to do that kind of thing. A lot of people were used to nursemaids. It was tough, but of course we didn't go out very much. There were some teenagers. They were looking for something to do. We formed a babysitting group, with rules and regulations, and those kids earned money hand over fist.

I remember the reaction when we heard about the first bomb. My husband and I talked long into the night about it. I think we had a party that night, an awful lot of people in my house. We felt relief that we could talk about it. But I remember my greatest feeling was shame. I couldn't believe they had dropped the second bomb, I thought why did they have to do it again? I didn't stay at the ceremony, later on, when they awarded us the pins. That's another thing I remember about Groves. He made this long speech and I remember it was hot. I didn't stay. Everybody was more or less expected to go, to receive their pin. It was a big outdoor meeting, on the ball field. I felt real ashamed, because of the loss of life, and I wished I had had nothing to do with it. Maybe I am too much of a pacifist. I feel very sure that if the bomb hadn't been dropped, we would have had a lot more casualties.

I think really I tried to put it out of my mind. It was such an awful, AWFUL, thing for all of us. I remember a big argument about the bombs over drinks one night at a cocktail party, at the Engineers Club. Our friend, Bill, he was very tight that night. Such a dear guy. And he made the statement, it was either them or us. And I got really angry about it. I wasn't doing any drinking. I got very upset and left the table and went down into a room off the ladies' lounge and stayed there the rest of the evening until everybody was ready to go home. I thought there has to be some other answer.

BILL AND LOUISE CEASE

The Ceases were interviewed at their home in Richland. Bill's brother, a navigator on a B-17, was lost when his aircraft was shot down in 1942 over the Java Sea. Mr. Cease talked first.

BILL: When I came here I was 27 or 28 years old, and I've been here 42 years. My previous job was at Bridgeport, Connecticut, at a Remington plant, making ammunition, anything from .22 caliber up to 20 millimeter. I went into operations in the 300 Area, where we were canning the uranium for shipment to the 100 Areas. By then, it was June, '44, they were breaking their butt in the

300 Area to get enough uranium metal to charge these reactors. They had beaucoup trouble. I was kind of a flunky the first month. Then I went on the autoclaves. Each slug, let's see, there were 240 slugs, placed in a series of baskets and put in the autoclaves and cooked for 24 hours, to see if there were any defects in the can.

I stayed at the 300 Area until Halloween night, '44. After the 300 Area, I went back to B as a "D" operator, the lowest level there is. I worked in the 115 Building, which provided the gas atmosphere for the reactor. It was helium. My job was kind of sitting around taking readings because it was fairly automatic. After you were an A operator, you did control room work, they called them pile operators.

Later, I was a pile operator, controlling the rods, taking readings, taking your turn at the control console. At the console, you keep the reactor at a certain level. It wasn't difficult but you couldn't go to sleep. You had a galvanometer in front of you, any minor movement of a control rod would move it. That measured the reactivity. You would look at it, and if the meter went to the left, you were losing power, so you would pull a rod. And if it went to the right, you would poke a little in. After you got up and leveled out the power, the reactor was pretty stable. Somebody watched the panel with the couple of thousand process tubes. Each tube had a light and if a light came on there was something wrong. That didn't happen very often. If a light came on, it could be a malfunction of the gauge, maybe an indication of a fuel element rupture and the tube was blocking up. If the tube blocked up, the pressure would go up. If a fuel element ruptured, you would shut down the reactor and try to push that tube. If you couldn't, you would call in maintenance. The training for reactor operation was on-the-job, there was no other way.

I didn't have any idea what we were doing. It didn't bother me. I had a job, it was a war effort. That's the way it was. Aw, people used to talk, saying we were making Kleenex or clothes pins. My wife and I and another couple were walking down a hill in Bridgeport, Connecticut, on a Sunday, going to the movies when we heard about the war being declared. That had more effect on me than hearing about the bombs. It was one of them things, you took it in your stride.

LOUISE: When we first came here, it was kind of wild. There was nothing here. The sand was knee-deep. We picked out our first house, a one-bedroom prefab. We rode the bus out from Pasco and came out what is Lee now and cut across a big sand dune, which is now a junior high school. We walked up

The control room at the B reactor, photographed in 1993. *Tony Midson*

that and came down and picked out our one-bedroom prefab. At the time it was half built. We were the only ones on that street who had two plum trees.

The city gave us the grass seed. Before that we had bulldozers running back and forth in front and back. We had the best lawn in the neighborhood. There was lots of irrigation water, we got it out of a ditch. Our little house had a little porch. You walked in the front door, and took a left. That was a combination living room and dining room. To the right, was the kitchen and off the kitchen was a bedroom, and a bathroom. Only it just had a shower, no bath. The rent was $27.50 a month, for everything. Heat, water, furniture. Our little house is still there.

Bill would work shift work and go to bed in the morning and leave the windows open. When he got up you could see his imprint in the bed. The sand wasn't really a problem, though, because it was easy to pick up. We came from the East, and back there you had dirt, but you had greasy dirt. It would stick to everything and you had to scrub it. Here, all you had to do was get the sweeper and sweep it up. We had no humidity.

When I got to Pasco on the train from the East, it was terrible. If Bill hadn't been there at the station to meet me, I'd have gone on some place else, maybe California. The station was all the time crowded with men. The men never shaved, it was hard to get laundry done. Construction workers would wear their overalls until they couldn't wear them any more and then they would buy a new outfit. We had one friend that made a fortune doing laundry. She came from South Dakota and she happened to have a beatup second-hand Maytag.

We had a lot of fun in that one-bedroom prefab. Everybody was from all over the country and didn't know anybody. So, you got acquainted real easy. The neighbors would come in for breakfast when Bill came home from the graveyard shift. They would come in at night when he was on the swing shift. We would have dessert together. There wasn't any entertainment, so we would play cards. Out in the camp, they had a big dance hall, and we would go to those, and dance to big bands. We considered ourselves kind of like pioneers.

JACK MILLER

Jack Miller, slim and slow-speaking and very organized in his recollections, was interviewed in his Richland home across the street from the Columbia River.

I started in running a lathe at the 300 Area, turning down the uranium fuel elements. The uranium billets ranged from 250 to maybe 325 pounds. They were round, and were not very big since uranium is heavier than lead. The uranium was extruded first into rods, through an extrusion press. These rods had to be turned down to a proper diameter and cut into proper lengths. Then they went to another lathe and they faced them, cut off the ends and put a slight radius on. From there, they were encapsulated in aluminum cladding, which was quite a process in itself. I had jobs in the tool crib, grinding and making cutting tools to be used in the lathes, and also at the Hanford test reactor. The test reactor was quite small, roughly 15 feet by 15 feet and about that high. It was dismantled eventually. The building is still there, and I understand is now being used for office space and storage.

I remember Leona Marshall. At the test reactor, we had a very small crew. Four of us. We communicated on a PA system from the control area to the work area floor back and forth. And the talk got rather bawdy, I'll have you know. Good Lord, I walked around the corner and there sat Mrs. Marshall counting some foil samples. And, you know, I felt just as guilty as if I had been saying those bad nasties. She never turned a hair.

I went out to the 100 Areas to the production reactors and I stayed there for 33 years. I went to F Reactor first, in early 1945. At F, I was a reactor operator. Now, what is a reactor operator? We didn't have the same type of classification you have now. Then, we did anything you were capable of doing. We had a lot of guidance, including from the world's most knowledgeable physicists. You didn't just go in there and run the darn thing up to full power. We followed procedures. We were told if you don't know what you're doing, DON'T do it.

The worst thing about the control room job was staying alert. As a supervisor said, it was no job for a bonehead. When you were working night shift, about four or five o'clock in the morning, it was awfully hard to sit there and stay alert. There were never less than three of us in a control room, and if it got too bad you asked someone to relieve you for a few minutes. We had a whole bank of instruments to watch, and each was pertinent. It required so much instrumentation that the guy at the board was limited, so you had other people monitoring other instruments. The control supervisor was there to insure that you stayed awake and that he stayed awake.

I remember one incident when I was a chief operator. We were having a little difficulty with heat distribution through the reactor. We had thermocouples inside the graphite moderator itself that you kept track of. I told the fellow to move one rod a tenth of an inch in and another one a tenth of an inch out. We had a hard-nosed character in there, with a belligerant attitude toward the world. He looked at me and said "My God, there isn't anyone who can move one of those a tenth of an inch." The operator at the board said "I won't argue about it," and he barely moved the rods. The belligerent fellow was monitoring the temperature and he couldn't believe the response from the slight movement. This could be done if you had the right touch, the right experience. You didn't want to shake the reactor up.

Originally they planned all of this to be automatic by instrumentation. The electrical rods would be run by instruments. But the response between the instruments and control rods was such that we didn't use the feature. It worked, but the rods were banging back and forth. The instruments were not delicate enough.

By monitoring the radioactivity of the exit water, you would know when you had a fuel element rupture. You got a nose for the thing, and could almost select an individual tube before it went down. You could smell it.

At unloading, the slugs were pushed through the fuel tubes and then fell into the storage basin pools behind the rear face. They were loaded into lead casks. Each cask was lowered into the basin, and arms extended out and removed the lids. The slugs were loaded with a long pair of tongs into buckets and then when the bucket was full it was dumped into a cask. The water was 20 feet deep. Everything was designed so that the slugs could not form a critical mass. The casks were raised, and loaded into a special rail car. All done remotely. The rail car was equipped with water-cooling also. These slugs were generating heat because of the radioactive decay. It did happen that the rail cars occasionally left the rails, but we had plenty of safeguards.

The biggest risk we had was during charge and discharge of the reactors. It would take two men to shove a column of fuel into the reactors, later we had a pneumatic charge machine. The fuel coming out was highly radioactive, so you wanted to make sure everybody was clear of the rear face. And you always wanted to make sure you had reduced water pressure at the front before you uncapped any tubes at the rear, so the irradiated water wouldn't get on you. That got a little hairy once or twice, because communications weren't always good between front and rear. I can remember being on the rear face, wearing coveralls, cloth boots, cloth gloves, rubber boots and rubber pants, rubber hat and jacket and rubber glove and an assault mask. It's difficult to talk into the communications mike when you're wearing an assault mask, which is like an Army gas mask. I was trying to raise the front face, "rear to front, rear to front," no response. Then I tried "rear to control," there's always somebody there. No response. I got so damned disgusted. I started to slam that mike down and noticed I only had a foot of cord on the mike, one of the pieces of machinery coming by had cut the cord. I got my hands contaminated a number of times, because of a leaky glove. We would wash off with soap and water.

In 1945, the Germans were getting well into their rocketry program and in my own opinion I thought we were making a solid rocket fuel competing with the Germans. So, I was way off base. But, obviously, I had to have some idea what we were working with, not being entirely stupid and I had a little physics, and the weight of the damn stuff alone was a clue. And all the radiation checks was another. I used the wrong word once. When they spoke of radiation during that time they referred to it as "activity." I made the mistake in the hearing of one of our managers, I used the word radioactive, because I knew what I was talking about. But, oh my, I was taken into an office and security people told me that word is a No-No, NEVER say that again.

We had frequent checks for radiation. We had hand and shoe counters. Before you smoked, you checked your hands. You checked your hands and feet before leaving work. We had medical inspections. Urinanalysis and blood counts. They also examined your skin closely. Nobody I knew of ever asked what these checks were for.

The idea of splitting the atom was not a new idea. I heard about that in high school, in the 30s. We would have untold sources of energy if we could and so on, and would be the greatest thing since motherhood, which turned out to be not entirely true. I was greatly surprised by the bombs, especially when I began to comprehend the damage that occurred. I did not have any guilt feelings, and don't have to this day. I'm sorry it had to make its announcement to the world as a big bang. I think that has hurt the nuclear program.

The general opinion was that ending the war was worthwhile. How you kill people, that is immaterial. It is just a matter of efficiency. That sounds very brutal. But if this saved a number of deaths and casualties, that of course relieves me of guilt. I do regret there is such a thing as an atomic bomb. I would much prefer that our wars be settled with clubs.

LOMBARD SQUIRES

Lom Squires went out to Hanford in June, 1944, as a chief supervisor in plutonium separations. Squires was interviewed by telephone at his home in Naples, Florida.

I was one of the four young engineers that Crawford Greenewalt took on when he became head of the technical division under Roger Williams. There were Hood Worthington, Dale Babcock, myself and Bill Kirst. I was a chemical engineer, so was Worthington. Babcock was a physical chemist and I think Kirst was a chemical engineer.

My job was to interface with the University of Chicago Metallurgical Lab chemists, and that turned out to be principally with Glenn Seaborg's group. That, I might say, was a fortunate thing, Glenn Seaborg, a very broad-based guy. Of all the other academics at Chicago during that period in the Met Lab, I think he understood best what was required. We had a very smooth working relationship. His chemist, Stanley Thompson, invented the bismuth phosphate process to separate plutonium.

The key to the success of the separations operation was really Ray Genereaux' inventions. He and a guy named Stanley Handforth, who worked for Ray in the design division at Wilmington, developed a technique for remote

When talking to old-timers about Hanford, they usually ask if you have read a piece of verse by Du Pont engineer Charlie Wende, poet laureate of Hanford. The ballad was an inside joke about the Du Pont stalwarts who made plutonium, and featured Hanford legends like Johnny "the Genie" Wheeler and Lom Squires, "the brave and the bold."

The Ballad of Lom and the Bomb

It was back in the Roaring Forties, that me and a guy named Lom
Went out to the Hanford desert and built an atom bomb.
Back of a door on the old Sixth Floor, we hatched a mighty scheme,
With a bunch of guys quite savvy and wise — a remarkably potent team.
There were Johnny the Genie and Roger and Greenie —
*   also on that mission,*
Were Dale and Paul, and Tom and Milt Wahl, the experts on atomic fission.
We were sure we could bust 'em, and it was our custom that every day at
*   noon, We saluted the sun with a shot of rum in an Orange Street saloon.*
And so the clan foregathered at the sign of the TNX,
A gang of moral, spiritual, mental and nervous wrecks. Westward by rail,
*   we blazed our trail from the haunts of the Mystic Brothers,*
And in our track, by horse and hack, came ninety thousand others.

maintenance of highly-radioactive facilities that had never been done before. Stanley Handforth was a design-engineer working for Ray. The two of them put together this idea of remote maintenance using a shielded crane, remotely operated connectors and the standard cell design. I think that was one of the most innovative things Du Pont engineering ever did. It has been the basis of all major chemical reprocessing plants in this country ever since, and for processing of radioactive materials.

When the separations process began, I think we had a very smooth startup. People felt that end of the plant could take care of itself. The reason for that was, first, the job that Seaborg and his people had done in laying the basis for the process, and second the experience we had had at Oak Ridge with Os Greager and Frank Vaughn and those people at the pilot plant down there in demonstrating the chemistry of the process on a semi-plant scale.

The only glitch we had was the fact we had some Teflon gaskets in the pipe connectors. Teflon is not very rigid and the gaskets crept under pressure and we had to replace them with asbestos gaskets. The reason Teflon was in there is because Genereaux had to design that plant to take care of a couple of different process alternatives. In June '44 we had to make a decision which process we would use, and the Met Lab said we have given you all the data, you make up your mind. We decided to go with bismuth phosphate. But, they also had to design the plant to take care of conditions for the lanthanum-fluoride process, which used very corrosive acid. So the gasket material was selected that would be resistant, and Teflon was. It wasn't an ideal material for the bismuth phosphate process which was much less corrosive. So we went back to the good old standard, blue african asbestos. The Teflon extruded, and didn't make a very tight seal.

Start up, as I say, was smooth. Operations people were well trained. We had some breakdown of equipment but that was no problem because we had spares to install and number two we could take the bum equipment out and replace it remotely by this Genereaux-Handforth remote maintenance. We were never in any trouble that way. We had a very experienced group of chemical supervisors on that job. They had been running dynamite plants and smokeless powder plants for years and they knew what it took to start up a new plant. They had been on the military explosives circuit, and starting up one plant and moving on to start up another one was a way of life with that crowd.

I left in '46. They were scaling back. The war was over, gas rationing was over, people were getting back to commercial work. I went to Du Pont's Belle Works, near Charleston, West Virginia.

W.K. AND VERA JO MACCREADY

Mac and Vera Jo MacCready lived in Kennewick overlooking a orchard. MacCready wore western garb, including cowboy boots and a big bronze belt buckle. A Missourian by birth, MacCready held undergraduate and graduate degrees in physical chemistry from the University of Alabama. The Alabama-born Mrs. MacCready, an amateur painter of landscapes, had a gentle southern manner.

MAC: The first shovel was stuck in the ground at Hanford in the early summer of 1943. All of the buildings, all of the facilities, all of the roads, railroads, all of the interim structures necessary to carry on construction, were built, the Hanford plant was finished, all of the temporary stuff was cleared out and construction gone by the 6th of February 1945. Three reactors were built, three major separations plants, and all of the affiliated stuff, all were built in less than two years.

I came out here in mid-April of 1944, when I was 31. Another fellow, by the name of Sam McNeight, and I were chosen to become familiar with the design and to be out here as liaison between the operations folks and the construction folks. Later, I was chief supervisor at B-Plant, in separations.

At the separations areas, see, they originally were going to build four plants. They decided at some stage before they got that far that three would be enough. So, two were being built in the West Area and one was being built in the East Area. The first one was the T-Plant and it was about 10-12 feet above ground when I got here.

Along about the time T was finished, we came to the conclusion from research work that actually the output from the three reactors could be processed by two separations plants. U was 85 percent finished, so they went ahead and finished it, but the determination at that stage was that the two we would actually operate would be T and B. In those days, we did a lot of precautions because we didn't know. All of this process, you see, was designed on the basis of work done in the laboratory with a few micrograms of plutonium.

So we were going to put one plant in one area and one in the other. If we had troubles with one, it shouldn't bother the other one. On the other hand, T and U were close together and trouble at one might make trouble at the other. Trouble might be something about the process that didn't function. There could have been radiation problems that would require heroic efforts and would not make it reasonable or feasible to work conveniently in that region.

In February, 1945, we began shakedown runs in B-Plant. We took 30 days to run through shakedown and then into the actual processing. Nowadays you can't even unlock the front door in under six months. In the shakedown, the first thing we did was run a water run, to see that all the valves and all the pumps and the instruments and suchlike did what they were supposed to do. After that we ran an acid run, to check the same things to see to it that acid versus water would not cause leaks.

One of the three chemical plants, called "221 buildings," which separated plutonium from uranium fuel slugs. More than 800 feet long, they were nicknamed "Queen Marys of the sagebrush." *U.S. Department of Energy*

As I have said many times, by a combination of circumstances in the period between the time I started with Du Pont and came out here, a matter of about nine years, I had been involved with liaison with construction and startup at about 15 plants, and none of those plants, which were relatively small and simple by comparison, started up as easily and in as trouble free a fashion as these out here did. I think that was because although the amount of specific information was limited, the amount of general information about chemical processes and chemical plants was very very large. And they were impressed with the significance of the fact they were going a long ways here on very little information. So everything was most carefully considered as we went along and most carefully checked. Every step was double-checked. As a consequence there was essentially nothing that had not been accounted for.

In those days, at the beginning, we were not afraid of plutonium concentration that might lead to a critical amount. The bismuth phosphate process was a batch process. You dissolve a batch of fuel and you ran that batch through the various steps, as an entity. Compared to the continuous process where you keep stuff feeding all the time. Then you would have more reason for concern because of the possibility that some place things can accumulate that you are not aware of. But, with a batch process, where the material went through tanks and centrifuges and the like, it was pretty easy to run through flush systems for each batch and be assured the stuff was out.

To run a batch through took about 12 hours, through 221-T building, the big rascal with the thick concrete walls, and 224 building, a more normal building of concrete blocks. By the time you ran through 221-T building, you had separated most all of the fission products as well as the uranium from the plutonium. By the time you got to 224, it was 99 percent plus pure. The radiation exposure was very low, so they could run through the next stages of purification in a more normal building without all the shielding or the remote operation. Eventually, the product was a 99.99 percent pure solution of plutonium as a nitrate salt in solution.

During the period before the bombs were dropped, there were no significant contamination accidents in final plutonium handling. They didn't have a complicated process, buildings 221 and 224 having taken most of the fission products and uranium out. You went a step and a half more to continue purification and reduce the volume. They might get in a 27-gallon batch and send out two or three gallons. All of these figures are approximate, it's been 43 years ago.

VERA JO: I came in June of '44. That was in the beginning of getting houses. Mac got a little house in Richland. He got some friends in and they put everything together. The draperies were up, everything was perfect, he thought. He came over at 3 o'clock in the morning and picked me up at the Pasco train station and we drove to Richland, and it was a bright moonlight night, and here sat this little red square thing in the middle of piles of dirt that were much higher than it was, and we sat down and I died laughing. I thought that was the funniest thing I ever saw in my life. And Mac was so mad, he was so proud of it. It was a three-bedroom one-story house.

People got confused, what with the new streets and the way the houses looked a lot alike. Several times I would be in the kitchen and a man would come in the back door, and usually I would know him and knew he just got in the wrong house.

I was one of the few people in that area who had a vacuum cleaner. Everybody used it. You could go in and there would be sand an inch and a half deep along the baseboard. I didn't mind it. I came from New Jersey where you scrubbed your woodwork, everything in the house, every month. You came out here, and you went around with your vacuum cleaner and picked the sand up and that was it. We had greasy dirt in New Jersey, and colored dirt, because every once in a while the Dye Works would let go with blue or whatever.

We made friends very quickly. We have friends we have had for 40 years who are closer than family. We came out here, and everybody was away from their families. You made friends in a hurry. The men were working anywhere from 14 to 18 hours a day, sometimes more than that, sometimes they didn't come home at all. So the women were left pretty much on their own. We had to do things together because you didn't get much gas in those days, so we shopped together. Because men didn't talk about their jobs, we could even get the husbands to come into the living room at parties and talk to the women.

You didn't hear too many complaints, but we had some women who absolutely hated the place. Everything about it. I came out and loved it the minute I saw it, I loved the desert. Lots of things some women didn't like. For one thing, there was one very small store, John Damm's store, that probably was two-thirds the size of this room. That's where we stood in line to get things like thread. At the post office, we stood in line for two to four hours.

Most everybody who came out here was real young, and not had a chance to accumulate things, like washing machines. I got, I think, the last washing machine that Montgomery Ward had in the country, so everybody came to my house to do washing. But I didn't mind any of it, because Mac was in this country, he was not overseas, I might not see him tonight but I at least would see him tomorrow night. So, I could take anything, and there were a lot of us who felt the same way.

WILLIAM D. NORWOOD

Dag Norwood was interviewed at his Richland home, in a room with a big view of the Columbia. It was a room filled with trophies from a big game safari to Tanzania years ago, including lion, impala, leopard, hartebeest, antelope, and some tall ivory tusks. A physician, Norwood specialized in occupational health and radiation.

I came to Hanford in March, 1944, as Du Pont's medical director. When we arrived, we stayed in a hotel, and felt sand in our teeth, sand on the bed. Richland had 200-300 people and one grocery store. At first, I was involved in all medical care, later it was mostly occupational health and radiation monitoring.

We used all types of measuring instruments, for different types of radiation. The worst possibility was plutonium. The amount allowed, total whole body, was .04 microcuries, an amount equal to what you could put on the point of a very sharp pencil. People wore a pencil-type monitor, and also a badge with X-ray film. At first the pencils were checked every day and the badges checked weekly.

Plutonium is an alpha emitter, and internal deposition is dangerous because it goes to the bone and liver and can cause malignancies. The people at greatest risk were working in the separations plants. We did urine tests, at first, some were done daily. After that, weekly and, finally, I think, monthly. We were looking for plutonium. Plutonium did show up, but well below the permissible limits.

FRED AND DIANA VANWYCK

The VanWycks, Van and Di, were interviewed in their living room, front door open on a spring day, the sound of a sprinkler going in the yard. They were Richland boosters and had never regretted their decision to move there in 1944 from Charleston, West Virginia, where Van worked at Du Pont's Belle Plant as a technician. The couple had known Richland when it was a raw, new, wind-blown, almost treeless town. They had watched it change to a pretty city of more than 30,000, with shade trees in abundance and grass that halted the sand storms of the 1940s. Richland had been a government-owned town, and remained so until 1957 when the Atomic Energy Commission allowed private ownership of residences.

VAN: I'm sure the Richland Players, which we helped found, was instrumental in our early adjustment to life here, because it gave us something to do. Di right away won the lead in a production.

DI: The play was "The Male Animal." We did it here and then took it to Walla Walla to the hospital, for the wounded. Van got involved then, and that was our recreation, except for going to the park and the pool. We used to take our dinner at night and go on the bus to the park. We didn't have a car. Everything was so new and clean and fresh, except for the wind. There's so much green now.

VAN: After I got here, I was supposed to get a duplex house, a two story. They had a big lumber strike in the Seattle area and they were cutting back here. But, I could get a brand-new three-bedroom prefab and that's what I took at 1706 Lee Boulevard. It cost $37.50 a month, furnished, with utilities and grass seed, tons of grass seed.

DI: I used to stand out with a hose on fine spray, with a book in my hand while the children were in school and spray this lawn. It came up very nicely. It happened that we had a faulty pre-fab. It had some construction problems they tried to repair. I came home one day and there was a man under the house in the middle of a terrible windstorm. I asked him what he was doing and he said he was trying to get this house fixed so it won't blow away. "We lost two of them last night," he said. We moved into another house.

VAN: I came here as an operator in 1944. To be perfectly honest, we weren't real sure where we were going. We received our tickets to Chicago, on the train, there were four fellows and we went to the Union Station in Chicago. There we received tickets to Pasco. On our trip, we were contacted by men interested in where we were going. We were non-committal. One guy said, "I'll bet you're going to Pasco. What did you ever do to get sent there?"

DI: Let me interject, this is really strange. Just before Van left for Hanford, we were driving out to the plant at Belle with a friend, a very bright fellow, a keen mind. Van was going out to do some last minute work and Jim was driving us out. And he said, "So you're going out to the Northwest. You know what they're doing out there, they're splitting atoms." Van asked him what he was talking about? "Yeah I read it in Time magazine two weeks ago." So much for secrecy.

VAN: Course, if he had said splitting bananas it wouldn't have made any difference to me at that time. At the Belle plant, I was a chemical operator. At that plant, we made 235 different products, but mainly alcohol, ammonia, nylon, brake fluid, anti-freeze. I was transferred out here as a power operator. We operated pumps, steam turbines, anything in the power phase. We operated things like compressors. We were at 100-B, in the 190 building, operating pumps for the cooling system, for one thing.

When I got to 100-B, well, the operating buildings didn't contain any windows, they were concrete block. The building was large, had lots of equipment. I was a pump operator, a compressor operator, a steam power plant operator. Our building was right across from the reactor building.

I also worked as a chief operator in the 190 building, which was the power plant. The chief operator controlled all the pumps. The operators started them up and shut then down. I was also a chief operator in the water treatment plant, which included the river pump plant, the filter plant, the water storage plant.

DI: Before the war was over, I was involved in the League of Women Voters. I taught Sunday school, was chairman of the Junior Red Cross, which was a going thing at that time because of the war. We had four boys, two born in West Virginia and two in Richland.

VAN: I did not have any idea what was going on before the bombs. The day the first bomb was dropped, I was on swing shift. We heard it on the radio, I believe around noon. That it had happened and what we were doing here.

DI: I was going home to West Virginia at that time, and in Cincinnati they had a man doing interviews with the train passengers and he walked up to me with his mike and he said, "And where are you from lady?" I said Richland, Washington. He said, "That's where they are splitting atoms. Come on, tell me about it." I turned my nose up and walked away.

VAN: Everybody was excited and very proud. It was the same thing when the second bomb was dropped. I had a brother with the First Marine Division on Guadalcanal. I had a brother in the Navy who was due to land in Japan two days after the bombs. He told me, "Let me tell you something. If we ever had to go ashore, the number of people we lost would be unbelievable." He was grateful for the bombs.

After the war when Du Pont was leaving Hanford, we were offered a transfer back to Charleston. My boss, the power superintendent, said he would like for me to stay here.

DI: I immediately called West Virginia and told mother we were coming home. We've got to find a house to live in, and I had no idea when we would be there but we were coming. Van came home from work that day and said, "Let's sit down and talk about this." We decided to stay. I've never been sorry. Have you ever been in West Virginia, and Charleston? It's the Kanawha Valley and it's damp, and it's very dirty and it's full of chemicals. It's closed in. Richland was so wide open and so clean and we liked it. We thought it would be a good place to raise children and as it turned out it has been a good place. We were such a young, fresh, enthusiastic group of people. Attractive too.

VAN: We were young, it was an adventure.

WAKEFIELD WRIGHT

Wakie Wright was a neat man with a crisp style. Born in Ohio, he had a degree in biological sciences from the University of Louisville. At Hanford, he supervised workers called "chemical operators."

The first day of September, '44, in a nice howling dust storm, I arrived at Hanford. I drove out from Oak Ridge, my wife could not come because there was no housing. Russ Chapman and I went to the ration board, and the ration board gave us four new tires, S3 Goodrich tires, and a whole wad of C tickets for gas. Russ had a Ford and I had a Chevy.

At separations, I worked at T Plant, somebody had to make up the run books, what I call cookbook chemistry. You gotta remember our manpower was chosen, frankly, out of the ranchers that had been dispossessed of their land and construction people who stayed on.

You have a crew of say 10 people. You look at this outfit and you say, "Now you do as I say or get hurt, because what we're dealing with, you can't see it, you can't feel it, you can't eat it, and so on and so forth." And you sit down and you have to train people how to read the run books.

You see, that type of operation was controlled by gang valves and the supervisor had a key to the gang valves. You have, let's say you have finished dissolving, you have to move the liquid, you have to jet the liquid from the dissolver cell over to, we'll say, an E-1 tank. Now, that solution could not be moved until, first, I look at the run book to see if everything is done, and secondly, I open the gang valve and then they say, "Jet dissolver to E-1 tank," for instance. Then when it is done, I come back and I lock the valve. Then it had to be centrifuged, let's say. Okay, so the operator comes down and says "I'm ready to centrifuge." I look at the run book. Okay, everything's fine. I open the gang valve.

That's what I call cookbook chemistry. Anybody who never saw a chemistry book in their life could do it because everything was labeled. All the piping was remote controlled. Everything was remote control maintenance, with remote control wrenches.

The equipment worked very well. In fact, the first run as I remember it at the T Plant was something like durn near 99 percent pure. It was a good process. Most of the time, things went fairly smoothly. Oh sure, we had our problems. We might have a leaky connector, or a jet that didn't work right, those normal kinds of problems. When I was there we had four to five really

The interior "canyon" of T Plant, one of the three separation plant
buildings. Each contained dozens of separate cells under the floor in which
the hotly radioactive material from the reactors was processed to obtain
plutonium.   *U.S. Department of Energy*

qualified crane operators to handle remote repairs and maintenance. These
guys could drop a pipe through a hole in a tank from 40 feet and never miss it.

The fuel slugs on well cars could be backed right into the tunnels and
unloaded into the dissolver. In those days we had only aluminum cladding on
the fuel slugs, not like now with zirconium. So nitric acid was used to dissolve.
Also before you could dissolve in those days you had to worry about wind
conditions, because nitric oxide fumes, on a first cut, would be practically
brown. They didn't want the wind to be in the direction of the Tri-Cities,
even though they were 30-35 miles away. We had a big meteorological tower
outside the West Area and we worked closely with them. If we started dissolving and the wind got bad, we would have to quit, so we were at the vagaries of
the wind. That's before we had sand filters and all kinds of purifiers. Right
now you go to PUREX (the post-war separations plant) and when they dissolve
you have to look hard before you can discern a slight light brownish smoke.

The radiation danger was always with us. We were taught to obey our instrumentation, like flying an airplane. If your instrument says you are flying straight and you think you are upside down you better think you are flying straight. In the early days, we carried Geiger counters with us, we didn't have fancy pencils and badges.

When we first came out here, for years, they would come by and leave a bottle on the porch. And you were required to urinate into that bottle and then they would come and pick it up. We were tested once a month, during the war and afterward. We had yearly physical examinations. And, every day somebody would check your feet for radioactivity.

We were taught about radiation at Oak Ridge. And on top of that we had to train our people too. It was much easier after they dropped the bombs. Before the bombs, you would have to tell them, "Put your confidence in me, because I am not letting you go somewhere where you would be hurt but at the same time I can't tell you what you are doing either." Not many of them guessed. I couldn't say anything about radioactivity, not until after August 6.

ORVILLE F. HILL

Chemist Orville Hill joined the Met Lab at the University of Chicago at the end of May, 1942, three months after it was created. After the war, he worked at Los Alamos and, in 1946, studied bomb debris from the Bikini atomic bomb tests. Eventually, he returned to Hanford, still looking for better ways of separating plutonium from irradiated uranium. When interviewed, he was retired and lived in Vancouver, Washington.

While I was in Oak Ridge, they chose the so-called bismuth phosphate process, as the way to separate the plutonium from the irradiated uranium. The inventor of it was a fellow named Stanley Thompson, who, incidentally, was my supervisor at Hanford. Stanley was told it wouldn't work, the wrong crystal structure for one thing. Nevertheless, he tried it, and it worked. Stan always said you can know too much, sometimes.

A crew of us went to Hanford in 1944 to study problems that might arise. We were troubleshooters in the separation process. It turned out we weren't needed for that, so we spent our time looking at variations of the process, how we might improve the decontamination, how we might do things to the process to increase its capacity at the plants being built, get the process down to fewer cycles. I think the separations plants worked well from the beginning. Our trouble-shooting chores never really developed. Occasionally, the plant operating staff had to rework batches but it was because of an operator error, or an engineer gave a wrong instruction or something like that.

I wasn't really concerned about radiation in those days, but I had respect for it. When I look back, we did a lot of foolish things. We took risks, to get results rather than spend days and weeks designing equipment so that you could do everything without getting very close or taking any risks. We went ahead and did the work.

In those days we didn't have good instrumentation to tell us how much radiation we were getting. Most people can take a fair amount of radiation. I am sure some of us got exposures higher than we should have. We did things quickly, and we were careful. We could have had accidents. Fortunately, we didn't. In the Manhattan Engineer District, we were on the frontier. We felt a tremendous pressure. We believed the Germans likewise were doing this. And we had to beat the Germans because if they got there first they would win the war. There was no question about it. I averaged 60 hours a week, at Chicago and Oak Ridge, and no overtime pay. We worked those long hours to get the information and the process.

That's why the designs for the reactors and for the separations plants were ahead of the technology, because that was a risk we felt we had to take, to get the plants designed and built and operating as fast as possible. You could not wait until you had all the knowledge. There was not time. We had to get there.

OSWALD H. GREAGER

Os Greager was the most eminent of the Manhattan Project old-timers still living in the Richland area. Before the war he was a high-ranking Du Pont chemist, but after the war began he was placed on leave from Du Pont so he could join the Army's chemical warfare service. Later, he was transferred to the Manhattan Project. At Hanford, as a major, he was the Army's representative at the plutonium separation areas. He returned to Hanford after the war to work for General Electric as a technical manager in the separation areas. He stayed in Richland after retirement.

I was in charge of the division at Oak Ridge which developed the separations process used at Hanford. I had 100 people, divided between Du Pont people, those hired by the Metallurgical Laboratory and soldiers who had scientific or engineering training.

At Hanford, my job was to keep the local Manhattan District office informed of what was going on in the separations area. Groves' advice to all of his people was to stand back and let the contractor do the job, and not to get in his way. As far as I was concerned, I didn't really feel I had anything I had to do. Du Pont was running the show, and that's the way Groves wanted it. Groves said "Stand back and let them run the job."

To run a batch of irradiated fuel through the cells in the canyon building, then to the concentration building, was a series of 12,13,14 operations, then it went to the isolation stage where the concentrated solution of plutonium was converted into a more or less pure plutonium compound for shipment. All this took a couple of weeks.

At the end, it was a semi-solid of jelly-like consistency and was put into a sample can, a strong spherical container of stainless steel. This was shipped to Los Alamos and they converted it into plutonium metal and made the parts for a weapon.

Now, plutonium is very, very toxic. You don't fool with plutonium. The lethal body burden was supposed to be a microgram. You don't have to worry about being exposed to penetrating radiation, because the alpha rays of plutonium can be stopped with a piece of paper. What you had to be concerned about was toxicity. You couldn't breathe it or swallow it, or have a wound or puncture of the skin.

It is hard to remember today what we got in the way of yield of plutonium from the irradiated fuel. One thing that sticks in my mind was they were worried if we would recover as much as 50 percent of the plutonium in the separations process. I bet a couple of bottles of scotch we would get 90 percent at Hanford with our first runs. We did better than that.

There was one big development that took place, involving implosion. In 1943 before they got to the implosion design (based on a technique of squeezing the plutonium, resulting in a more "efficient" and powerful explosion), the people at Los Alamos were asking for purity of plutonium that we didn't believe was feasible. They wanted purities down to 10-thousandths of a percent, you know, 99 and about three more nines. We said there was no way we

Before the plutonium was transported to Los Alamos, it was stored in these vaults, here shown under construction, built into the side of Gable Mountain at Hanford.   *U.S. Department of Energy*

could make that sort of thing. It's tough just to carry it out of solution, all the other stuff in the mess, we just can't do it.

When implosion came along, then the matter of purity sort of dropped out of the picture, because with the implosion technique, any reasonable purity would do. Say, 99 percent pure plutonium, they were satisfied. I do know that eventually we had 9s after the decimal point. The gun-type bomb (where one chunk of U-235 is fired into another) is inefficient, because the uranium pieces get close enough for the reaction to occur prematurely. The competing impulses make the bomb pull apart again. They had to put tremendous explosive charges in it to make the pieces come together and get some kind of a yield.

But the implosion device where everything is pushed down and pressed together at the core, this seems to have a very much better effect and there were high explosive yields. High, for those days, was about 20 kilotons.

I was the one who received the plutonium from Du Pont for the military. The man I received it from was Du Pont's operating head man in the isolation building, Lou Larson, my lab mate back at Du Pont's experimental station at Wilmington in 1930-31. He signed for Du Pont and I for the Manhattan District.

I don't know if anyone has ever told you how this was done, what happened after the Army took custody of the plutonium in those sample cans. We had a building that was back in the side of Gable Mountain. The doors on this thing were great big Mosler safe doors, tremendous things. Inside we had shelves and racks. We were very careful to keep the plutonium separated in an anti-critical mass geometry.

When Du Pont was ready to give the Manhattan District some plutonium at the 231 Building, we would make up a little caravan of one car with the plutonium, one car ahead of us and one car behind us, with Army personnel with .45s and I think machine guns. It was about 10-12 miles from the 231 building to the storage building. The vault doors at the storage building required two combinations to open. As I recall, nobody was supposed to know both combinations.

Before shipment to Los Alamos, the plutonium was in a quite viscous syrupy form, it was evaporated down. We didn't want it to splash around in the stainless steel shipping cans, very rugged containers designed to stand a lot of punishment, about the size of a volleyball. These sample cans were inside another steel container.

I never had any misgivings about working on the bomb. I had a brother who would have been in the first wave landing in Japan. He was in the 33rd Division, an infantry officer then in the Philippines. Even without the brother thing, well, I do know some in the Metallurgical Lab expressed reservations afterward, but I don't recall any of the people I worked with at the time saying anything except it was something we had to do, that's all there was to it.

There was a great question in the minds of the people in the Metallurgical Project as to how far along the Germans were. Even after the Germans surrendered, there was some worry that they had transferred a lot of their know-how to the Japanese. In my own case, I was in the chemical warfare reserve, and that's why I was in uniform in 1942. Chemical warfare isn't very pretty either. You get conditioned to the idea that if there will be a war, the important thing is to win it. Or, not to lose it, anyway.

A replica of the plutonium bomb, called "Fat Man," the bulbous implosion bomb used against Nagasaki. The bomb weighed 10,800 pounds, which included 5,300 pounds of chemical explosives and 13^1/$_2$ pounds of plutonium.

U.S. Army

A replica of the Hiroshima bomb called "Little Boy," a weapon using uranium as its explosive force. It was 10 feet long and weighed 9,700 pounds. Unofficial estimates say it contained 132 pounds of U-235.

Los Alamos National Laboratory

L O S   A L A M O S

On February 2, 1945, the first Hanford-produced plutonium was handed over by Du Pont to the Army. The next morning, Colonel F. T. Matthias took it to Portland by car with a military intelligence escort. From there, Matthias and an agent went by train to Los Angeles where the package was given to an officer from Los Alamos. Matthias described the container as a wooden box wrapped in brown paper about 14 inches on a side and 18 inches high. It had a carrying handle and the syrupy plutonium, weighing about 100 grams, was carried in a flask suspended between shock absorbers.

"This was one of the few times I had direct contact with Los Alamos. They called and said to hurry up, they needed it bad. I think it was February 3, we started out," Matthias said.

"In Los Angeles we met the agent from Los Alamos, but he didn't know what we were giving him. I asked him if he had a compartment back to New Mexico and he said he didn't, that he had an upper berth. I said you better go in and get that changed to a locked compartment. I said this is a very important thing, and it cost $350 million to make it. He got a locked compartment."

For a time, that was the pattern for shipping the plutonium. By March, 1945, Hanford's three 250 megawatt reactors were running under a full-scale production schedule which, in theory, meant daily production per reactor of an estimated 250 grams of plutonium. However, General Groves knew that soon the scientists at Los Alamos would need even larger quantities of plutonium. He asked Du Pont to operate two reactors, 100-D and 100-F, above their rated operational levels during the spring and early summer months. This speed-up, which was done at some risk, increased output and produced sufficient plutonium for the Trinity test bomb and one of the bombs used against Japan in August, 1945. One of the risks involved concerned the irradiated slugs . With the production speed-up the cooling time for slugs was shortened. The normal process, called lag storage, allowed some fission products to decay and become relatively harmless before slugs were sent to the separations area. When slugs went through the separation process during the speed up period, high radioactive gaseous emissions resulted.

As larger amounts of plutonium became available, it was realized shipping small amounts by train was too slow. The Army wanted an unremarkable means of transporting larger shipments that would not call attention to a link between Hanford and Los Alamos. Before long, it was decided to use olive drab panel trucks of a type usually associated with Army ambulances. The delivery operation was turned over to military intelligence.

Up to two dozen containers were carried in each vehicle, with a stainless steel flask inside each of them. Originally each flask held 80 grams.

2ND LT. O. R. "BIG" SIMPSON

O. R. "Big" Simpson was a second lieutenant in military intelligence in charge of convoys carrying plutonium from Hanford to Fort Douglas, Utah. On a summer morning, sitting on his porch next to the Columbia in Richland, eating newly-picked apricots and snapping new string beans, he talked about his days as a classified materials courier and how he finished the war riding converted ambulances to Utah. He retired in 1972 as deputy director of security at Hanford.

I am going to guess we started the convoys in May, of 1945. They took some of it by car for a couple of trips but I think it was May when we started the convoys. We had to get the trucks from Detroit, and get them all set up, with the racks and stuff in them. The containers we carried were wooden boxes about 16 inches square. They built a rack which the container would fit in, and the top would come down over it. The trucks were ton and a half vans. They were Chevrolets. Or were they Fords? Like field ambulances. No windows. Olive drab, no markings.

We loaded them ourselves. There was a metal container inside the boxes. I think, I don't know this, but I think a piece like a test tube was placed inside the metal container. The boxes were not heavy.

In a convoy, we had three panel trucks with a lead car and a rear car. The cars were ordinary Ford sedans. There would be two people in a truck and two people in each car. We drove directly through. In the trucks we had a bed in the back where a guy could sleep. Each convoy included 10 men. Everybody was armed. We carried shotguns and .38-caliber revolvers, and we had a submachine gun for each vehicle. When we stopped for chow, one guy would stay with each vehicle while the other guy ate.

A typical trip was we picked up the boxes at Gable Mountain, where they were stored in two concrete vaults tunneled into the mountain. We would take off for Pendleton, gas in Pendleton. We took U.S. 30, back in those days, we would go down through Idaho, Boise, to Mountain Home, into Bliss, and then we went down through the Hagerman Valley, by Twin Falls. From Twin Falls, we would go to Burley, Idaho, from there we cut down into Utah through Snowville, Brigham City, into Fort Douglas, which is in Salt Lake City. From here to there was something like 707 miles.

We had people ask us what we were doing. We ignored them. One time, in Payette, Idaho, a guy at a service station said "For Christ's sake, don't let those damn things go off in here." He had a pretty good idea what we had. With all the secrecy, they still gave us credit cards to charge gas with. They said U.S. Army. We weren't fooling anybody.

We were lucky. We seldom had any wrecks or breakdowns. We had a damn good record, because we were really careful. We had radio communications between all the cars. We were told what to do in case of fire, or wreck. Get the hell out of the road and get up wind.

I think I knew what was in them. We all carried health badges. We were checked every time. We had monitors. When we unloaded at the other end, we put on protective clothing. Gloves, shoe covers, coveralls and gloves. We always wore the monitoring devices. I have always thought they were over-cautious at Hanford. I think we handled it more carefully than Los Alamos. The Los Alamos people never took the precautions we took. We even laid paper down every time we unloaded.

We tried to make the run all at once at first, all the way to Los Alamos. But we decided that was not the way to do it. So Los Alamos came to Fort Douglas to meet us. The Los Alamos crew would arrive a day ahead of us so they could get their rest. We switched vehicles, unloading our containers into their vehicles. We maintained our own vehicles. We liked ours better than theirs. It didn't take long to switch the 20 to 24 containers in each vehicle.

We never had any adventures. It was the dullest thing in the world. It was the most routine deal I have ever run across in my life. No one tried to steal it, or cause any problems. The roads were not too good, not too bad. For the speed, about 55, they weren't bad. It was sparse country, miles and miles of desert. I think then Boise was about 15,000 people. When we got to Salt Lake City we took the main drag right past the Mormon Temple on the way to Fort Douglas which was near the university.

We never worried about sabotage or hijackers. We had a capable crew, there was quite a few of us and we were all armed. They worry about it now, I don't think they should worry about it as much. What were you going to do with it, in the shape it was in?

We flew two shipments, I think, in July or August, to Santa Fe in C-47s. We took the containers, and tied them down. No racks. It was rushed. I know it was hotter than hell because the pilot was worried about getting over the bluffs out there.

Once, during the convoy stage, we had a wreck near the Snake River, some gal hit a fender, on our way back from Fort Douglas. And once in the Blue Mountains coming back, we were coming up out of La Grande on ice and we were coming good and the traffic ahead stopped and the kid in the last Ford sedan stopped and slid backwards into the brush.

We had a guy from Iowa, Cec Bell, who was one of the best truck drivers I had ever seen. We got soldiers who were ex-truck drivers, over the road truckers. We had a five-day turn around. We left here, get there, rest a day, and come back and rest a day here. It took 18 to 22 hours to get to Fort Douglas, depending on the roads and the weather. One stretch we went every week, later three times a month. I recall it was really busy just before the war ended.

CYRIL S. SMITH

In Manhattan Project jargon, Hanford was the producer and Los Alamos the customer. Hanford was a place that sent an unfinished product to a finishing plant, as wheat goes from mill to bakery. At Los Alamos, Cyril Smith was the man responsible for transforming the Hanford product into something that would work in the bombs which Los Alamos designed. In 1942, Cyril Smith, 39 years old, a native Englishman, was with the federal wartime committee on metallurgy and hating his work. Early in 1943, when the Los Alamos staff was being assembled, chemist Joe Kennedy, a co-discoverer of plutonium, asked Smith if he wanted another job. He accepted immediately, and was appointed chief of metallurgy at Los Alamos. One of his responsibilities was refining plutonium metal for the Trinity test bomb and the Nagasaki weapon. Smith occupied a unique place in atomic bomb history. At Trinity Site, he was the last person to touch the plutonium pieces before they were sealed inside the bomb's core. He called them, "Those portentous bits of warm metal."

The plutonium we metallurgists received was actually a fluoride, a dry powder. It came to Los Alamos from Hanford as a kind of syrupy nitrate, which was treated by the chemists in a series of ingenious purification processes. I had essentially nothing to do with that. The powder, being color blind I never notice these things, but it was kind of a pinkish color, a pale pink.

On the plutonium the job was to take the fluoride, and convert it to solid metal, and later we discovered these amazing transformations in the metal, which it undergoes with the crystal structure change, with a very big difference in volume.

We had to be very careful from the health standpoint, which complicated matters a bit. At first our health precautions were nothing more than wearing masks and being careful. When we realized what we were up against, which we didn't in the beginning, we built glove boxes, sealed containers where you work with rubber gloves. These served rather well.

Plutonium is an alpha emitter, with no long-range penetrating gamma radiation. The main danger was simply getting particles of it around, because you might breathe them. By the time it was a lump of metal it wasn't so bad, even then though it was a little dangerous because you were afraid little bits of it would abrade off.

The first thing we did, we worked on a scale of one gram. Mostly, we got tiny ingots. and with these we were able to find out a little bit about the strength, the hardness, the density. And we heated it, and noticed how it changed length. At about 125 degrees C. there was a 20 percent increase in volume. That's extremely unusual.

Tin changes by 18 percent, in its low temperature form, but tin falls apart into a powder when it changes. Plutonium, for reasons I still don't quite understand, doesn't. It will crack, and deform: If a little flat sheet goes through this transformation it warps and ends up in a highly-distorted form. So, obviously we were in for a great deal of trouble in shaping it accurately. It was our job to first find out how to do it, then do it.

Many alloys of plutonium were made to study the effect on the transformation temperature as well as to find out about their strength and the ease of working them at various temperatures. Every bit of plutonium that arrived on the Hill was reused many times in a carefully scheduled series of metallurgical, chemical and physical experiments, being recycled through chemical purification and reduction. Before Hanford came on line, we were getting these little bits from Oak Ridge.

Plutonium in its high temperature form is a very plastic material, beautifully easy to shape. The alloy can be shaped easily by rolling, extruding or pressing in dies. At first we avoided machining because we wanted to get every bit of available metal into the bomb cores, not in turnings.

Before we got to the hemisphere shaping phase, for the bomb core, we had to do a lot of work with plutonium alloys. We had to be very careful, you see, if you get this volume change, because you could get a lot of the lower density material in the bomb, and that material would compress to a higher density. It was more efficient as an explosive device to use the lower temperature form.

It was desirable to have it alloyed because it was more easily shaped, to get all these things to fit together. So we wanted to find some means of retaining this high temperature low density form. It is a bit like trying to retain the high temperature form of iron, steel actually. You quench steel in order to make it hard and you quench plutonium in order to make it soft. It is still the same kind of change of structure with temperature, you see. Anyway, as with steel, if you put in enough nickel you can retain the high temperature form at room temperatures. With plutonium if you put enough of various things in you can retain this at low temperatures.

So, the actual plutonium core of the bomb was not pure plutonium; it was an alloy of plutonium. The first thing we found that did what we wanted, metallurgically, was plutonium-aluminum, but aluminum was bad because it reacted with the alpha particles arising from the natural radioactivity of plutonium and generated enough neutrons to produce premature explosion on compression.

We looked around for something that might have the same metallurgical effect but which wouldn't saturate the thing with neutrons. We made alloys of plutonium with almost all the metals on the periodic table. We did it purely empirically. There was no theory to guide us. We made the alloy to see what would happen. I have no idea what they use nowadays, but the one we ended up with was gallium. Plutonium and gallium. Gallium is an element quite like aluminum.

These days, of course, theory is in such a state that one could get a fairly good guidance as to what to try. Back then, we simply followed hunch, not science. That was in a stage where science didn't help much. You did something empirically and observed what happened.

We knew fairly early how big the bomb's core would be. Of course, we also knew that if we got a little bit too much in our crucibles we would be in for trouble — it would react, and undergo fission. We played safe. We worked with a very small amount, so that even getting two pieces together under the worst conditions it could not form a super-critical amount. There was a group responsible for the safety: plutonium was taken from one operation to another by these people. It all worked like a railroad switching operation, in fact the plan was worked out by a man who had been a railroad switcher. We had no trouble. We arranged it so the stuff was always stored where there was plenty of boron around in plastic containers, to absorb any neutrons. I think we were excessively cautious, but after all we did not want to spend our time finding out under what conditions you could get a chain reaction. That was the physicists' job.

The first stage for making the core was making little plutonium buttons, the second was melting plutonium, alloying it, and the final end was to produce a couple of hemispheres like this [see sketch next page].

The initiator was a special little device which when compressed released neutrons and caused the chain reaction. The core would fit rather easily, and even rather pleasantly, in the hand. It was warm, and felt like a piece of warm metal.

Although the metallurgical preparation of the plutonium had been completed a week before the Trinity test, I was unexpectedly involved intimately with the actual assembly of the core. The hemispheres had been shaped by hot-pressing to exact shape. Then they had to be coated by electroplating with silver to prevent corrosion and to avoid contamination of the environment, including the fingers of anyone who handled them. A clean plutonium surface has a slightly dark steel-gray color, but when exposed to air it rapidly develops a dark gray tarnish.

There was a tiny imperfection in one of the pieces and some plating solution had become entrapped; it slowly reacted to form a little blister so that the two parts didn't fit exactly together. This would have caused trouble during

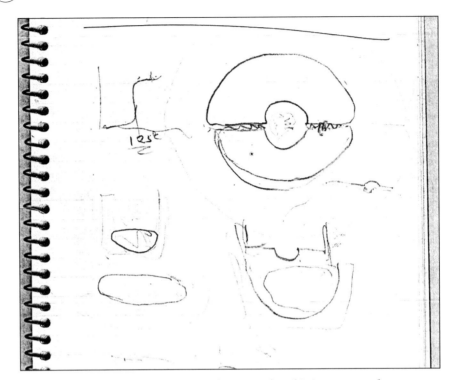

Cyril Smith's pencil drawing of the plutonium bomb's inner core, drawn about actual size. The two hemispheres each about as large as half an orange, were a blend of plutonium and gallium. In the center was the initiator, an arrangement of beryllium and polonium, probably about the size of a hazlenut, which provided a burst of neutrons to spark an explosive chain reaction in the plutonium.

the implosion because of the phenomenon known as jetting—an explosive wave encountering a cavity actually causes some of the material to squirt out ahead of the main compression. If, in the implosion of the final Gadget, that squirt had hit the initiator before the main mass of plutonium had reached maximum density, the premature burst of neutrons could have resulted in a very low-grade explosion.

Someone hit on the idea of filling the space around the blister with specially crinkled gold foil to stop the jet, and it was up to me to personally make the foils and insert them carefully into the assembly. Toward the end of the project I had been telling other people what to do and, since I'm an experimentalist at heart, I was pleased to have some task for my own fingers.

Another thing we were doing was making the uranium to go around this core, a massive sphere of uranium which served both a nuclear and mechanical function. It was between the core and the explosive lenses. I suppose it was a matter of between one and two hundred pounds, but I have forgotten. It was reasonably pure natural uranium metal.

Two things had to be done to assemble the core. The center of the thing was essentially a solid, but split in two. One plutonium hemisphere was put in, the initiator was put in, these little gold foils were put on, then the top hemisphere was put in place. My only memento of the project is one of these little gold foils which was there to go into the bomb but wasn't needed and ended up in my personal collection. Anyway, the foil was put in, and the second half of the cylindrical part of the uranium tamper was put on and locked with rings, and this whole thing was lowered later into the rest of the assembly. My job was over after the appropriate amount of gold foil had been fitted in and the core assembled.

We put the core together at the McDonald ranch house. The core ended up as a cylinder, as I remember it, approximately, four inches in diameter and 12 inches long with spherical ends because it was part of the larger sphere of uranium which had the explosive lenses around it. It was like a large Polish sausage with rounded ends.

When the time came for the final assembly in the tent at the base of the test tower, the core wouldn't slide into place for it had expanded partly because of the heat generated by the plutonium and partly because of the desert heat. However, it cooled when in contact with the massive tamper and eventually went in smoothly. I no longer had anything to do at this stage, but I watched the assembly and saw it hoisted to the top of the tower.

Later in the day, when all the electrical connections had been made I climbed the ladder and spent a minute or two alone looking at the portentous device. I had been intimate with many of the components but had never seen the whole thing. There were a large number of wires going all over the place. I suppose it looked a little bit like the earlier sea mines, a sphere with little things sticking out here and there. One had a kind of feeling of doom. Then I went back down and back to the base camp, where I watched the test the next morning.

Smith was interviewed in the living room of his small two-story brick house on quiet Madison Street in Cambridge, across the street from the Harvard Observatory. After he had detailed his part in the metallurgy and assembly of the New Mexico test bomb, he still was talkative and asked his wife, historian Alice Kimball Smith, to join the conversation. A courtly, friendly man who taught at the Massachusetts Institute of Technology, he asked if anyone wanted a drink, and brought from the kitchen a tray of foreign beers. After that, the talk ranged widely, from the question of using the bomb against Japan to the subject of implosion, which turned out to be a supremely critical factor in the making of the plutonium bomb. Another question which interested Smith was whether the Plutonium Project was necessary to the war effort, and if, in a sense, the plutonium bomb was irrelevant.

Speaking of America's first use of nuclear weapons, Smith said, in retrospect, he thought the first bomb was necessary. "In order to educate the world, and I think it had to be used in anger, too, because a demonstration in an uninhabited area would have done no more than the test in New Mexico, where there resulted a rather pretty little green bowl in the desert. I think it had to be used in a way it would destroy something." He thought the Nagasaki bomb was completely unnecessary.

Another subject was implosion. Without this explosive technique, plutonium likely would not have been usable in a nuclear weapon. Basic questions about plutonium's usefulness in a bomb threatened to make Hanford's plutonium production almost a waste of time. Scientists at Los Alamos had discovered that neutron emission in plutonium was different from uranium. Plutonium, unlike U-235, would fission spontaneously. This information meant a plutonium bomb likely would go off prematurely, unless it was designed differently from the so-called "gun-type" uranium bomb, the Hiroshima design.

In a gun bomb, one subcritical piece of U-235 was placed at one end of a cannon-like tube and another subcritical piece at the other. High explosives fired one piece into the other, which resulted in one supercritical explosive mass.

Plutonium was known to be more readily fissionable than uranium and thus much less of it was required to make a bomb. The trouble with plutonium was it contained the unstable, spontaneously-fissioning isotope Pu-240. Pu-240's stray neutrons could spark a premature chain reaction unless the bomb reached supercritical mass more quickly than was possible in a gun-type bomb. It only takes one-thousandth of a second to assemble (bring together) the two chunks of material in a gun-type bomb. Even this rate was not quick enough to prevent a premature chain reaction caused by the unstable Pu-240's neutrons. Premature detonation would work against the process of combining the pieces and would blow the weapon apart before assembly. Pre-assembly detonation would result in a very low energy-yield bomb, which the physicists called a "fizzle."

When this information was digested at Los Alamos, it was realized plutonium likely would not work in a bomb unless the bomb's components could be assembled faster. In 1943, Los Alamos physicist Seth Neddermeyer had suggested implosion as an alternative to the simpler gun-type approach. The young physicist, who later was a professor at the University of Washington, recommended placing non-nuclear high explosives around the plutonium core and detonating them in an imploding (inward) direction. This explosive wave would compress the plutonium to a supercritical mass in one-millionth of a second.

Neddermeyer was put to work on his idea, but it was not taken seriously until it was realized implosion apparently was the only way plutonium could be used in a bomb. Others took over the assignment. John von Neumann, a mathematician, and British physicist Rudolf Peierls provided key theoretical information about the effect of shaped chemical explosive charges. Edward Teller showed that implosion would transform subcritical (not chain reacting) material into a supercritical (nuclear explosive) mass. George Kistiakowsky, a chemist and explosives expert, was called in by Los Alamos director J. Robert Oppenheimer in February, 1944, and he and others developed the "lenses" which surrounded the plutonium core, whose purpose was to focus the chemical explosives' effect on the plutonium. When detonated absolutely uniformly, these explosive charges would implode, squeeze the plutonium in three dimensions and set off a nuclear bomb.

The explosive qualities of U-235 and Pu-239 varied greatly. In the gun-type Hiroshima bomb, Little Boy, the two pieces of U-235 were said to have weighed 132 pounds total while the sphere of Pu-239 in each of the Trinity and Nagasaki implosion bombs weighed about 13.5 pounds. Little Boy's explosive yield was estimated to be 12.5 kilotons, and the yield for Fat Man, the Nagasaki weapon, was estimated at 22 kilotons. The Trinity Gadget was a bit less powerful, about 19 tons. These figures are estimates. and usually are expressed with a range of one or two kilotons plus or minus.

A kiloton is equivalent to 1,000 tons of TNT, a chemical explosive. A comparison of nuclear yield to TNT, however, is misleading. The explosive, or blast, energy is equivalent. But, a nuclear bomb has the added factors of very intense heat and radiation. In an exploding atomic bomb, the maximum temperature reaches several million degrees Centigrade compared to about 5,000 degrees C. for a conventional explosive. In addition, radiation adds a major component to the killing power of a nuclear bomb which does not exist in a conventional explosive.

Another way of describing the power of the implosion-plutonium design was expressed in *The Curve of Binding Energy* by John McPhee (Farrar, Straus and Giroux, 1974). The amount of plutonium which changed into explosive energy in the Nagasaki bomb was one gram, a third the weight of a penny.

During an interview in Seattle with physicist Robert R. Wilson, director of research at Los Alamos during the war, he suggested that development of the plutonium-implosion bomb really was not needed to end the war. The Hiroshima bomb, he said, was a gun-type bomb, and this design was known and considered reliable before Los Alamos existed. Furthermore, he said, the gun-type used U-235, not plutonium.

Asked about Wilson's feeling that the Plutonium Project may not have been needed to end the war, Smith said he was surprised to hear that, "but the more I think about it the more I agree with him." If more bombs had been needed after Hiroshima, U-235 production at Oak Ridge would have provided the fissionable material, not as fast as Hanford's plutonium production but fast enough, Smith said.

He went on to say, though, that there was a good reason for the decision, in 1942, to pursue the theory that plutonium would work as bomb fuel. No one knew for sure, he said, which method would be successful, whether obtaining U-235 from the various methods at Oak Ridge or getting plutonium from the Hanford reactors. Smith called the two-headed approach to bomb fuel "a necessary and wise policy."

On another topic, the context of the wartime period, he said, "It is so hard today for youngsters to reconstruct those times. The students at MIT by and large think anybody who had anything to do with the Manhattan Project is some kind of moral outlaw. I think at the time with the threat of Hitler one was anything but that. I sometimes think I have essentially done what science I wanted to do because I was interested in it, and that hasn't made me a good citizen always, I suppose. But one time I was a good citizen doing what my country demanded, and that was working on this damned bomb."

The plutonium Gadget atop the tower the day before it was exploded at Trinity Site. The man is Norris Bradbury, a physicist at Los Alamos laboratory, later the lab's director. A twin of this bomb enclosed in a streamlined bomb casing with tailfins and radar antennae was dropped on Nagasaki.

Los Alamos National Laboratory

CHAPTER 7

TRINITY

Trinity is the point at which the project changed from a technical and scientific research endeavor to weaponry and instrument of national policy.

WALTER SIMON[*]

The memory I do have is when I took the dark glasses away, of seeing all the colors around and the sky lit up by the radiation, it was purple, kind of an aurora borealis light, and this thing like a big balloon expanding and going up. But, the scale. There was this tremendous desert with the mountains nearby but it seemed to make the mountains look small.

I believed it would go off, I bet that way, but until I saw it, it was an academic possibility, a little like talking about the existence of God. It can be very real for some people and very unreal for other people, but I'm sure if God did something, made a miracle out there, it would speak to me, and I would feel much differently about God than I do.

I had been working on this since the fall of 1940, so I thought I was very accustomed to everything. But there's a difference between something that's intellectual and almost academic. However well you can deal with it and describe it, you have not really seen it and sensed it in an existential fashion. It doesn't really exist, and that's when it existed for me, not just a dream or something you had been working on or something terrible, it was something that existed. Suddenly, that changed my life, I think.

ROBERT R. WILSON[*]

---

[*] All quotations are from conversations with the author.

I saw the most brilliant flash and knew instantly that the whole thing was a success. The mushroom cloud went on forever in the sky and everything was enormous and brilliant. The most impressive thing was the ionization effects. It looked like a living thing with a blue glow. The mountains stood out like old science fiction paintings of sunlight on the moon.

WARREN NYER

The beauties of nature have endured in the high desert of southern New Mexico. A couple of miles to the east of Ground Zero and curving to the south are the San Andres Mountains, starkly bare and slightly purple in clear sunlight. The Rio Grande is 25 miles west. The early Spaniards called it Jornada del Muerto, this region of Apaches and no water, wind and limitless distance. Journey of Death, Route of the Dead Man.

Where the tower stood is a black lava monument, with a plaque that says: "Trinity Site, where the world's first nuclear device was exploded July 16, 1945." Nearby is a stub of one of the tower's concrete and steel foundation supports. That's all that remains of the 103-foot tower, and its metal shed on top where the five-ton test bomb rested on a cradle. It was nicknamed "the Gadget" and was a dark steel egg five feet in diameter containing 5,300 pounds of chemical explosives and 13.5 pounds of plutonium. With detonation, the tower vaporized and became part of the fireball. Quarter-sized bits of dull greenish rock are scattered about in the reddish sand, pieces of the once glassy-green trinitite, sand that was melted, fused and turned green by the sun-like heat of the nuclear explosion.

The morning after the blast, physicist Robert Wilson drove to where the tower had been. The crater was disappointingly small, something like 30-40 feet in diameter and only slightly dished and perhaps a foot deep. "The concrete of the tower foundations was there, with some steel sticking out of them. I seem to remember four of them, but I was very excited and maybe only one was left," he said. In aerial photos made after the explosion, the blackened area is about one mile in diameter. Today, the entire blast location would be grown over with yucca and creosote brush if the Army didn't cut the vegetation to discourage shade-loving rattlesnakes.

In 1944, Los Alamos director J. Robert Oppenheimer and his advisers had decided that the plutonium bomb, because it was a tricky and highly theoretical implosion device, would have to be tested before it was used as a

The Trinity test tower, 103 feet high with a tin shed on top to shelter the Gadget. The tower was vaporized by the heat of the explosion.   *U.S. Army*

weapon. Usually, the test is linked with Alamogordo, New Mexico, probably because the Manhattan Project borrowed the site from the Army's Alamogordo Gunnery and Bombing Range, now the Army's White Sands Missile Range. The town itself is 60 miles south. The closest towns of any size are Socorro and Carrizozo, 30-35 miles away. Physicist Kenneth Bainbridge, director of the test, selected the site in 1944 and for months it was called only "the test site." By March, 1945, Bainbridge said a code name was necessary, and his best recollection was that Oppenheimer is the person who named it Trinity.

Various stories have been told about the origin of the name. Oppenheimer said he suggested Trinity, although precisely why was not clear even to him. He mentioned a poem by John Donne which included the line "So death doth touch the Resurrection."

"That still does not make Trinity: but in another, better known devotional poem Donne opens, 'Batter my heart, three person'd God,' beyond this I have no clues whatsoever," Oppenheimer wrote in a letter to General Groves in 1962.

Part of the core of the test bomb is unloaded at McDonald's ranch house. The core was assembled in the house, which still stands about two miles south of Ground Zero.   *U.S. Army*

The whole section he referred to goes like this:

"Batter my heart, three person'd God; for you

As yet but knock, breathe, shine, and seek to mend…"

Said Bainbridge, "With all due respect to others, I am willing to buy J.R.O.'s story and go with Donne's three-person'd God."

The scientists and technicians stationed themselves at three bunkers, north, south, and west, each 10,000 yards from Ground Zero. The base camp was about nine miles south. McDonald's ranch house, where the plutonium core was assembled, was about two miles south of the tower. Today, nothing remains of the bunkers or the base camp. McDonald's ranch house stands. Otherwise, a few concrete shelters for instruments and cameras and low wooden posts, well weathered, are the only remnants.

In the early morning of the dawn of the age of nuclear weapons, the most pressing question was the weather, which Oppenheimer called "whimsical."

It was windy and rainy and lightning flashed, making people nervous about accidental detonation. Physicist Victor Weisskopf recalled that the intercom system connecting scientists with the control bunker at S-10,000 was on the same frequency as a New Mexico radio station, which that morning was playing Tschaikowsky. "When the final countdown started, 10, 9, 8, you heard background music, The Nutcracker Suite, da, da, dum, dum. Whenever I hear that melody the whole thing comes back to me, and then zero and the explosion."

At 15 seconds before 5:30 in the morning, the Gadget exploded, with a rapidly expanding fireball, white, then yellow and finally red. "And then the sight, the cloud, of the bomb going up, which reminded me of the medieval picture of Christ's Ascension," Weisskopf said.

MARVIN H. WILKENING

Professor Wilkening, lanky and friendly, was interviewed on his 67th birthday in his office at the New Mexico Institute of Mining and Technology in Socorro, a dusty town northwest of Trinity Site. Wilkening, a physicist, traveled the Grand Circuit of the Manhattan Project, pursuing his speciality of measuring neutron intensity. He was at the first chain reaction in Chicago, then moved to Oak Ridge, next to Hanford, Los Alamos, and Trinity. Before the Army restricted visitors, he regularly took his New Mexico Tech physics students on field trips to Trinity Site. In a corner of his office was a cardboard box filled with pieces of trinitite, some as big as a man's hand, artifacts of the nuclear age.

So there we were the night before the test, in one of those little huts, with thunder and lightning and the promise of a storm. Fermi called us together in a corner and told us no major problems were anticipated, but it's always possible we have not calculated right. The winds may bring some fission products over us, he told us. They were prepared to evacuate us. I was at base camp, about nine miles south of Point Zero. It was scheduled to go at 4:30 a.m. but was postponed for an hour subject to further delay, because of the storm.

There was a countdown by Sam Allison, the first time in my life I ever heard anyone count backwards. We used welder's glass in front of our eyes, and covered all our skin. My feet were toward Mockingbird Gap, Point Zero

0.100 SEC.   100 METERS

Trinity bomb explodes and a fireball forms less than a second after detonation. The photo was taken from an instrument bunker six miles away.

U.S. Army

was to my left. The countdown ended, and it was like being close to an old-fashioned photo flashbulb. If you were close enough you could feel warmth because of the intense light, and the light from the explosion scattering from the mountains and the clouds was intense enough to feel.

Immediately we turned around, and looked toward the blast, and the cloud was a white spot through the welder's glass. Terrific as it was, the blast was an anti-climax compared to the feel of the flash of light which traveled so much faster than the sound wave. We heard it, too far away to be like a close lightning stroke, but that kind of phenomenon. We followed the fireball as it rose, white, then light orange. What was fantastic to me was the development of what, under other circumstances, would have been a beautiful purple color that was the result of the intense radiation from this ball of fire. Radiation interacting with air molecules. We had seen it in a laboratory, but here it was on a massive scale. That was the clue to the intensity of the radiation that was present. And we were almost 10 miles away. Yeah, okay, that was a signal that spoke volumes. It went, it worked. That purple light, and we were so far away.

Fermi was close by, he was dropping little pieces of paper into the blast wave to measure the explosive power. I didn't notice a lot of what was going on because we all had a job to do and it was up to you to do it. But Allison was there, and Oppenheimer and General Groves. I tuned in on Fermi; I had a tremendous admiration for him.

What do I think of the bomb, the rightness and wrongness? The thing that I can remember that was pretty deep in our minds was that our friends, some of them, were killed in the war, including a very close friend of mine from college killed in Europe. We had considerable concern. Suppose the Nazis had succeeded, maybe not in making a bomb, we didn't know that was possible either earlier. But suppose they had a reactor device that could sow the beaches with high-intensity fission products? Any reasonable person had to deal with it in a rational framework, and, well, you can't always win them all. Wars, that is.

We thought whatever it is, this atomic energy was a thing that had to be worked on. As far as the actual use, I think it was regrettable, but it had to be done. When it was announced, in August, Hiroshima and Nagasaki, the thing was, well, we had participated. But we felt if it hadn't been us, it would have been someone else.

EXTRA # The Villager EXTRA

VOLUME 1   Richland, Washington, Monday, August 6, 1945   NUMBER 22—A

IT'S ATOMIC BOMBS

News Spreads Slowly, Surprises Everyone Here

Jubilation And Satisfaction Follows Revelation Of Product Manufactured Here

Richland was about the last place in the country to hear the news of the atomic bomb. As in other parts of the country it was the housewives who first heard the news over their radios, and broke it to their husbands in a flurry of telephone calls which kept the switchboards humming.

In town, the stores were all closed until noon and few people were on the street. It was THE VILLAGER reporter who spread the word to most of those encountered. Disbelief was soon followed by enthusiasm. Everyone felt the same reaction—"It's nice to know what this project is all about" and "Maybe the war will end promptly."

To nearly everyone the news of what Richland was helping to make came as a complete surprise. Even those who may have been in the know would not admit it. The old habit of secrecy was strong upon them.

Said J. T. Minard who was downtown doing some shopping: "They did the most marvelous job of keeping a secret. I just didn't think it would be possible."

Patrolman W. N. Gasway, who was enjoying a day off with a stroll through the village, had no idea what was being made. "I didn't want to know," he explained. "If a person knew too much he might land in jail. I don't care what it is as long as it smashes the Japs."

Kenneth E. Jensen who's been on the project almost two years, heard the news first from a hotel porter and was on his way to check with Military Authorities to see whether there was anything to it. "I'm sure glad it's out," he said. "If you don't get in the Army, you can hope to help win on the job here." Said his companion who refused to give his name, "I still don't believe it I'd like to find out for sure"

Mrs. S. F. Schlecht of Kennewick was in Richland waiting for the hardware store to open. Said she when told that a bomb had been dropped on Japan: "Good! I've never seen a job where things were kept so secret. My husband works here, but he didn't know anything about it."

James Fagg was one of the few encountered in the streets who had heard it on the radio: "I felt it must be important for them to interrupt a broadcast I hope this means the war will be over in a hurry."

The night clerk in the Transient Quarters, Dell, refused to give anymore of his name or discuss the matter at all. Said he, "I've been secretive for two years. Why should I change now?" John Ferns was encountered at the hotel desk. It was his day off. He has worked on the project two years in October, but said he knew little of what they were doing out there. "I thought they were making some awful explosive," he said. "Now I'm glad to know for sure and especially glad to know that I've been doing some good for the war"

Jack Wilson, assistant manager of the bank, heard it like most of the men, from his wife. Every customer to enter his bank after it opened at noon came in with the

(Continued on Page 2)

Development Of Bomb Traced

Begun In 1939; Plant Expanded In June, 1942

The energy of the atom has been harnessed to produce the deadliest weapon ever devised, the atomic bomb, the War Department today announced shortly after the first of the aerial missiles cascaded upon a Japanese military target.

The initial combat use of the bomb culminated three years of intensive effort on the part of science and industry, working in cooperation with the military. It is heralded as the greatest achievement of the combined efforts of science, industry, labor and the military in all history.

President Truman and Secretary of War Henry L. Stimson made the first announcements of the new weapon, declaring that the atomic bomb has an explosive force such as to stagger the imagination. Improvements were revealed as forthcoming which will increase several fold the present effectiveness.

While the use in combat has permitted a slight relaxation in the security that has cloaked the project, the War Department declined for security reasons to disclose the exact methods by which the bombs are produced or the nature of their action and requested that the press and radio refrain from disclosing other information as well as all those connected with the Project, other than that information released.

In broad outline, the War Department made the following disclosures:

Late in 1939 the possibility of using atomic energy for military purposes was brought to the attention of the President, who appointed a committee to survey the problem;

In June 1942 sufficient progress had been made to warrant a great expansion of the project and the assumption of its direction by the

(Continued on Page 2)

What is Atomic Bomb?

The details have not yet been released, but information reveals that it contains more power than 20,000 tons of TNT. It produces more than 2,000 times the blast of the largest bomb ever used before. It is the greatest force ever harnessed—and may change the entire course of civilization.

President Truman Releases Secret of Hanford Product

Information Is Made Public This Morning

SPECIAL—Today President Truman, in an offical White House release, broke the biggest secret of World War II—and perhaps the greatest secret of any war—when he informed Americans that the U. S. Army Air Forces had released on the Japanese an Atomic bomb containing more power than 20,000 tons of TNT—and that the Hanford Engineer Works is one of three plants in the country manufacturing the new bombs.

How Much Damage?

How much damage was done by the bomb dropped this morning on Japan was a question in everyone's mind today in Richland.

Japanese news sources, while admitting the raid, did not reveal the extent of the damage.

THE HANFORD ENGINEERING WORKS Bring V-J DAY CLOSER!

The bomb, made in the Hanford Engineer Works, in Oak Ridge, near Knoxville, Tennessee, and an unnamed installation near Santa Fe, New Mexico, produces more than 2,000 times the blast of the largest bomb ever used before.

Richland Gets Ready To Entertain Press

Richland, the quiet, the secret, was getting ready today to entertain the Press. In the former dining room of the Transient Quarters, forty typewriters were in place on 29 desks and the lunch counter.

A switchboard was being installed with eight phone booths to go with it. Couches for weary newshawks took up every square inch of floor space. Closed dormitories were open to house the expected influx of newmen.

To the last, the cloak of secrecy hung about preparation. Miss Kelma Kennedy, manager of the Transient Quarters, didn't know until this morning that the press was expected. "They told me," she said, "that the government was going to move in. You know we're not supposed to ask questions."

Dave Haley, who had spent busy days, scouting for typewriters and installing them, had no inkling of why. "I heard something was going to break. What is it? They told me we needed 40 typewriters. We haven't had much explanation for a couple of years."

Two operators brought in from Kennewick to help handle the switchboards, were equally surprised. Mrs. Helena Evett and Mrs. A. Westermeyer said they had heard plenty of rumors, as to what had been going on in Rich-

(Continued on Page 2)

The bombs blast even the landscape out of sight. Nothing is impossible. The first bomb was dropped on Hiroshima a few hours ago. Observers report that the explosion was thousands of times greater than an earthquake and may change the course of civilization.

Atomic power was released against the Japs in answer to their refusal to the ultimatum issued last week. Source of the power is said to be coal, oil and power produced by the great dams in the Northwest and Tennessee.

In making the announcement, President Truman said that the atomic bomb has added new and revolutionary increase in destruction on the Japanese. Mr. Truman went on that "it is an Atomic bomb. A harnessing of the basic power of the universe, the force from which the sun draws its power."

CHAPTER 8

EPILOGUE

The Manhattan Project was probably the most important, certainly the most exciting, thing I ever did.

GLENN SEABORG*

I have been asked again and again, if I have regrets. Will you please excuse me, this is one of the most idiotic questions, except for the fact that apparently others do have regrets. I may suffer from some moral insufficiency, but I don't have regrets. I didn't put the world together and if you had the choice that something simple that was in the long run unavoidable should be first done by the United States or the Nazis or by the Soviets or by someone else, would you have regrets to make sure we did it first?

EDWARD TELLER*

anford's World War II role ended at Nagasaki, August 9, 1945, when a plutonium bomb exploded 1,600 feet above the city, killing perhaps 70,000 of the industrial seaport's 280,000 population. This bulbous five-ton weapon was a duplicate of the Trinity test bomb placed inside a streamlined tail-finned casing five feet around and almost 11 feet long.

---

* Quotations are from conversations with the author.

Opposite: **The front page of Richland's weekly newspaper, August 6, 1945, the date of the Hiroshima attack. The information, although inaccurate and incomplete, was the first official announcement of what had been going on at Hanford.** *U.S. Department of Energy*

Tatsuichiro Akizuki was in Nagasaki that day, and wrote a book about the experience:*

> There was a blinding white flash of light... A huge impact like a gigantic hand smote down upon our bodies... Looking to the southwest I was stunned. The sky was dark as pitch, covered with dense clouds of smoke; under that blackness, over the earth, hung a yellow-brown fog. Gradually the veiled ground became visible, and the view beyond rooted me to the spot with horror.
>
> All the buildings I could see were on fire... Electricity poles were wrapped in flame like so many pieces of kindling. Trees on nearby hills were smoking, as were the leaves of sweet potatoes in fields...
>
> It seemed as if the earth itself emitted fire and smoke, flames that writhed up and erupted from underground. The sky was dark, the ground was scarlet, and in between hung clouds of yellowish smoke. Three kinds of color—black, yellow, and scarlet—loomed ominously over the people, who ran about like so many ants seeking to escape...
>
> It seemed like the end of the world.

A ship-building center on the west coast of the island of Kyushu, Nagasaki was the location of the Mitsubishi naval arsenal which had manufactured torpedoes used in the attack on Pearl Harbor. The city was the home of Japan's largest colony of Christians, and was said to have been the site of Puccini's opera "Madame Butterfly."

Fat Man's yield, an estimated 22 kilotons, was almost twice that of the Hiroshima bomb, but the death toll and damage in Nagasaki were limited by the city's hilly terrain which protected many areas from the full force of the weapon. Even so, much of the city was destroyed, including the Mitsubishi factory. On Aug. 10 the Japanese government offered a conditional surrender, and on the same day President Harry S. Truman ordered a halt to the atomic bombings because he did not like the idea of killing "all those kids."

Japan surrendered on August 14. The next day, in a broadcast message to the nation, Emperor Hirohito, who was allowed to remain as Japan's spiritual leader, said "The war situation has developed not necessarily to Japan's advantage, while the general trends of the world have turned against her interest." This comment probably was a reference to the Soviet Union's declaration of war against Japan, August 8, and the subsequent invasion of Manchuria and Korea by Soviet troops. Hirohito continued: "Moreover, the

---

* Nagasaki 1945, London: Quartet Books Limited, 1981.

Fat Man shortly before being loaded into a bomb bay of a B-29 for departure early on the morning of August 9, 1945, from the island of Tinian to the Japanese mainland and the eventual target, Nagasaki.

Los Alamos National Laboratory

enemy has begun to employ a new and most cruel bomb, the power of which to do damage is indeed incalculable, taking the toll of many innocent lives... This is the reason why we have ordered the acceptance of the provisions of the Joint Declaration of the Powers... "

Henry L. Stimson, Secretary of War during 1940-45, was a critical voice in the decision to use atomic bombs against Japan. In 1947, an article by him appeared in which he explained the decision. The final paragraph:

> In this last great action of the Second World War we were given final proof that war is death. War in the twentieth century has grown steadily more barbarous, more destructive, more debased in all its aspects. Now, with the release of atomic energy, man's ability to destroy himself is very nearly complete. The bombs dropped on Hiroshima and Nagasaki ended a war. They also made it wholly clear that we must never have another war. This is the lesson men and

leaders everywhere must learn, and I believe that when they learn it they will find a way to lasting peace. There is no other choice.

When the Manhattan Project began its leaders were aware of the terrible hazards associated with radioactivity. Radiation was one of the most deadly aspects of a nuclear weapon; it also was a danger for those persons who manufactured the weapons material and for those who lived in the vicinity of the weapons plants.

At Hanford and throughout the Manhattan Project radiation protection was an early concern. Chicago's Met Lab set up a Health Division in 1942 that was a full partner to the other scientific divisions. Although radiation hazards were taken seriously the main work was to build a bomb. As Colonel Matthias, Hanford's commanding officer, said: "Our first requirement is the early production of some material, and…our second requirement is a large quantity of material." He meant plutonium.

In his book on Manhattan Project radiation safety procedures, Barton C. Hacker wrote that uranium processing, such as the work done at Oak Ridge, was not considered particularly hazardous because uranium was relatively benign. Plutonium was another matter. Every stage in the manufacture of plutonium posed a radioactive hazard, particularly the often highly radioactive "fission products" of the plutonium process. The challenge of protective safeguards against plutonium and its byproducts "explains the early and lasting stress on radiation safety" of the Chicago Met Lab operation, Hacker said.

Wartime needs were urgent, and workers took risks, but these risks, as Hacker noted, were "far smaller than those routinely faced by frontline soldiers." There was a war on and peacetime safety standards might not be reasonable. This pressure likely was the main reason not enough emphasis was placed on longterm safety of the ground storage of nuclear waste, which contributed to a legacy of immense problems at Hanford.

In May, 1943, a meeting was held at the Met Lab in Chicago to discuss concerns about radioactive contamination of air and water by the Hanford plutonium plant. Construction of the main plant had not started yet, but Manhattan Project leaders wanted to do all that was possible to prevent serious trouble from radiation discharges into the atmosphere and the Columbia River.

Effects on plant workers also were considered, although it was believed safeguards such as concrete and lead shielding, monitoring by instruments and periodic physical examinations would suffice to keep people at the facili-

The Nagasaki atomic bomb raid was carried out by this B-29. The usual commander was Frederick Bock, but the strike aircraft was piloted on this raid by Maj. Charles W. Sweeney. The bomber usually is identified as "Bock's Car," but the Air Force official name is "Bockscar." The aircraft is on display at the U.S. Air Force Museum, Wright-Patterson Air Force Base, Ohio. The nose art with name was added after the mission. At the time of the Nagasaki attack, the airplane was referred to as No. 77.   *USAF Museum*

ties safe from dangerous radiation or poisoning by toxic substances. A complication of Manhattan Project secrecy was that workers could not be told in detail about the invisible menace of radiation. Du Pont, a pioneer in industrial medicine and safety, was allowed to operate its own careful medical program with a minimum of supervision from the Army.

During World War II, the atmosphere's greatest risk was from radioactivity in the form of gaseous emissions from the fuel fabrication areas, the reactors and, most of all, the plutonium separation plants. A University of Washington professor, meteorologist Phil Church, was in charge of early studies designed to reduce the danger of emissions of radioactive gases. These studies confirmed, quoting a letter from Colonel Matthias to Groves, that gaseous radioactive material from the separation process could drift long distances relatively undiluted, especially during temperature inversions.

Although care was taken to prevent radioactive contamination by separation plant emissions, the pressure of the wartime emergency meant that manufacturing plutonium was the top priority. This pressure, combined with inexperience with radioactivity, resulted in dangerously large quantities of radioactive iodine-131 being released from the 200 Area stacks on several occasions from late 1944 until the end of the war. The fuel slugs were removed from the reactors and run through the separations facilities too fast to allow the iodine fission product to diminish through radioactive decay. The half life of iodine-131 is only eight days, and a longer lag time between reactor and separations, as well as improved filtration on the exhaust stacks reduced these emissions.

John W. Healy, a chemical engineer in charge of environmental monitoring for Du Pont at Hanford during the war, said that in later years the iodine emissions would be considered "very dangerous" because of the threat of thyroid irradiation in children.

> But, we were very cautious during that period. Du Pont always was a very safety-conscious company, and they were putting their reputa-tion on the line in operating this plant. They were not about to have anything happen if they could help it. As far as the iodine goes, the cooling time for the metal was increased as soon as we discovered it. Nobody had ever predicted that iodine would deposit the way it does. They dissolved the metal, and iodine, which is a fission product, was volatilized, and it went up and out the stack.

Daniel Grossman, who has studied Hanford's early atmospheric emissions, has noted that the health and safety of plant operators and the public were genuine concerns from the beginning of the plutonium project. However, efforts to protect shifted eventually "from prevention of, to alleviation of, hazards." Pressure to produce plutonium was critical, and public discussion of radiation dangers never was allowed during World War II because of very strict secrecy.

Another concern was the Columbia River. General Groves worried in particular about the fish. Groves had spent part of his youth in the Pacific Northwest because his father was an Army chaplain stationed at Seattle's Fort Lawton, and he was sensitive to the importance of fish—especially salmon—to the economy and culture of the region. Groves was admonished by the man who had designed the fish ladders at Bonneville Dam: "Whatever you may accomplish, you will incur the everlasting enmity of the entire North-west if you harm a single scale on a single salmon."

During the summer of 1943, Dr. Lauren R. Donaldson, an assistant pro-fessor of fisheries at the University of Washington, was asked to take charge of studies on the effects of radioactivity in the river. Hanford Thayer, a civilian employee of the U.S. Corps of Engineers, was responsible for the design of special intake and discharge facilities at the reactors which protected the Columbia River fish.

Studies showed that radioactive products could concentrate in river life and enter the food chain, but that discharge of cooling water from the wartime reactors had not done significant harm to the Columbia River or the life within it. One safeguard was to retain reactor cooling water in large retention basins which allowed a reduction in heat and the decay of short-lived radioactive substances.

Healy said a close eye was kept on the river, partly because some drinking water supplies depended on it. Radioactive concentrations were noted during the pre-1946 period, with one of the main constituents being sodium-24. But, he said, sodium-24 has a very short half life of about $2^{1/2}$ hours, which means every $2^{1/2}$ hours it lost one-half of its remaining radioactivity. In contrast, plutonium has a half life of 24,400 years.

One of Donaldson's original research associates was Dr. Richard F. Foster, a fisheries specialist. In June, 1945, Foster took charge of a fish laboratory at Hanford's F-Reactor to study radiation effects on salmon and steelhead trout. In 1970 he wrote that research done over a 25-year period showed radiation doses received by the public were well within guidelines and no discernible radiation or thermal effects occurred to fish and other wildlife.

Foster's laboratory studies determined that the dominant source of fission products released to the river resulted from the fissioning of "tramp" uranium, which is uranium occurring naturally in the river water. In passing through the reactors this uranium was affected by neutrons in the same way neutrons affected uranium inside the fuel slugs. Besides the "tramp" uranium, the other main source of radiation was fuel slug ruptures inside the reactor. During an interview by telephone from his retirement residence at Sunriver, Oregon, Foster said these ruptures occurred only occasionally, but until the reactor was shut down after detection "there were more than normal releases that went into the river."

Lower levels or river life, such as algae and insects, concentrated levels of radioactivity that were considerably higher than the water itself, a condition which, in turn, led to very high levels in the tissues of larger fish farther up the food chain. As more reactors were built after the war, radioactivity increased.

Hanford's World War II activities engendered an ongoing risk to the river and surrounding area from the threat posed by ground storage of nuclear and chemical waste from the separation plants during and after the war. Huge amounts of "hot" liquid waste were stored in World War II era single-wall tanks, some of which began to leak during the early 1950s. Other low level waste was poured directly into the ground. One fear is that a portion of waste from these sources eventually will reach the Columbia.

Michele Stenehjem Gerber, a historian of Hanford, has described Hanford as "a battlefield of World War II and the Cold War." One casualty was the natural environment, a reality which persists to the present day.

After 1945 Hanford continued to be a source of plutonium for nuclear weapons. The new Atomic Energy Commission took over in 1947, and under AEC direction 28,000 workers built five more reactors and two additional chemical processing plants along the Columbia. In 1963, a ninth reactor was completed, the dual purpose New Production Reactor, N-Reactor for short, which made plutonium but also used the by-product heat to make steam to generate electricity. By 1971, all Hanford reactors except N were retired.

From the 1950s on, when the Savannah River, S.C. reactors added their production, Hanford manufactured from a quarter to a third of the plutonium used in America's nuclear weapons. But, in 1987, as the Cold War began to wind down, Hanford's last working reactor, N, was shut down for safety improvements, and in 1988 the U.S. Department of Energy said the N Reactor would not be restarted unless national security required it. With closure of the N-Reactor, Hanford's days as a plutonium manufacturer ended.

Over the years, Hanford also became more than a military facility. The Fast Flux Test Facility was built at the south end of the reservation, a scientific research complex designed for testing materials that could be used in advanced nuclear power plants. Other nuclear research laboratories moved in as part of a diversification effort. Also located on the Hanford Site, but separate from the Department of Energy's operations, was a working civilian nuclear power reactor owned by the Washington Public Power Supply System.

The three World War II reactor buildings stood gray and deserted behind high fences. All nuclear fuel has been removed, but the reactors remained radioactive. After a period of "safe storage" to allow radioactivity to decrease, the Department of Energy planned to remove the reactors from the buildings for safer storage at the chemical separation area on the Hanford Site. The B Reactor, retired in 1968, the last of the three Manhattan Project units to

The Nagasaki mushroom, a lethal pillar of smoke and fire which rose to
above 45,000 feet. Lt. Col. Fred Olivi, the "Bockscar" co-pilot, said the
boiling cloud came within 1,500-2,000 feet of the bomber before the pilot
turned to escape it.   *National Atomic Museum*

stop production, has been designated a National Historic Mechanical
Engineering Landmark and may become a museum.

Two World War II-era chemical plant facilities, T and B, remained in
use, mostly as part of the continuing decontamination process at the site. In
the 300-Area, where the fuel was fabricated for the reactors, some buildings
were abandoned, while others were being considered for possible commercial use.

On the south side of Gable Mountain, the vaults where the plutonium
was stored in 1945 had been used in recent years in more prosaic ways, such
as storage of contaminated sodium from the Fast Flux Test Facility and soil
samples from radiation monitoring work. During the mid-1990s, though, a
Department of Energy spokesman said the vaults were empty except for "snakes
and other crawly things."

World War II-era single steel wall tanks for storage of liquid nuclear waste under construction in 1944. Some of these undergound steel tanks, surrounded by concrete, began to leak in the early 1950s causing concern that Hanford radioactivity would pose a health threat to the general public.

U.S. Department of Energy

HANFORD'S POSTWAR VOICES

By Bruce Hevly
University of Washington

After World War II, and the events described by those whose memories are presented here, Hanford and the Tri-Cities of Richland, Pasco, and Kennewick underwent a transformation. The voices of those who had helped produce the fuel necessary for the two plutonium fission explosions of July and August, 1945, began to be heard publicly for the first time. As time has passed, more and more voices have been heard: explaining, examining, condemning and justifying Hanford's mission and its conduct.[1] Even when ostensibly concerned with the events of World War II, these stories were often formed in reference to contemporary issues. Hanford's postwar history included three important strands: the continuing development of production reactors, the establishment and growth of distinct communities whose existence centered on the federal commitment to Hanford, and emerging concerns over Hanford's environmental impact.

With the end of the war, physicist Henry D. Smyth described Hanford's existence and its contributions in the federal government's official account of the Manhattan Project, *Atomic Energy for Military Purposes*.[2] The Smyth report represented an attempt to inform those capable of understanding the basic workings of nuclear weapons of the secret work done by the Allies

---

[1] Notes to this chapter are appended in References, p 245.

during World War II, so that "engineers and scientific men" could in turn educate their fellow citizens and prepare them for the responsibilities of active participation in the political debates of a nuclear-armed republic. The wartime commander of the Manhattan Engineer District, Major General Leslie R. Groves, saw one function of the Smyth report as defining the limits of acceptable discourse on nuclear weapons. "Obviously military security prevents this story from being told in full," Groves wrote in a preface to the report. "All pertinent scientific information which can be released to the public at this time…is in this volume…Persons disclosing or securing additional information by any means whatsoever without authorization are subject to severe penalties under the Espionage Act."[3] These introductory statements symbolize the terms under which Hanford, and the nuclear weapons policy of the United States, were to be discussed from 1945 on: a vital matter of national policy, about which most Americans could have only superficial or very general knowledge.

Of course, the discussion quickly transcended the straightforward account written by Smyth, and more and more voices joined the chorus. Atomic bombs and associated science fiction weapons popped up immediately in comic books and on radio programs, where pre-war tropes about the mysterious power of the atom were amplified by the war's realities.[4] Some scientists and other thinkers began to discuss the necessity of world government in a nuclear age.[5] On another level, in late 1945 MGM began work on a movie version of the atomic bomb story. It reached the screen in April 1947 under the title *The Beginning or the End*. Despite the cooperation of some of the Manhattan Project's principals, the result was "a cultural, historical, and artistic flop," in the words of historian Nathan Reingold.[6] The public's information continued to come from a broad spectrum of popular and official sources, all more or less reliable on occasion.

The Hanford Engineer Works had been built quickly in order to meet a strategic goal: the production of nuclear weapons to realize the Allies' war aims. The facility's postwar prospects, and those of the new community which had been established to support it, were unclear, and Hanford's workers were left briefly wondering whether it was "the beginning or the end" for the site. Soon, though, plutonium became an essential strategic material as America entered the Cold War, and Hanford's graphite-moderated piles represented a crucial, reliable system for producing the substance. By 1947 a major building program was under way at Hanford under the direction of the Atomic

Energy Commission, an agency created by Congressional legislation the previous year. General Electric had taken over from Du Pont as the operator of the site. In 1955 there were eight reactors dispersed along the Columbia River at Hanford, including the three intended for only months of wartime service, which instead remained active for two decades.

Concerns over the dangers of nuclear weapons came not just from comic books. The Smyth report explained the hazards of radiation and of radioactive fission products, while pointing to the successful work of the health and safety units attached to the various Manhattan Project facilities to protect the project's staff; confidential reports agreed that Hanford had run acceptable hazards in the context of emergency wartime operations.[7] Still, some vivid reports from Hiroshima and from the postwar U.S. nuclear weapons tests in the Pacific raised concerns about the hazards of the atomic age. But in the context of the Cold War, Hanford's production mission was deemed essential to the nation's defense; in the spring of 1950, a memorandum designated NSC-68 formalized the Truman Administration's view that the competition between the United States and the USSR represented a state of emergency, which would last for some years and which required a peacetime mobilization of the nation's resources.[8] The Korean War affirmed the American view of communism's expansionist threat.

During the Cold War, Hanford ran at full steam, releasing large amounts of radioactive contaminants into the environment, but in a manner that the staff believed would disperse them sufficiently so that they would not pose an unacceptable danger to the public.[9] Most local feeling against the AEC centered on Hanford's continuing withdrawal of potentially rich, irrigated farmland from the reclamation effort begun during the New Deal and continuing after the war. Against this economic loss, in addition to Hanford's substantial payroll, many in Washington saw Hanford as the potential cradle of industrial development for the Inland Empire—the center of the "nuclear progress state" and the Grand Coulee of the atomic age.

In his recollections of Hanford, physicist John Wheeler made a striking statement. "I never thought of Hanford in terms of being a factory," he told Stephen Sanger. "There was a sense of adventure about it."[10] Why should these two images contradict? Hanford's adventure, its challenge, the issue in doubt, was a drama of production: the all-out effort to fulfill Colonel Matthias' orders to produce plutonium in "whatever quantities are necessary."[11] The commitment to production shaped Hanford's history from then on, as did the perception of those who came to work on the project that they were pioneers, joining the geographical expansion of America's history with a march into new intellectual territory.

Models for how to occupy and hold the new ground of high technology also came in abundance after the war. World War II was perceived as "the physicists' war," the importance of radar and nuclear weapons pointing to the importance of investing in intellectual capital as a strategic asset.[12] Vannevar Bush, who directed the Office of Scientific Research and Development during the war, wrote *Science—The Endless Frontier*, a widely circulated argument for government support of science after the war. The vital, creative work of scientific thinking, Bush argued, could only go on under circumstances of independence for those doing the thinking.[13] Chiming in to confirm this view was Samuel Goudsmit, a physicist assigned by the Manhattan Project to follow in the wake of the Allied invasion of occupied Europe, assess the German nuclear weapons program, and secure records and materiel related to the German effort.[14] Working in the environment of a dictatorship, Goudsmit explained, under government regimentation, German scientific work had suffered and ultimately failed. The ethereal image of Albert Einstein, the most prominent scientist in the public's eye, confirmed a popular idea of scientists as abstract thinkers requiring a large amount of artistic freedom.[15]

Given these assumptions, Hanford was an anomaly. Its new operator, General Electric, called not for theoretical physicists as it took over operations, but for chemical engineers, mechanical engineers, and electrical engineers; also electricians, plumbers, and building tradesmen to maintain the wartime facilities and build new ones.[16] The industrial adventure of the war set the pattern for expansion at Hanford; if many of the wartime staff represented a group of new West cowboys—"starting up one plant and moving on to start up another one was a way of life with that crowd," one of Sanger's informants tells us—construction crews became a familiar sight at Hanford after the war as well, moving from one area to the next on the reservation, setting up new reactors and new chemical separation plants.[17] Presidential administrations, Congress, the AEC and Hanford's staff operated under the assumption that the United States faced a threat in Stalin's Soviet Union as severe as that posed by Hitler's Germany.

At first the AEC's planning for new reactors at Hanford was spurred by the danger that the reactors built during the war might have nearly reached the end of their useful lives. Each reactor was a stack of graphite bricks, drilled from the front of the pile to hold pipes, the pipes in turn carrying aluminum cans of uranium fuel and cooling water; holes drilled from one side allowed control rods to slide into the reactor, controlling its activity, and others running vertically through the pile made space for rods to drop from above, shutting down the reactor in case of an emergency. After the blocks of neutron moderating material had been exposed to the radiation and high temperatures for several months, they began to manifest a condition called "graphite creep," some blocks expanding and bending. The center of the pile, where heat and radiation were the most intense, began to buckle upward, threatening the alignment of the channels for fuel elements, control rods and the safety system. [18]

Faced with this problem, one of the reactors was put on standby, to preserve its useful life and to ensure that it would be available if needed to produce weapons components. Hanford's staff began work to solve the problem, and new reactors went on the drawing boards, designed to follow the proven pattern of the site's original production piles; two were approved for construction in 1947. To save time and money, the AEC contemplated building two replacement piles, to be set near wartime reactors and taking advantage of the already-built water processing and pumping equipment in place there. In the end, one of these, designated "DR," was built in the original D reactor area, and completed in 1950. Another, designated H and completed the year before, sat on another site downstream.

A second plutonium production facility using heavy-water moderated reactors, a design explored but not pursued for production purposes during the war, went up at Savannah River, South Carolina. Reactor operations began at Savannah River in 1953; in contrast to these new facilities, Hanford's were always devoted to the tried-and-true wartime design, with improvements. For example, engineers and craftsmen developed a bag of techniques to defeat the graphite creep problem, changes which drew little on the high art of physics represented by the hortative accounts of Bush and Goudsmit and the public image of Einstein. Like most developing technologies, progress came through hands-on work and from engineering the details.[19]

These improvements and new facilities, along with work to improve the efficiency of processing operations, represented Hanford's first generation of expansion, undertaken to assure a steady supply of plutonium to postwar defense planners. Some of the material was needed for test explosions, to explore new weapons designs and investigate the conditions under which military units might have to operate if nuclear weapons were again used in war. The construction of Hanford's H and DR piles represented America's strategic commitment to nuclear weapons in the aftermath of World War II. A second round of expansion came in response to the shocks and decisions of 1949 and 1950: the Soviet Union's detonation of a fission weapon of its own, atom spy revelations in the United States, the Korean War, the crystallization of Cold War policy in NSC 68, and the U.S. commitment to build fusion weapons—the so-called "Supers"—first contemplated in 1941.[20] In addition to the construction of five new reactors at Savannah River between 1951 and 1955, three more were built at Hanford: C, which reflected improvements in cooling based on accumulated experience, and so was designed to be operated at higher power levels than the earlier reactors, and the "jumbos", KE and KW.

Two important general points characterized the development of reactors at Hanford in the decade following the war. First, the steady advancement in reactor power, and so in plutonium output, came about because of hands-on experience accumulated by the engineers and craftsmen who worked with the reactors on a daily basis. Second, the importance of Hanford's product and the reliability of the graphite-moderated reactors dictated that the Atomic Energy Commission would continue to invest in this proven wartime technology. In terms of reactor technology, Hanford represented a distinct tradition, followed by no other institution, which veered away from the developing stream of reactor development.

In an effort to rejoin that stream, Hanford, the AEC, and local politicians worked to establish Hanford's ninth production reactor, the N reactor, as a dual-purpose facility. The jumbo reactors, KE and KW, had been designed to make use of some of the heat generated by the fission process in their piles, extracting it from the cooling water and using it to heat the voluminous reactor buildings. The N reactor would take this plan one step farther: the heat produced as a by-product of plutonium production would be extracted by means of a heat exchanger and used to turn water in a separate plumbing system into non-radioactive steam. That steam, in turn, would be used to turn a generator, producing electricity which might be sold via the Bonneville Power Administration.

The BPA, established during the New Deal to distribute the electricity produced at a series of dams on the Columbia River, knew Hanford mainly as a customer. The N reactor proposal suggested that Hanford might return electric power to the grid, as well as consume it, generally following the outline of power industry planners who saw dual-purpose reactors as important steps in the development of civilian nuclear power. Ideally, in their view, such plants would be operated not by the government, but by power companies. If the federal government agreed to provide civilian reactor operators with uranium fuel, and then pay them for the plutonium produced in the process of their operations, plutonium sales might partially underwrite the tremendous expense of building nuclear power plants as the operators learned the business.[21]

Senator Henry Jackson of Washington became the project's congressional champion; it spoke to his commitments as both an ardent anti-communist, concerned with building up the United States weapons stockpile, and a believer in public power and the development of the Columbia's resources to spur Washington's economic development. Jackson's first proposal for a Hanford dual-purpose reactor failed. On a second attempt, in 1958 it passed in a burst of post-Sputnik concern about American technological competitiveness, although without federal support for a generating facility. The latter was provided by the Washington Public Power Supply System (WPPSS), which represented a consortium of the state's public utility disticts for the purpose of developing electrical generating sites.[22] With a fence separating the federal reactor from the utilities' generator, the heat from the N reactor passed from the military to the civlian economy, creating steam to turn turbines in electrical generation plant. While WPPSS went on to make a major investment in nuclear generation of electrical power, including construction of civilian power reactors on the Hanford site, the history of production reactors at Hanford ended with the N reactor, which began operations in 1964.[23]

In addition to four generations of plutonium production reactors—Manhattan Project, postwar supply assurance, Korean War expansion, and dual-purpose—the federal presence at Hanford also fostered generations of residents who understood that the continued existence of their communities rested on the work which went on inside the reservation. Though the construction workers who built the reactors and fuel processing facilities were a transient population—their construction camp was demolished once their work was completed during the war—Hanford also required a permanent population of operators, managers and maintenence personnel, as well as police officers, fire fighters, and storekeepers. "We're here to stay," was the motto of Richland Day in 1947, as the annual civic festival staged a welcome to General Electric, the new operating contractor at Hanford and celebrated Richland's continuing existence.[24] Who "we" were, in turn, depended on a communal interpretation of Hanford's history and its meaning for the future.

The past and the future intersected in the image of the pioneer, a theme running through the memories of those interviewed for this book. As Franklin Matthias recalled, Hanford came into being in "an area with almost no people, very undeveloped," and one of his fellow Manhattan Project veterans reported that "we considered ourselves sort of like pioneers."[25] (Of course, many of the newcomers did not know about the families displaced to build Hanford, or about the New Deal plans for the growth of the area's agricultural base with electricity and irrigation supplied from the Grand Coulee project.) In becoming a permanent community, those who came to Hanford during the war and remained after it saw themselves as playing out the continuing drama of American settlement in the West: they came to a strange, empty, in many ways inhospitible land, built a community and a made the landscape productive. What distinguished Hanford was that it also represented pioneering at an intellectual frontier, the boundary to the high-technology future. The logo for Richland's first "Atomic Frontier Days" in 1948 showed a wagon train moving to the west, leaving behind smoke-filled industrial cities and headed toward a clean, futuristic community by the light of a nuclear dawn.[26]

As western pioneers always had done, the residents of Pasco, Kennewick, and especially Richland expected that the government would support their efforts. Those living in Richland grew accustomed to having federally-built housing, to seeing the government collect their rents and provide city services, even to the incongruity of having corporate security officers exercise police powers in town. Congress and the Atomic Energy Commission, though, grew increasingly disenchanted with the expense, and the political implications, of the federal government running small communities.[27] As early as 1949 congressional overseers began to urge the AEC to get out of the business.

Washington State was willing to incorporate Richland as a city, but the citizens initially resisted the move. Some believed that local politicians would never deliver services as efficiently as General Electric or the federal government, and while many were happy to have the opportunity to buy their homes, sale prices set by federal assessors did not seem to reflect the sacrifices that had been made by many of them as pioneers in the new community. One Richlander, describing how she had "pioneered it with the rest of the oldtimers" a decade before, reminded the Joint Committee on Atomic Energy of the conditions faced by Richland's early residents and the work they had invested in the town.[28] Others pointed out the long period many of them had paid rent, the need for expensive remodeling faced by many would-be owners of wartime housing, and the hazards of home ownership in a one-industry town. Most assessed values were reduced substantially, and the AEC agreed to another decade of financial aid to the new city, which came into existence on December 12, 1958.[29]

If images from the frontier past helped to shape the residents' sense of their community, other historic images animated Hanford's early critics, as well as political allies from western Washington. While merchants in Richland, Pasco, and Kennewick oriented themselves to serving an industrial workforce at Hanford, local agricultural interests objected to the amount of potentially productive land removed from farmers' use by the AEC. Part of the land surrounding Hanford's buildings, kept empty as a safety measure, represented acreage scheduled to be reclaimed with irrigation water from the Grand Coulee project, as well as a main right of way for the water to flow elsewhere in the project. Even after an initial release of lands from Hanford's control in 1953, agricultural interests pressed for more, indicating that they were willing to accept the associated hazards. The AEC, noting that, while their safety systems had improved, the reactors were running at ever-higher powers, insisted on keeping the existing exclusion zone.[30]

Jackson had seen the N reactor as an intermediate step between Hanford's production reactors, and a future center for the production of electricity by nuclear power in eastern Washington. A nuclear industrial park, in this view, would continue the great work begun during the New Deal: to develop the Columbia as a central resource for the economic progress of the state. Power for industry, and to pump irrigation water throughout the region, might flow from civilian reactors as plutonium came from the AEC's graphite-moderated piles.

This vision, shared by Democrats and Republicans alike, caused the state's leaders to advocate the policy of creating in Washington the "nuclear progress state" well into the 1970s. It led to the broad reactor construction plans pursued by WPPSS; three of the consortium's first five planned reactors were sited at Hanford. Only one was taken to completion and has produced power, while the rest fell victim to poor design, construction management, and (so far) unrealized predictions of the region's demand for electricity. Through support for WPPSS and other non-defense projects and by encouraging continued investment at the site, those leading the increasingly self-aware, Hanford-centered community fought for its economic interests.

Efforts to develop Hanford as a high-technology industrial center were thwarted by first the federal government's disengagement from Hanford, and then the state's. As a factory, Hanford's liability was that it produced a substance which, ideally, was never consumed. Failing the use of nuclear weapons, their plutonium components were more than durable: the substance decays slowly, with a half-life of over 24,000 years. After a point, United States stockpiles were considered adequate, and the government set about shutting down Hanford's reactors, beginning during the Johnson administration. While the pace of this process varied with national and international political trends, it tended increasingly toward the reduction of Hanford's role in the nuclear economy. At the same time, with the rise of a more active environmental movement in the early 1970s, one often allied with antimilitary sentiments, the idea of Washington as the nuclear progress state became a controversial one. An unsuccessful initiative campaign was mounted in 1976 to curtail reactor construction in Washington (part of a multi-state campaign), but the second half of the decade brought increasing pressure on WPPSS. The Three-Mile Island accident reduced confidence in the safety of nuclear power, while economic slowdowns reduced the demand for electricity in the northwest. Washington's voters declared themselves against nuclear power on economic grounds, a year after voting by a three-to-one ratio to ban the importation of out-of-state nuclear wastes, a measure quickly overturned in federal court.[31]

Beginning in the early 1960s, as the federal government began to close Hanford's production reactors, the Atomic Energy Commission and its successor agency, the Department of Energy, began to see the economic future of the Tri-Cities as distinct from the future of nuclear technology, and worked to make the community around Hanford see it that way, too. With most of its own advanced-technology investments elsewhere, the federal government began to promote economic diversificaton for the Tri-Cities, to wean the local economy at least in part away from nuclear technology. Rather than a single operating contractor, Hanford's operations were divided among several; each, in its bid for a contract, had to agree to contribute to the process of building new employment opportunities for those who had worked on the reservation. Some, such as Batelle's Pacific Northwest Laboratories, worked to expand the opportunities for technical employment on the site. Others met the diversification goals by sponsoring a new hotel, a cattle feed lot, and the expanded Port of Benton County—not all businesses which provided jobs and wages of the kind to which skilled, unionized workers were accustomed.

All of the government's single-purpose plutonium production reactors, the last of which had been completed in 1955, were shut down between 1964 and 1971, a series of events which made the citizens of the Tri-Cities exceptionally sensitive to their economic dependence on Hanford. Much of the opposition to the work done at Hanford centered on the environmental threats posed by operations at the site, complaints dismissed by Hanford's defenders as based on ignorance.

Strictly speaking, they were. Most discussions of safety at Hanford, including the establishment of acceptable levels of radioactive releases into the environment, were carried out in secret, even when they involved representatives of federal and state agencies outside of the AEC. After the Commission took over all the Manhattan Project sites, it empanelled a group of health and safety experts to investigate Hanford's operations, along with those of the other facilities. Reporting in the spring of 1948, these auditors found that Hanford's safety planning, and its record over the course of the war, compared favorably with the other Manhattan District sites, probably because Du Pont had extensive experience with industrial safety programs.

Still, in contrast to the Smyth report's assurances about the lack of dangerous emissions from Hanford, as well as the other laboratories and production sites, the Safety and Industrial Health Advisory Board warned that Hanford's "sins of emission" would "soon be public property," reducing the public's confidence in the government's operation of Hanford. Inevitably, the board believed, a "municipal or state health department" would review waste-stack building practices, and find them not up to industrial norms.[32] There were too many untested assumptions, the board believed, not only about radioactive emissions from the plutonium separation facilities, but also about the ability of the site's soil to hold wastes dumped into dry wells or storage cribs, and about the dilution of wastes which reached the Columbia River.[33]

Local authorities took an interest in Hanford's releases into the Columbia, and a wartime program to monitor radioactive isotope uptake in salmon was continued through the postwar period. But the Board raised two other, long-term problems: the carrying capacity of the soil to hold low-level wastes, and the dispersion of radioactive gases, especially iodine-131, into the surrounding environment. The former, as it turned out, was based on a faulty understanding of the chemical process which dictated how the wastes stuck to the soil. By the late 1950s, Hanford scientists began to question whether liquid wastes would remain out of the Columbia, or whether the underground plumes of waste were moving relatively rapidly toward the river.[34]

The major points of contention over Hanford's history are the extent to which its staff allowed radioactive iodine to leave the site, the damage those emissions have done, and the federal government's policy of carrying out such releases with no notification to Hanford's neighbors. It was a problem recognized from the time the processing facilities were built during World War II; after the war, when General Electric won the operating contract for Hanford, the company was charged by the AEC with responsibility for eliminating iodine releases. At the same time, even as they voiced concern over the stack emissions problem, the members of the Industrial Health and Safety Board pointed out that almost any industrial facility releases pollutants, which may be harmful to the plant's neighbors. In the case of Hanford, public announcement of the composition and magnitude of the plant's releases would have given the Soviet Union crucial information about the plant's rate of production and the techniques used there, and, by extension, data about the probable size of the United States nuclear weapons stockpile. Also, standards for environmental exposure to radioactivity were only being defined in the period during and after World War II, many remaining ill-defined until the mid-1950s.

The argument must turn on two governmental determinations: first, that building America's nuclear stockpile, and testing new weapon designs, was more important than an indeterminant threat to the public health represented by radioactive emissions, and, second, that the public could not be consulted about the decision. America's commitment to the external threats of the Cold War weighed most heavily in calculations of policy related to safety at Hanford, as demonstrated by any number of events which occurred during operations in the 1940s and 1950s. The filters installed by GE in the stacks of the separation plants were occasionally overwhelmed and failed during peak production. In 1949, the government ordered the deliberate release of a massive amount of radioactive material from the plants, during the so-called "Green Run." Michele Stenehjem Gerber has made a persuasive argument that one reason for this release may have been to calibrate devices for monitoring the Soviets' nuclear weapons program in the aftermath of their first nuclear test.[35] (She has also described some of the efforts made by Hanford's staff to protect Richland's population from exposure to some of the ecological niches where radioactive isotopes tended to concentrate, including sagebrush, mosquitoes, and milk from dairies under the main plume from the separation plants.) Documents more recently aquired by researchers from the Department of Energy suggest that the Green Run was part of a program of releases conducted in different parts of the country as radiological warfare tests.[36]

To take another example, while the AEC Reactor Safety Committee endorsed retaining extensive empty lands around the reactors and the separation plants despite the complaints of local farmers, decisions to place two reactors at a single site (D and DR, B and C, for example) and to build the "jumbos" (KE and KW) violated the Committee's own guidelines for the size of Hanford's safety zone, which should have increased further with the increase in reactor power concentrated at those points. The committee also expressed concerns from the late 1940s to the early 1960s about the lack of containment buildings around the eight Hanford production reactors. Yet the AEC's Director of Production felt that, in the context of the Cold War demand for Hanford's product, he could not justify the expense or delay of making changes. "The contribution to national security through gains in plutonium-production...appear to outweigh the...consequences...[of] the unlikely event of a major reactor accident," he wrote.[37] The perceived urgency of Hanford's defense mission overrode all these concerns.

If the public was not privy to the details of Hanford's operations, or their dangers, there were still a number of incidents and influences which created pockets of opposition to nuclear technology. Spencer Weart has shown how images of atomic power going back to the turn of the century touched on profound chords of anxiety in Western culture, and after World War II these concerns took more specific forms.[38] In 1948 the book *No Place to Hide* appeared, written by David Bradley, a physician who had participated in the 1946 Bikini tests in the South Pacific.[39] The most fearsome image in Bradley's account was not the bomb's explosion, but the fallout and contamination left in its aftermath. Invisible, insidious, and deadly—unaccountably absent in one place and concentrated in another—it was the bomb's latent threat that Bradley found most worrisome.

Similarly, concerns about the safety of Hanford's reactors—only partially provided with surrounding structures able to contain the results of an accident in one of the piles—built up over time, mainly as the result of problems elsewhere: the Windscale accident at a British plutonium production facility in 1957, the anti-fallout campaigns which focused on milk contamination as a result of above-ground testing, Three-Mile Island, an emerging downwinder movement around continental test sites, and finally Chernobyl, which contributed to the decision that the N reactor be closed in 1986.[40]

By the mid-1980s, outside criticism began to focus on a seemingly less dramatic danger among Hanford's facilities: the over one hundred waste storage tanks which had been built on the site since the beginning of World War II. Carrying millions of gallons of radioactive waste, failure of the tanks through either degradation of their metal walls or an explosion of the exothermic mixtures they held would release the contents into the environment.[41] Pressed by a series of journalistic investigations on the storage tanks, as well as continuing pressure from eastern Washington families concerned about the possible effects of radioactive gaseous releases, and facing a stream of pending Freedom of Information Act requests, the Department of Energy in 1986 began the release of tens of thousands of pages of formerly restricted documents. These confirmed that Hanford had indeed allowed a tremendous amount of radioactive contamination to leave the reservation. The *Tri-Cities Herald*, a leading voice defending Hanford against both environmentalists and government cutbacks, declared that the AEC and the DOE had betrayed and lied to the community.

But in 1995, employment and government spending at Hanford are at postwar highs. Hanford's new mission is to clean itself up, a process expected to take decades and tens of billions of dollars. It involves locating and properly disposing of large amounts of slightly contaminated materials, many of which were buried in casual, unmarked barrel dumps on the reservation, as well as confronting the continuing progress of contaminants through the ground and toward the waters of the Columbia, the bubbling tons of liquid high-level waste, and the problem of disposing of the reactors themselves, which are, technically, building-sized blocks of solid waste.

These are challenging problems for craftsmen and technical professionals, the equal of those posed by the Manhattan Project. The clean-up is conducted under the supervision of the Department of Energy, the Environmental Protection Agency, and the Washington State Department of Ecology, which monitor not only the process of collecting, repackaging and storing contaminants, but also that of assessing the damage done by Hanford's operations over four decades of secret operations. A 1991 preliminary study by the Hanford Dose Reconstruction Project estimated the ammount of radioactive iodine released into eastern Washington, while a study published in the spring of 1994 estimated the dispersion pattern of the material, focusing on the existence of areas where the substance tended to concentrate, many of them distant from the site.[42] Epidemiological research is continuing, to look for anomalously high rates of cancers associated with the substances Hanford released.

At least temporarily, Hanford's defenders and critics are in general agreement about the work being done at the site. There are, and will be, sharp disagreements about the extent to which information on the site's operations is forthcoming, on the course taken by the public health investigations (for example, whether to focus on the effects of iodine 131 or less abundant, but even more virulent, substances), and, especially, over the question of whether or not the DOE ought to supervise the clean up. The goal of cleaning up, at least, has gained general assent.

It has also created a new community identity for Hanford's workers. Rather than the pioneer technicians of the nuclear progress state, they will identify themselves with a new set of esoteric, specialized skills, related to the long-term task of policing up after the Cold War. The companies and workers who develop this expertise will be eager to expand their market, and there are potential clients in many of the western states. Over the question of importing more such work onto the Hanford reservation, voices will be raised in disagreements as sharp as any which have taken place so far. The community's response to Congressional threats to funding for the clean up reveal the importance of this new mission to Hanford workers and their families.

Further, a heated discussion will continue over the establishment of the Columbia's Hanford Reach as a National Wild and Scenic River, along with the creation of a wildlife sanctuary on the surrounding hill sides. Hanford's presence made the stretch of river running past the reactors the last free-flowing, undammed section of the Columbia in Washington state, the last part of the river which reflects its character before the reclamation projects of the New Deal. Long-frustrated local farmers insist that the land might be put to better use by putting it into agricultural production; others have not given up on the prospects of taking barge traffic upstream to the rich orchard country above Hanford, which would require dredging the channel. Even better, in the view of the Army Corps of Engineers, would be another dam. "We are in the business of building projects," a spokesman explained. "And that's the last major dam site left on the river. However, we are having a little trouble selling that dam."[43]

Discussing the use of Hanford's product to bomb Nagasaki in 1945, Eugene Wigner admitted to Stephen Sanger that while he realized it had been debated ever since, he had not been inclined to engage in any post-hoc analyses. "You see, though," he said, "it is not a question which interests me, because we cannot change the past."[44] That is true. But the debates over Hanford's history and meaning, and the forms they have taken, will shape all the discussions of the site's future yet to come. History will continue to be a powerful and contested resource for those engaged in debates over Hanford's future.

This essay is based on work conducted with support from the U.S. Department of Energy, Richland Operations Office (Cooperative Agreement No. DE-FC06-91-RL12260), the University of Washington Graduate School Research Fund, and the University of Washington Department of History. I am especially obliged to my collaborator in a longer study of Hanford's history, Professor John Findlay, as well as to Terri Traub of the DOE Public Reading Room in Richland, Washington, and to Dr. Roger Anders, Archivist-Historian and Dr. Benjamin Franklin Cooling, Chief Historian, Department of Energy, Germantown, Maryland.

REFERENCES

NOTES TO INTRODUCTION

1. For Groves's life see William Lawren, *The General and the Bomb* (New York: Dodd, Mead and Company, 1988); and the general's somewhat self-serving autobiography, Leslie R. Groves, *Now It Can Be Told: The Story of the Manhattan Project* (New York: Da Capo, 1962; 1983).

2. Groves, *Now It Can Be Told*, 69.

3. Lenore Fine and Jesse A. Remington, *The Corps of Engineers: Construction in the United States* (Washington, D.C.: USGPO, 1972), 667/ 673.

4. Michele Stenehjem Gerber, *On the Home Front: The Cold War Legacy of the Hanford Nuclear Site* (Lincoln and London: University of Nebraska Press, 1991), 12. On the selection process, see also, Mary Powell Harris, *Goodbye, White Bluffs* (Yakima: Franklin Press, 1972), 150-152; and Lisa Scattaregia, "The Disappearance, How Did Two Entire Years Vanish?" *East Benton County Historical Society, The Courier* 13 (April 1991), 5-11.

5. Stephane Groueff, *Manhattan Project: The Untold Story of the Making of the Atomic Bomb* (New York: Bantam Books, 1967), 152.

6. Barton C. Hacker, *The Dragon's Tale: Radiation Safety in the Manhattan Project, 1942-1946* (Berkeley: University of California Press, 1987), 45.

7. F.T. Matthias, "Building the Hanford Plutonium Plant," *Engineering News-Record, 135* (Dec. 13, 1945), 118-124.

8. Groueff, *Manhattan Project*, 156-159.

9. Groves, *Now It Can Be Told*, 90.

10. Richard G. Hewlett and Oscar E. Anderson, Jr., *The New World, 1939-1946*, Volume I of *A History of the United States Atomic Energy Commission* (University Park, Pennsylvania: The Pennsylvania State University Press, 1962), 215.

11. Interviews with Walter Knowles, 1969-1975.

12. Lawren, *The General and the Bomb*, 114.

13. F. T. Matthias, "Building the Hanford Plutonium Plant," *Engineering News-Record*, 135 (Dec. 13, 1945), 118-124.

14. Eugene P. Wigner, *The Recollections of Eugene P. Wigner* as told to Andrews Szanton (New York and London: Plenum Press, 1992), 233.

15. Arthur Holly Compton, *Atomic Quest: A Personal Narrative* (New York: Oxford University Press, 1956), 192.

16. Lenore Fine and Jesse A. Remington, *The Corps of Engineers: Construction in the United States* (Washington, D.C.: USGPO, 1972), 696-693; Hewlett and Anderson, Jr., *The New World*, 692; *The Recollections of Eugene P. Wigner*, 233.

17. Leona Marshall Libby, *The Uranium People* (New York: Charles Scribner's Sons, 1979), 168; Groueff, *Manhattan Project*, 354.

18. K.D. Nichols, *The Road to Trinity: A Personal Account of How America's Nuclear Policies Were Made* (New York: William Morrow and Company, Inc., 1987), 140-141.

19. On Trinity, see Ferenc Morton Szasz, *The Day the Sun Rose Twice: The Story of the Trinity Site Nuclear Explosion, July 16, 1945* (Albuquerque: University of New Mexico Press, 1984); for the role the British played, see Ferenc Morton Szasz, *British Scientists and the Manhattan Project: The Los Alamos Years* (New York: St. Martin's, 1991).

20. Rhodes, *The Making of the Atomic Bomb*, 741-742.

21. Patricia Nelson Limerick, "The Significance of Hanford in American History," 1990 Pettyjohn Distinguished Lectures at Washington State University.

22. Gerber, *On the Home Front: The Cold War Legacy of the Hanford Nuclear Site*. One should probably also include journalist Michael D'Antonio's impassioned *Atomic Harvest: Hanford and the Lethal Toll of America's Nuclear Arsenal* (New York: Crown, 1993). Excellent studies that have only the briefest mention of Hanford include: Robert C. Williams and Philip L. Cantelon, eds., *The American Atom: A Documentary History of Nuclear Policies from the Discovery of Fission to the Present, 1939-1984* (Philadelphia: University of Pennsylvania Press, 1984; Allan M. Wigner, *Life Under a Cloud: American Anxiety About the Atom* (New York: Oxford University Press, 1993); and Spencer R. Weart, *Nuclear Fear: A History of Images* (Cambridge: Harvard University Press, 1988).

23. For examples of Hanford doggerel, see Groueff, *Manhattan Project*, 329, and Compton, *Atomic Quest*, 192-193; Marilou Awiakta, *Abiding Appalachia: Where Mountain and Atom Meet* (Memphis: St. Luke's Press, 1978; 1986), 95.

NOTES TO AFTERWORD

1. In addition to this volume and the work of Michele Stenehjem Gerber, cited below, a sample of works on Hanford's history includes Paul R. Loeb, *Nuclear Culture: Living and Working in the World's Largest Nuclear Complex* (New York: Coward, McCann, and Geoghegan, 1982); Patricia Nelson Limerick, "The Significance of Hanford in American History," in *Washington Comes of Age: The State in the National Experience*, edited by David H. Stratton (Pullman, Wash.: Washington State University Press, 1992); Daniel Grossman, "Hanford and Its Early Radioactive Atmospheric Releases," *Pacific Northwest Quarterly* 85 (1994): 6-14; Michael D'Antonio, *Atomic Harvest: Hanford and the Toll of America's Nuclear Arsenal* (New York: Crown, 1993); and Glenn T. Seaborg, *The Plutonium Story: The Journals of Professor Glenn T. Seaborg, 1939-1946*, edited by Ronald L. Kathren, Jerry B. Gough, Gary T. Benefiel (Columbus, Ohio: Battelle Press, 1994).

2. Henry D. Smyth, *Atomic Energy for Military Purposes* (Princeton, NJ: Princeton University Press, 1948), ch. 7 and 8. Smyth's account was first prepared as a Manhattan Project report in 1945.

3. Smyth, *Atomic Energy*, vi, 266 (Smyth on informed citizens), p. v (Groves on the limits of security).

4. On the shaping of popular attitudes toward nuclear energy, see Spencer R. Weart, *Nuclear Fear: A History of Images* (Cambridge, Mass.: Harvard University Press, 1988), especially part 1 and ch. 6.

5. Alice Kimball Smith, *A Peril and a Hope: The Scientists' Movement in America, 1945-1947* (Chicago: University of Chicago Press, 1965). See also, Daniel J. Kevles, *The Physicists: The History of a Scientific Community in America* (New York: Knopf, 1977), ch. 21 and 22 on the physicists' lobbying for postwar legislation, including the Atomic Energy Act passed in 1946.

6. Nathan Reingold, "Metro-Goldwyn-Mayer Meets the Atom Bomb," 334-350 in Reingold, *Science American Style* (New Brunswick, NJ: Rutgers University Press, 1991), 345, 337.

7. Barton C. Hacker, *The Dragon's Tail: Radiation Safety in the Manhattan Project, 1942-1946* (Berkeley and Los Angeles: University of California Press, 1987), is the most thorough study of radiation safety and health physics work during World War II; on Hanford, see 44-58.

8. Daniel Yergin, *Shattered Peace: The Origins of the Cold War and the National Security State* (Boston: Houghton Mifflin, 1978); Ernest R. May, ed., *American Cold War Strategy: Interpreting NSC 68* (Boston: St. Martin's Press, 1993).

9. Michele Stenehjem Gerber, *On the Home Front: The Cold War Legacy of the Hanford Nuclear Site* (Lincoln, Neb: University of Nebraska Press, 1992) presents a summary of the routes taken by radioactive substances into the environment, and the fate of the dilution assumption as applied to each.

10. See page 157.

11. See page 42.

12. Kevles, *The Physicists* (n. 5), ch. 20.

13. Vannevar Bush, *Science—The Endless Frontier* (Washington DC: Government Printing Office, 1945), and *Modern Arms and Free Men: A Discussion of the Role of Science in Preserving Democracy* (New York: Simon and Schuster, 1949).

14. Samuel Goudsmit, *Alsos* (second edition); Los Angeles: Tomash, 1983. See also, Goudsmit, "Secrecy or Science?" *Science Illustrated* 1 (1946): 97-99. The best account of the German nuclear weapons effort during World War II is Mark Walker, *German National Socialism and the Quest for Nuclear Power, 1939-1949* (Cambridge, England: Cambridge University Press, 1989).

15. Helen Dukas and Banesh Hoffman, eds., *Albert Einstein: The Human Side* (Princeton, NJ: Princeton University Press, 1979).

16. On the mixture of specialists working at Hanford after the war, see Milton R. Cydell, AEC Hanford, to Jack Curtis, Chief—Industrial Relations Division, AEC, "Professional Personnel, Hanford Engineer Works," 25 July 1945. Box 45, Record Group 326, Accession 67A803, National Archives, Southeast Region, East Point, Georgia. One trade journal argued that "capable chemical, electrical, electronic, and mechanical engineers can acquire the small amount of nuclear physics necessary" to solve the problems of advanced reactor designs; *Nucleonics* 2, 6 (June, 1948), 2.

17. See page 179.

18. Minutes of Executive Session, Joint Committee on Atomic Energy, U.S. Congress, 10 March 1949, pp. 3-4, in folder 2, box 5312; "Operation of Hanford Piles at Higher Power Levels," attached to Carleton Shugg to Brien McMahon, 25 July 1950, folder 412.14, box 4944, both in AEC Secretariat files 1947-1951. See also "Division of Production—Monthly Status and Progress Report, December 1948," p. 3, folder 18, box 74, AEC Production Division files.

19. Several AEC reports testify to what the headquarters staff referred to as this "stepwise approach" to raising the power levels in Hanford's reactors, including AEC 40/8, *Improvements to Hanford Reactors*, 15 September 1952; Box 4933, AEC Secretariat Files. Also, Planning and Scheduling Branch, Production Division, *Power Level Changes in Hanford Reactors*, 1960; Box 5439, AEC Production Division Files. Both in Record Group 326, National Archives.

20. On the development of fusion weapons, see Peter Galison and Barton Bernstein, "In any light: Scientists and the decision to build the Superbomb, 1952-1954," *Historical Studies in the Physical and Biological Sciences* 19 (1989): 267-347.

21. Charles Allen Thomas, "What Are the Prospects for Industrial Nuclear Power? Good—Here's a Plan to Consider," *Nucleonics* 6, 2 (February, 1950): 73, 77-78; C.G. Suits, "Power From the Atom: An Appraisal," *Nucleonics* 8, 2 (February, 1951): 3-9; Carroll A. Hochwalt and Philip N. Powers, "Dual-Purpose Reactors: First Step in Industrial Nuclear Power Development," *Nucleonics* 11, 2 (February, 1953): 10-13. The following cite Hanford's piles as a model for the future development of dual-purpose reactors: J.R. Menke, "Reactor Designs for Commercial Power," *Nucleonics* 12, 1 (January 1954): 66, 68; "U.S. Power Reactor Program...Goal: Economic Power in 10 Years," *Nucleonics* 12 (July 1954): 48-51. In practice, the N reactor operated under one set of conditions for the efficient production of steam for electricity, and another for the production of plutonium.

22. On the process of funding Hanford's N reactor, see Bonnie Baack Pendergrass, "Public Power, Politics, and Technology in the Eisenhower and Kennedy Years: The Hanford Dual-Purpose Reactor Controversy, 1956-1962," (Ph.D. dissertation, University of Washington, 1974). On the controversies surrounding implementation of the ideals of the transfer of nuclear technology to industry under the 1954 Atomic Energy Act, see Richard G. Hewlett and Jack M. Holl, *Atoms for Peace and War, 1953-1961: Eisenhower and the Atomic Energy Commission* (Berkeley and Los Angeles: University of California Press, 1989), ch. 5 and 425-429.

23. In addition to the nine plutonium production reactors, several small experimental reactors have been built on the Hanford site. One overview is Hans Toffer, "Evolution of the Hanford Graphite Reactor Technology," 237-243 in James W. Behrens and Allan D. Carlson, eds., *50 Years With Nuclear Fission* (La Grange Park, Il.: American Nuclear Society, 1989).

24. "Richland Day Souvenir Program," 1 September 1947, Richland Public Library Clipping Files, guidebook file.

25. See pages 20, 174.

26. "Atomic Frontier Days: A New Light on the Old Frontier, Richland, Washington, Sept. 4-5-6, 1948," (Richland, Junior Chamber of Commerce, 1948). "Richland—Richland, Washington: A Key city of the Atomic Age; 2nd Annual Atomic Frontier Days," (Richland, 1949), cover.

27. Paul John Deutschmann, "Federal City: A Study of the Administration of Richland, Washington, Atomic Energy Commission Community," (M.A. Thesis, University of Oregon, 1952).

28. Joint Committee on Atomic Energy, *Disposal of a Government-Owned Community at Richland*, 89-90.

29. U.S. Congress, Joint Committee on Atomic Energy, "Disposal of Government-Owned Community at Richland, Wash.: Hearings before a subcommittee on disposal of government-owned communities of the Joint Committee on Atomic Energy, Congress of the United States, Eighty-Fourth Congress, First Session, on disposal of government-owned community at Richland, Wash., June 18 and 19, 1954" (Washington, D.C., 1955), gives a thorough overview of the process of disposal. Also, JCAE, Subcommittee on Communities "Stenographic Transcript of Hearings Before the Joint Committee on Atomic Energy," held June 11, 19, 20, 21, 1956; 4 vol., copies in Fred Clagett Papers, Manuscripts and University Archives, University of Washington Library.

30. "Testimony Taken at Public Hearing Concerning Wahluke Slope," in Ted Van Arsdol, "The Wahluke Slope and Hanford," ms. 1980, University of Washington Library Pacific Northwest Collection. "The Wahluke Slope—Secondary Zone Restrictions," Hanford Operations Office, (n.d., c. Aug-Oct 1951), 30-31. AEC General Manager files, box 5440, file 7, Department of Energy Archives, Germantown, Maryland.

31. The shifting response of Washington voters to issues related to nuclear power is discussed in Daniel Pope, "Anti-Nuclear Activism in the Northwest: WPPSS and its Enemies," in John M. Findlay and Bruce Hevly, eds., *The Atomic West* (Seattle: University of Washington Press, forthcoming).

32. "Report of the Safety and Industrial Health Advisory Board," 2 April 1948, 64, 35, 44-45, 73, and principal recommendation 5, np. AEC Secretariat Files, 1947-1951, "Health and Safety Program" file.

33. Report of the Safety . . . Board., 69-70, 74; Gerber, *On the Home Front* (n. 9), 148-150, 117-127, 133-141.

34. Federal and state health authorities from Oregon and Washington took part in the Columbia River Advisory Group, created by Hanford's AEC management in 1949. Gerber, *On the Home Front*, (n. 9), pp. 121-125; ch. 6, especially 152-157.

35. Gerber, *On the Home Front*, (n. 9), 77-79, 90-92.

36 Karen Dorn Steele, "1949 Radiation Release Linked to Tennessee Experiment," *Spokane Spokesman-Review*, 18 December 1994.

37. The concerns of the Reactor Safeguards Committee (later the Advisory Committee on Reactor Safeguards) and the Division of Production's decision are summarized in "ACRS Report on Modifications to Hanford Reactors," 4 February 1958, AEC Report 172/22, 1-2. AEC Secretariat Files, box 1284, file 8, Department of Energy Archives, Germantown, Maryland. Edward J. Bloch, also quoted in Gerber, *On the Home Front*, 102-103.

38. Weart, *Nuclear Fear* (n. 4).

39. David Bradley, *No Place to Hide* (Boston: Little, Brown and Company, 1948).

40. Eliot Marshall, "End Game for the N Reactor?" *Science* 235 (2 January 1987): 17-18. On the changing political processes and public perceptions of nuclear regulation, see George T. Mazuzan and J. Samuel Walker, *Controlling the Atom: The Beginnings of Nuclear Regulation, 1946-1962* (Berkeley: University of California Press, 1985); Walker, *Containing the Atom: Nuclear Regulation in a Changing Environment, 1963-1971* (Berkeley: University of California Press, 1992); Barton C. Hacker, *Elements of Controversy: The Atomic Energy Commission and Radiation Safety in Nuclear Weapons Testing, 1947-1974* (Berkeley: University of California Press, 1994); and Dan O'Neill, *The Firecracker Boys* (New York: St. Martin's Press, 1994).

41. Department of Energy, "Final Environmental Impact Statement: Disposal of Hanford Defense High-Level Transuranic and Tank Wastes," (Richland, Wash.: Department of Energy, 1987), appendices A and B lists the history of tank construction at Hanford.

42. L.L. Burger, "Fission Product Iodine During Early Hanford-Site Operations: Its Processing and Behavior During Fuel Processing, Off-Gas Treatment and Release to the Atmosphere," (Richland, Wa.: Pacific Northwest Laboratory Report PNL-7210 HEDR, May 1991). The body of official reports on Hanford's environmental impact is ever-growing; among the best places to begin for an accessible overview is a set of summaries of the initial work: "Columbia River Pathway Report," (PNL-7411 HEDR, July 1991), "Air Pathway Report," (PNL-7412 HEDR, July 1991), and "Summary Report: Phase I of the Hanford Environmental Dose Reconstruction Project," (PNL-7410 HEDR, August 1991).

43. Noel Gilbrough, quoted in *Seattle Times*, 2 July 1992. See also, "Hanford Reach of the Columbia River: Comprehensive River Conservation Study and Environmental Impact Statement" (2 vol; Pacific Northwest Region, National Park Service, June 1994).

44. See page 35.

BIBLIOGRAPHY FOR CHAPTERS 1 THROUGH 8 AND ADDITIONAL READING

Books

Clark, Ronald W. *Einstein, the Life and Times*. New York: The World Publishing Company, 1971.

Cochran, Thomas B., Arkin, William M., Norris, Robert S., Hoenig, Milton M. *Nuclear Weapons Databook, Vol. 2, U.S. Nuclear Warhead Production*. Cambridge: Ballinger Publishing Co. (copyright 1987 by Natural Resources Defense Council).

Coffinberry, A.S., and W.N. Miner. *The Metal Plutonium*. Chicago: The University of Chicago Press, 1961.

Compton, Arthur Holly. *Atomic Quest*. New York: Oxford University Press, 1956.

Dietrich, William. *Northwest Passage: The Great Columbia River*. New York: Simon and Schuster, 1995.

Du Pont Project, *History of the Hanford Engineer Works* (unpublished four volume work). Wilmington: E.I. du Pont de Nemours & Company, Inc., 1945. (on file at Hagley Museum and Library, Wilmington, Delaware)

Gerber, Michele Stenehjem. *On the Home Front: The Cold War Legacy of the Hanford Nuclear Site*. Lincoln: University of Nebraska Press, 1992.

Groueff, Stephane. *Manhattan Project: The Untold Story of the Making of the Atomic Bomb*. Boston: Little, Brown and Company, 1967.

Groves, Leslie. *Now It Can Be Told, the Story of the Manhattan Project*. New York: Da Capo Press, 1983.

Hacker, Barton C. *The Dragon's Tail: Radiation Saftey in the Manhattan Project, 1942-1946*. Berkeley: University of California Press, 1987

Hageman, Roy C. Hanford, *Threshold of an Era*. Unpublished manuscript, 1945.

Harris, Mary Powell. *Goodbye White Bluffs*. Yakima, Washington: Franklin Press, 1972.

Hewlett, Richard G., and Oscar E. Anderson, Jr. *The New World, 1939-46*. Washington, D.C., U.S. Atomic Energy Commission, 1972.

Hines, Neal O. *Proving Ground, An Account of the Radiobiological Studies in the Pacific, 1946-61*. Seattle: The University of Washington Press, 1962.

Hiroshima and Nagasaki, the Physical, Medical and Social Effects of the Atomic Bombings. New York: Basic Books, Inc., 1981.

Jones, Vincent C. *Manhattan: The Army and the Atomic Bomb*. Washington, D.C.: Center for Military History, the United States Army, 1985.

Lamont, Lansing. *Day of Trinity*. New York: Atheneum, 1965.

Laurence, William L. *Men and Atoms*. New York: Simon and Schuster, 1962.

Lawren, William. *The General and the Bomb*. New York: Dodd Mead & Company, 1988.

Libby, Leona Marshall. *The Uranium People*. New York: Crane, Russak & Company, Inc. Charles Scribner's Sons, 1979.

McPhee, John. *The Curve of Binding Energy*. New York: Farrar, Straus and Giroux, 1974.

Pruter, A.T., and Alverson, D.L. *The Columbia River Estuary and Adjacent Ocean Waters*. Seattle and London: University of Washington Press, 1972.

Relander, Click. *Drummers and Dreamers*. Caldwell, Idaho: Caxton Press, 1956.

Rhodes, Richard. *The Making of the Atomic Bomb*. New York: Simon and Schuster, 1986.

Glenn T. Seaborg. *History of Met Lab, Section C-I. Journal of the years 1942-1946*. Prepared for U.S. Energy Research and Development Administration, Lawrence Berkeley Laboratory, University of California, Berkeley, 1977-1980.

Seaborg, Glenn T. *The Transuranium Elements*. New Haven: Yale University Press, 1958.

Segre, Emilio. *Enrico Fermi, Physicist*. Chicago: The University of Chicago Press, 1970.

Smith, Alice Kimball. *A Peril and a Hope: The Scientists' Movement in America*. Cambridge: The MIT Press, 1971, 1970.

Smythe, Henry DeWolf. *Atomic Energy for Military Purposes (The Smythe Report)*. Princeton: Princeton University Press, 1945.

Splawn, Andrew Jackson. *Ka-Mi-Akin, the Last Hero of the Yakimas*. Caldwell, Idaho: Caxton Printers, 1917.

Szasz, Ferenc Morton. *The Day the Sun Rose Twice*. Albuquerque: University of New Mexico Press, 1984.

Szilard, Leo. *Leo Szilard: His Version of the Facts*. Cambridge: The MIT Press, 1978.

Tsipis, Kosta. *Arsenal: Understanding Weapons in the Nuclear Age*. New York: Simon and Schuster, 1983.

Van Arsdol, Ted. *Hanford, the Big Secret*. Richland, Washington: Columbia Basin News, 1958.

Wilson, Jane (editor). *All In Our Time*. Chicago: The Bulletin of the Atomic Scientists, 1974.

Wyden, Peter. Day One. New York: Simon and Schuster, 1984.

Articles

Babcock, Dale. "The Discovery of Xenon-135 as a Reactor Poison," *Nuclear News-American Nuclear Society* (September, 1964), 38-42.

Blackburn, Marc K. "Balloon Bombs & Submarines," *Columbia, The Magazine of Northwest History* (Winter, 1994-95), 11-12.

Burke, J.E. "Recollections of Processing Uranium Hydride and Plutonium at Wartime Los Alamos," *Journal of Nuclear Materials* (Vol. 100, 1981), 11-16.

Engineering News-Record (special number featuring "Construction for Atomic Bomb Facilities), Dec. 13, 1945.

Gerber, Michele S. "Hanford's Historic Reactors," *Columbia* (Spring 1995), 31-36.

Grossman, Daniel. "Hanford and Its Early Radioactive Atmospheric Releases," *Pacific Northwest Quarterly* (January, 1994) 6-14.

Sayle, Murray. "Did the Bomb End the War?," *The New Yorker* (July 31, 1995) 40-64

Smith, Cyril S. "Some Recollections of Metallurgy at Los Alamos, 1943-45," *Journal of Nuclear Materials* (Vol. 100, 1981), 3-10.

Snell, Arthur H. "Graveyard shift, Hanford, 28 September 1944—Henry W. Newson," *American Journal of Physics* (April, 1982), 343-348.

Stimson, Henry L. "The Decision to Use the Atomic Bomb," *Harper's Magazine*, (February, 1947) 97-107.

Weinberg, Alvin M. "The Sanctification of Hiroshima," Bulletin of the Atomic Scientists (December, 1985), 34.

Other

A History of the Manhattan Engineer District, a compilation of official Manhattan Engineer District records, filed on microfilm at the Federal Archives and Record Center, Seattle, Washington.

Findlay, John M., and Bruce Hevly. *Nuclear Technologies and Nuclear Communities: A History of Hanford and the Tri-Cities, 1943-1993*. Center for the Study of the Pacific Northwest, University of Washington, Seattle. A report to the U.S. Department of Energy, Richland Operations Office. 1994

Foster, Richard F. "Effects of Hanford Reactors on Columbia River and Adjacent Land Areas," presented to the State of Washington Ecological Commission, Richland, Dec. 15, 1970.

Foster, Richard F. "Some Effects of Pile Area Effluent Water on Young Chinook Salmon and Steelhead Trout," Aug. 31, 1946, Battelle Pacific Northwest Laboratories, File No. 7-4759

Mikesh, Robert C. "Japan's World War II Balloon Bomb Attacks on North America." *Number 9, Smithsonian Annals of Flight*. National Air and Space Museum, Smithsonian Institution Press.

Highlights of Historical Documents (Hanford), 1943-1948, U.S. Department of Energy.

Legend and Legacy: Fifty Years of Defense Production at the Hanford Site. Prepared for the U.S. Department of Energy by Westinghouse Hanford Company (M.S. Gerber), 1992.

Review of Hanford Historical Documents. Revised Final Report. State of Washington Department of Ecology, 1987.

Miscellaneous documents associated with Du Pont's Hanford period on file at Hagley Museum and Library, Wilmington, Delaware, including papers of former Du Pont president W.S. Carpenter, Jr.

Jay Haney papers, Hanford Science Center, Richland, Washington.

Personal correspondence: Kenneth T. Bainbridge, Stanley Goldberg, Franklin T. Matthias, and Walter O. Simon.

Video Documentary on World War II Hanford

A collaborator on the early stages of this book was Robert W. Mull, a documentary film maker. His one hour film about Hanford "Something to Win The War: The Hanford Diary" (1985) is available in VHS format. It contains rare footage of Hanford under construction and interviews with many of the people profiled in this book. To order send $25.00 (includes shipping and handling) to:

Sepia Productions
1501 East Jefferson
Seattle, WA 98122
(206) 323-7804

AUTHOR'S NOTE

My first sight of Hanford was in February, 1977, as I was driving east on Highway 243 along the Columbia River below Priest Rapids Dam. The steep, craggy Rattlesnake Hills were to my right, across the river, the lower and smoother Saddle Mountains to my left. As the valley widened, I could see vague smudges of gray across the river. They were buildings almost lost to sight in a sea of desert brown.

My interest in Hanford began as simple curiosity, but when I asked questions my curiosity was not satisfied. I was a reporter at the Seattle Post-Intelligencer and at times met men and women who had been part of the Manhattan Project. Two were Edward Teller and Glenn Seaborg, who became impatient when they noticed I was a nuclear novice. I needed background, and began with books by John McPhee and Leslie Groves.

In 1980, I attended an energy seminar in Richland and toured the inactive B Reactor, a ghostly mansion filled with echoes. As a tourist, I visited Los Alamos and Oak Ridge. Not long after, I became the newspaper's military reporter, which allowed me to write and learn more about nuclear weapons.

In 1984, I interviewed Franklin T. Matthias, Hanford's wartime Army commander. I had assumed that most of the key people from Hanford's wartime past were dead, but it dawned on me that perhaps others were alive and willing to be interviewed. I met Robert W. Mull, a Seattle filmmaker who was working on a documentary video about Hanford during World War II and we talked about a book.

During a six-month leave in 1986 I zig-zagged across the country interviewing Manhattan Project people who had been connected with Hanford. I found them in telephone books, history books, and Who's Who. Scientists and engineers often were reluctant to talk to me until I convinced them I was not planning to depict them as murderers. Physicist John Wheeler grilled me for 20 minutes before he shook my hand and spoke of "the romance and adventure" of Hanford.

One major problem was finding construction workers because usually they moved on after a job was done. One morning at a cafe in Richland I heard the men in the booth behind me talking fondly of Hanford during the war. I turned around and spoke to them. One man had come in 1943, and he told me of others.

Another difficulty was locating representatives of the thousands of black men and women from the south who had worked at Hanford, but I had no success in finding a single one until I found clues in a newspaper obituary.

While talking to the cement finishers, millwrights and carpenters, security officers, secretaries, messhall cooks and waitresses, steamfitters, and housewives, I realized World War II's immense effect on America's social and occupational life. These people had come from far away, earned high wages in war jobs and seemed to have cut most ties with their prewar homes and prewar lives. They were uprooted but seemed to enjoy it, and very few went home again.

The time finally came when I had enough interviews and knew I should start writing. Slowly, like untying a knot, I saw the way. I would let those who had been there tell the story, from the plutonium beginning to Nagasaki, in their own voices. My job would be to provide background commentary to guide the reader.

Since the first edition was published in late 1989, many of the Manhattan Project's veterans interviewed for the book have died. The dead include Robley L. Johnson, who shot many of the first version's wartime photographs, and Franklin T. Matthias and Walter O. Simon, whose assistance was crucial and much appreciated. Their voices and those of the others interviewed, however, are not stilled. Interview tapes and transcripts are on file at the University of Washington Libraries' manuscripts and university archives division.

S. L. Sanger
August 1995

INDEX